New Concepts in Latino American Cultures
A Series Edited by Licia Fiol-Matta & José Quiroga

New Directions in Latino American Cultures
Also Edited by Licia Fiol-Matta & José Quiroga

New York Ricans from the Hip Hop Zone
by Raquel Z. Rivera

The Famous 41: Sexuality and Social Control in Mexico, 1901
edited by Robert McKee Irwin, Edward J. McCaughan, and Michele Rocío Nasser

Velvet Barrios: Popular Culture & Chicana/o Sexualities
edited by Alicia Gaspar de Alba, with a foreword by Tomás Ybarra Frausto

Tongue Ties: Logo-Eroticism in Anglo-Hispanic Literature
by Gustavo Pérez-Firmat

Bilingual Games: Some Literary Investigations
edited by Doris Sommer

Jose Martí: An Introduction
by Oscar Montero

New Tendencies in Mexican Art: The 1990s
by Rubén Gallo

The Masters and the Slaves: Plantation Relations and Mestizaje in American Imaginaries
edited by Alexandra Isfahani-Hammond

The Letter of Violence: Essays on Narrative, Ethics, and Politics
by Idelber Avelar

An Intellectual History of the Caribbean
by Silvio Torres-Saillant

None of the Above: Puerto Ricans in the Global Era
edited by Frances Negrón-Muntaner

Queer Latino Testimonio, Keith Haring, and Juanito Xtravaganza: Hard Tails
by Arnaldo Cruz-Malavé

The Portable Island: Cubans at Home in the World
edited by Ruth Behar and Lucía M. Suárez

Violence without Guilt: Ethical Narratives from the Global South
by Hermann Herlinghaus

Redrawing the Nation: National Identity in Latin/o American Comics
by Héctor Fernández L'Hoeste and Juan Poblete

Hispanic Caribbean Literature of Migration

Narratives of Displacement

Edited by

Vanessa Pérez Rosario

HISPANIC CARIBBEAN LITERATURE OF MIGRATION
Copyright © Vanessa Pérez Rosario, 2010.

First published in 2010 by
PALGRAVE MACMILLAN®
in the United States—a division of St. Martin's Press LLC,
175 Fifth Avenue, New York, NY 10010.

Where this book is distributed in the UK, Europe and the rest of the world,
this is by Palgrave Macmillan, a division of Macmillan Publishers Limited,
registered in England, company number 785998, of Houndmills,
Basingstoke, Hampshire RG21 6XS.

Palgrave Macmillan is the global academic imprint of the above companies
and has companies and representatives throughout the world.

Palgrave® and Macmillan® are registered trademarks in the United States,
the United Kingdom, Europe and other countries.

ISBN: 978–0–230–62065–0

Library of Congress Cataloging-in-Publication Data

Hispanic Caribbean literature of migration : narratives of displacement /
edited by Vanessa Pérez Rosario.
    p. cm.—(New concepts in Latino American cultures)
    ISBN 978–0–230–62065–0 (hardback)
    1. American literature—Hispanic American authors—History and
criticism. 2. American literature—Caribbean American authors—History
and criticism. 3. Emigration and immigration in literature. 4. Displacement
(Psychology) in literature. 5. Caribbean Area—In literature. 6. National
characteristics, Caribbean, in literature. I. Pérez Rosario, Vanessa.

PS153.H56H57 2010
810.9'3552—dc22   2009049123

A catalogue record of the book is available from the British Library.

Design by Newgen Imaging Systems (P) Ltd., Chennai, India.

First edition: June 2010

D 10 9 8 7 6 5 4 3 2

Printed in the United States of America.

Contents

Acknowledgments

I would like to express my deepest gratitude to the contributors for their excellent chapters, for trusting me with their work, and for their patience.

To Luis Cruz Azaceta, whose work on the cover powerfully (and beautifully) speaks to the experience of migration, thank you for generously participating in this project.

I am grateful to the CUNY Faculty Fellowship Publications Program 2009 and my participating colleagues for their criticism and advice especially Natasha Gordon-Chipembere and my senior mentor in the program, Virginia Sánchez Korrol. I would also like to thank Inés Hernández-Avila, Riché Richardson, and Neil Larson for their critical comments and mentorship over the years.

Thanks are also due to Martha Nadell, James Davis, Laura Lomas, Natasha Lightfoot-Swain, Hlonipha Mokoena, Michael Ralph, Alan Aja, and Miranda Martinez for their valuable feedback and criticism.

Finally, I would like to thank my parents, Francisco and Carmen Pérez, my sisters Shelley and Karina and Rodney M. Miller for their endless love, friendship, and support.

Introduction

Historical Context of Caribbean Latino Literature

Vanessa Pérez Rosario

> *Most people are principally aware of one culture, one setting, one home; exiles are aware of at least two, and this plurality of vision gives rise to an awareness of simultaneous dimensions, an awareness that—to borrow a phrase from music—is contrapuntal.*
>
> —Edward Said ("Reflections on Exile")

In his essay "Reflections on Exile," Edward Said notes that the exile feels a sense of constant estrangement. The writer's life abroad is contrapuntal, precisely because of the constant interplay between two languages, geographies, traditions, and cultures. This awareness of at least two visions is what leads to feelings of perpetual alienation. For the moment let us suspend the distinction between the various reasons for migration such as exile and immigration, to focus on the experience of migration. The migrant lives a life outside of habitual order; it is a life that is decentered between two worlds. This contrapuntal vision or double consciousness allows the Caribbean Latino writer the ability to challenge national discourses from her or his country of origin while simultaneously critiquing U.S. hegemonic narratives and imperial power in the Caribbean region. The essays included in the collection *Hispanic Caribbean Literature of Migration: Narratives of Displacement* explore the lives and literature of intellectuals and writers of Cuban, Puerto Rican, and Dominican origins who cross barriers and borders of thought and tradition.

The collection opens with a look at three migrating writers from the Hispanic Caribbean: José Martí and Juan Bosch, who were exiled from their countries of origin, and Julia de Burgos, who left to escape a narrowly defined island national discourse. These authors' dissonant ideologies in relation to the national discourses in their countries of origin at the time are illustrated in this first section of the collection entitled *Migratory Identities*. José Martí was exiled for denouncing the Spanish colonial government in Cuba, and as expressed in his essay "Nuestra América," as well as in other writings, developed a keen understanding of U.S. imperialism during his extended stay in New York. On the other hand, Juan Bosch's contrapuntal doubling is revealed in his astute understanding of the role that the U.S. government played in its attempt to establish "democracy" in the Dominican Republic. Finally, nationalist leaders in 1930s' Puerto Rico challenge U.S. invasion of the island by clinging to a Hispanic legacy that served the recently displaced landowners, while silencing the African and indigenous voices on the island. The strengthening of contrapuntal vision for these three writers can be noted in further detail in the chapters included in this first section.

While Edward Said privileges the experience of exile in his essay quoted above, his reflections also shed light on other migratory experiences. However, here Said does not account for what comes after exile: diaspora. If the exile's vision is contrapuntal, Puerto Rican, Cuban, and Dominican diasporic communities in the United States find new ways to express this instability, disruption, and fragmentation which is exacerbated by extended time abroad, distance from the Caribbean island of origin, U.S. citizenship, and English or bilingualism in English and Spanish, as the mother tongue. The rest of the collection is made up of three sections with three essays in each that explore salient themes in Puerto Rican, Cuban, and Dominican diasporic literature: the question of belonging is examined in *Dislocated Narratives*; migration that is motivated by gender and sexual orientation is considered in *Gender Crossings*; finally, the experience that Caribbean Latina/os face upon migration to the United States of either being racialized into ethnic minorities and/or being fixed into a U.S. racial discourse is investigated in *Racial Migrations*.

While this collection is not meant to be a comprehensive examination of Caribbean Latino literature, the essays included study some of the prominent themes and notable authors who migrated to the United States from the Hispanic Caribbean or form a part of its corresponding diasporas. The Cuban, Puerto Rican, and Dominican shared cultural heritage and regional location, yet distinct political realities and migratory and diaspora histories provide fertile ground for contrast and comparison of the ways that Hispanic Caribbean literature written abroad confronts and challenges established cultural traditions and norms, and expands notions of national identity that are often exclusionary. Reading the literature of migration by writers originating from these three nations side-by-side, allows us to note parallels and draw preliminary conclusions. Indeed, Ana Belén Martín Sevillano argues (chapter 8) that Cuban queer literature written from abroad forms part of the national literary canon proving that exile is a territory of the nation. In addition, Caribbean Latino literature challenges and expands traditional notions of American literature (U.S. literature) as it disrupts the black/white racial binary in the United States and is often multilingual; written in Spanish, English, and/or Spanglish. Simultaneously, one can begin to describe a Caribbean Latino literary tradition as Laura Lomas argues in her chapter on José Martí as a foundational writer of deteritorrialized literature in the region (chapter 1). Opening with a chapter on José Martí as an early figure in this literary tradition of Caribbean Latino writing in the United States and as a writer who defined literature in Latin America as a discourse critical of state and other institutional discursive practices,[1] we close with an examination of Dominican born, Junot Díaz's 2008 Pulitzer Prize winning novel *The Brief Wondrous Life of Oscar Wao*. As this chapter reveals, Díaz continues the tradition of contrapuntal transnational discourses and uses his positioning of being both outside and inside the nation to critique master discourses both in the United States and in the Dominican Republic (chapter 12).

Understanding Hispanic Caribbean and Caribbean Latino literature requires an understanding of the history of migration and the historical, social, political, and economic circumstances that led to the movement of people in the region. The collection opens with the late nineteenth-century writer José Martí's works to provide historical depth to Caribbean Latino literature that is often misunderstood to be a mid-twentieth century phenomenon. The cultural expressions of writers from the region is erroneously thought to have emerged because of the Cuban Revolution of 1959, the end of the Trujillo dictatorship in the Dominican Republic in the 1960s and the economic policies and establishment of the Free Associated State in Puerto Rico in 1952. In reality, people from the Hispanic Caribbean have been migrating to the United States throughout the nineteenth century and growing in number as the United States became the main economic power in the region. Although laws governing the region were still made in the centralized governments of Europe, U.S. economic and political power were taken into account before setting policy.

From U.S. shores Cuban and Puerto Rican anti-colonialists took advantage of the freedom of the press by using the newspapers to establish the "imagined communities" Benedict Anderson describes to continue the struggle against Spanish rule. All publications were centralized in Spain and were heavily censored. The Cuban and Puerto Rican press in exile began because of the repression in the homeland that forced intellectuals to migrate.[2] By mid-nineteenth century, Spanish language newspapers were flourishing in the Northeast and have remained in

Hispanic communities since, preserving and advancing Hispanic culture and maintaining its relationship with the larger Spanish-speaking world. The newspapers were instrumental in organizing civil rights and in educating the communities in the States. They shared information about religion and cultural celebrations, and helped the communities to battle segregation and discrimination. They also published creative literature in Spanish during the nineteenth and early twentieth centuries. They helped to shape the identity and ethos of U.S. Hispanic communities as they developed. Spanish-language newspapers calling for independence and liberation continued to emerge in cities along the eastern seaboard of the United States throughout the nineteenth century. In New York there was *La Verdad* (1852), *La Revolución* (1869), and *El Pueblo* (mid-1870s). In New Orleans, *El Independiente: Organo de la democracia cubana* (1853), and in Florida *El Yara* (1878), to name a few. *La Voz de América* (1865), founded by Cuban Juan Manuel Macía and Puerto Rican José Bassora, helped unify the Puerto Rican and Cuban exile communities in their liberation from Spain.

Important writers, such as José María Heredia, Cirilio Villaverde, and José Martí, who are considered Cuban nationalists and were later adopted into the Cuban literary canon wrote for these papers and also published their poetry and prose there.[3] In these papers, Hispanic Caribbean writers in New York participated in the conversations about race, abolition, and Cuban, Puerto Rican, and Dominican annexation to the United States. From New York, Cuban exiles wrote militant poetry they believed would inspire Cubans on the island to fight against Spanish colonialism.[4] It is important to note that these writers are later rescued from exile and included in the national literary canon even though they spent significant time abroad. Villaverde's short-lived support for annexation of Cuba to the United States can be noted in his writings for *La Verdad*, although he later supported Cuban independence.[5] Founded by Cuban exiles and U.S. expansionists, John O'Sullivan and Moses Beach, *La Verdad*'s mission was to lobby support for Cuban annexation from both the U.S. public and Cubans. Slavery and abolition were central to the Cuban independence movements of the nineteenth century. *El Mulato* emerged in New York in 1854 and set out to unite the Cuban independence and abolitionist movements (Kanellos 13). Carlos de Colins, Lorenzo Alló, and Juan Clemente Zenea established the paper to unify the Cuban revolutionary movement with the U.S. abolitionist movement in direct opposition to the annexationist ideology espoused by *La Verdad*. The awareness of an Afro-Cuban identity and culture expressed in *El Mulato*, surfaced once again with Arturo Alfonso Schomburg's archiving of Afro-Caribbean and black culture in New York in the late nineteenth century. These themes were later revisited in the Hispanic journalism of Alberto O'Farrill and Jesús Colón's (chapter 10) writings for *Gráfico* in the 1920s. The racialization of Hispanic Caribbeans within U.S. racial politics remains an important theme of Hispanic Caribbean diasporic literature today.

The most important and well remembered writer who forms part of this exile community in the late nineteenth century is José Martí, and as with any great leader he had the gift of uniting people.[6] He encouraged Puerto Ricans to join efforts with Cubans. José Martí (1853–1895) studied in Spain where he obtained a law degree. He spent much of his life abroad working as a professor and a writer in Mexico, Guatemala, Venezuela, Spain, and in New York. He founded various papers and magazines throughout Latin America. He was able to bring "the various classes and factions together in the revolutionary cause" even "extending open arms to Puerto Rican intellectuals to unite their efforts with those of the Cubans" (Kanellos 19). In addition to his revolutionary efforts and his journalism, Martí is remembered as an early Latin American *modersnismo* poet, even though his books of poetry were first published in the United States. From New York he published a book of poetry dedicated to his son, *Ismaelillo* (1882). His poems included in *Versos sencillos* (1891) describe his love for freedom and for Cuba, echoing some of Heredia's poetry on Cuba written in exile. While the poetry he wrote in New York is included in canonical national literature in Cuba and read across Latin America, he also wrote numerous articles about the United States and North American literature during his fifteen years in New York. Abroad he developed a penetrating critique of U.S. imperialism and expansionism (Lomas 2008).

As in Cuba, discontent and a desire for independence grew in Puerto Rico during the 1860s. For the remainder of the century, Puerto Rican intellectuals joined Cuban brothers in New York in their struggle to overthrow Spanish colonialism. After the failure of the Grito de Lares in 1868, Puerto Rican intellectuals including Eugenio María de Hostos, Ramon Emeterio Betances, Lola Rodriguez de Tió, and Luis Muñoz Rivera moved to New York to continue the struggle for independence. In 1891, Francisco Gonzalo Pachín Marín (1863–1897) brought his newspaper, *El Postillón,* to New York from Puerto Rico. Marín later died in 1897 in battle in Cuba. Sotero Figueroa (1851–1923), the Puerto Rican writer, also migrated at this time as did writers such as Ramon Emeterio Betances (1827–1898), Manuel Zeno Gandía (1855–1930), Salvador Brau (1842–1912), Matias González, and Miguel Meléndez Muñoz, all leaders in the independence movement who contributed to exile publications in New York.[7] Lola Rodriguez de Tió (1848–1924) arrived in New York in 1895 and stayed until 1899. She was first exiled to Venezuela (1877–1880) and later Cuba (1889–1895). However, after the Spanish American War, she spent the rest of her life in Cuba. She strongly supported independence and refused to return to Puerto Rico. This nineteenth-century writing often consisted of letters, diary entries, and newspaper articles.

This early writing offers an inside view of U.S. society, one that is further elaborated by Puerto Ricans of the early twentieth century who were writing between the two world wars and formed part of the first wave of Puerto Ricans migrating to the United States.

Another important turn-of-the-century Puerto Rican writer in New York is Arturo Alfonso Schomburg who is remembered for his archive and book collection about black history and culture. In 1926 he sold his collection to the New York Public Library "laying the foundation for one of the world's richest archives for the study of black culture" (Hoffnung Garskof 3). Born in Puerto Rico in 1874 to a black West Indian mother and a father of German ancestry, Schomburg moved to New York in 1891 where he joined a small enclave of Puerto Rican and Cuban radical cigar workers who were involved in the independence movement. He founded the revolutionary club "Las Dos Antillas." Hoffnung Garskof notes that "Schomburg's gradual absorption into black North American social and intellectual life reflects an untold history of race within the small group of Puerto Rican migrants in New York between 1890 and 1900" (3).

Although the nineteenth-century history of the Dominican Republic distinguishes itself greatly from Cuban and Puerto Rican history, Dominican involvement with the United States during this period shares some similarities. Prior to the Dominican Republic claiming independence, Haiti had occupied the Spanish colony on two separate occasions. First, by Toussant L'Ouveture and Dessalines between 1801 and 1805, and once again by Jean-Pierre Boyer from 1822–1844. In 1844, Dominican independence leaders in search of "commercial and diplomatic credibility" sought recognition from the United States soon after independence (Torres-Saillant, *Before Diaspora*, 256). Torres-Saillant notes that Dominicans who had the ability to travel to the United States and Europe during the nineteenth century were of the educated class, and therefore it is not surprising that they would "have literary interests and aptitudes" (255). Manuel de Jesús Galván (1834–1910), author of *Enriquillo*, spent significant time in Paris and later in Puerto Rico, where he lived the remainder of his life.[8] Likewise Juan Pablo Duarte, Dominican independence leader studied English in New York before the Dominican Republic became independent on February 27, 1844. Duarte wrote plays, prose, and verse.

During the nineteenth century, the United States was a place where Dominicans who were exiled by political rivals traveled to. It was the home of Dominican writers such as Alejandro Angulo Guridi (1822–1906) who lived in the United States from 1840 to 1852, and Pedro Alejandro Pina.[9] Mid-century discussions about Dominican annexation to the United States also circulated. Although the Dominican Republic was never annexed, by the end of the century the United States became the primary influence in the newly independent republic as it had in all of the Caribbean region, strongly influencing all aspects of economic, social, and political life.

While the economic and political ties between the Caribbean and North America continued to grow during the nineteenth century, by the turn of the century their economies were enmeshed. Cuba, Puerto Rico, and the Dominican Republic all spent the twentieth century under U.S. imperial power; this led to massive migrations to the United States and the development of ethnic enclaves and diasporic communities. However, they differ greatly in nation formation—with Puerto Rico remaining a direct colony, and Cuba participating in a socialist revolution—and represent two extremes in their relationship to the United States. The Dominican Republic as a neo-colony rests somewhere in between. Economic, cultural, and political dependency for each nation has been negotiated differently. As ethnic enclaves emerged in metropolitan centers such as Chicago, New York, and Miami, writers of Puerto Rican, Cuban, and Dominican origins developed new ways to express their relationship to the past, their positioning in history, and the emergence of new cultural identities. The essays included in this collection explore multiple migratory experiences from Cuba, Puerto Rico, and the Dominican Republic to the U.S. and the diasporas that resulted, leading us to reflect on modern notions of citizenship, residency, and belonging.

U.S. occupation of Puerto Rico and the extension of citizenship with the 1917 Jones Act precipitated increased Puerto Rican migration to the United States. While most accounts of early migration explore the lives of men, Luisa Capetillo (1879–1922) traveled to the United States in 1912 where she organized tobacco workers in both New York and Tampa. She was a labor organizer, a women's rights activist and an anarchist. Written in 1911 on the eve of her departure for the United States, Luisa Capetillos's book *Mi opinión sobre las libertades, derechos y deberes de la mujer* (1911) was the first Puerto Rican book dedicated exclusively to questions of gender and women's rights (Ramos, *Amor y anarquía* 30). In her essay, "For the Sake of Love: Luisa Capetillo, Anarchy, and Boricua Literary History," Lisa Sánchez notes that Capetillo left the island after being "harassed by both colonial regimes in Puerto Rico and becoming discontented with the workers' movement" on the island (59).

By the interwar period, most Puerto Ricans settled in New York City where a vibrant community emerged.[10] Among the texts written by Puerto Ricans in New York between the two wars, there are two that stand out: *Memorias de Bernardo Vega* (written in 1940 and published in 1977), and Jesús Colón's, *A Puerto Rican in New York and Other Sketches* (1961). Their stories are compelling autobiographical and testimonial accounts of life for Puerto Ricans in New York in the early part of the century as well as important historical resources. Bernardo Vega

(1885–1965) and Jesús Colón (1901–1974) migrated from Cayey, Puerto Rico at a young age and were *tabaqueros*, members of the socialist party, labor organizers, and regular contributors to the various Puerto Rican and Spanish-language newspapers being published at this time in New York. Their writings highlight the need for improved living standards for Puerto Ricans in New York City, and provide a glimpse of every day life in the city. Vega's obsession with history as detailed in his memoirs and his desire to rescue Puerto Rican history from oblivion, also provides a contrasting perspective to the stories in the mainstream newspapers that criminalized the emerging *colonia*. Jesús Colón contributed regularly to the newspaper *Gráfico* (1927–1931) first edited by Cuban Alberto O'Farrill. Here, Colón explored his political perspectives on race and culture (chapter 10). Colón also published weekly columns in *The Daily Worker* (1924–1958), *El Nuevo Mundo*, *The Worker*, *Mainstream*, *Liberación* (1946–1949), and *Pueblos Hispanos* (1943–1944). His column "Puerto Rican Notes" appeared in *The Daily World* from 1968 to 1971, and "Lo que el pueblo me dice" in *Pueblos Hispanos* in 1943.[11] Colón was a worker and union organizer who made the transition to writing in English by the mid-1950s. Julia de Burgos (1914–1953) also wrote for *Pueblos Hispanos* during 1943–1944 (chapter 3). She wrote about art and culture and also published poetry in the newspaper. She too anticipated the language shift of the growing community, and wrote her final poems in English.

The second wave of Puerto Rican migration to the United States occurred mid-century, between the years 1950–1970. Often referred to as the Great Migration, it signals the peak of Puerto Rican migration and the first airborne migration. This time period also saw the first change in government policy on the island. Puerto Ricans elected their first governor in 1947, and became a Free Associated State in 1952, a situation that persists today and has been the topic of concern for many Puerto Ricans both on and off the island.[12] The second stage of twentieth-century Puerto Rican writing in the United States took place during the decades immediately following World War II. Fueled by policies such as Operation Bootstrap on the island, hundreds of thousands of Puerto Ricans came to New York and other parts of the United States in search of work. During this period, the experience of migration and the growing community in New York became major themes in Puerto Rican literature. There was also a shift in this literature from a rural to an urban focus. Puerto Rican writers such as René Marqués, Enrique Laguerre, and Emilio Díaz Valcárcel traveled to New York to witness the growing community. Other writers such as Pedro Juan Soto and José Luis González lived in the United States for extended periods of time however, many of the writers from this period are closely identified with the island and incorporated into that national literary canon. The literature of this period is clearly about Puerto Ricans in the United States, rather than literature of this community as can be noted in the language of these texts which does not resonate with the language of the community at the time. By the 1950s the Puerto Rican community in New York was already inclined toward bilingualism, language mixing, and code switching.[13]

The Great Migration of the middle of the century was followed by the emergence of the Nuyorican Movement, which we can recognize as the first true Puerto Rican literary movement of the diaspora. The Nuyorican writers grew out of the social movements of the 1960s and 1970s in the United States. Many of the writers were first generation born in the States or had migrated there when they were young. In this literature, there is an awakening of a Puerto Rican New York consciousness with pride in their Afro-Caribbean and indigenous Caribbean identity. This is an urban literature that gives expression to the hostility that Puerto Ricans faced in New York and their treatment as second-class citizens. Most notably, there is a language shift in the literature that is written in English, Spanish, and Spanglish, reflecting the language spoken by the community. The use of English, and a new articulation of a racial identity gave rise to tensions between island and Nuyorican writers. Nuyorican creative expression draws from the testimonial writing of the 'pioneer' stage as well as from the fictional approach of the mid-century writers, although it appears to have emerged with no apparent knowledge of this earlier literature.[14] The combining of testimonial and imaginative modes of expression can be noted in Piri Thomas' *Down These Mean Streets* (1967) and Nicholasa Mohr's *Nilda* (1973). Puerto Rican literature written in the States today remains a literature that straddles two national literatures and remains marginal to both.

The 1970s brought about a new phenomenon in the migration patterns of Puerto Ricans to the United States. From the 1970s to the present, there has been a great deal of two-way migration or return migration of Puerto Ricans born in the United States to the island. Although Puerto Ricans did begin to return in large numbers in the 1970s, little attention has been given to the impact of this return migration or "remigrants" as Juan Flores has noted in *The Diaspora Strikes Back: Caribeño Tales of Learning and Turning*. Flores explores these "cultural remittances" and determines that "it is in the language, music, literature, painting, and other expressive genres that the values and lifestyles remitted from the diaspora to homeland become manifest in the most tangible and salient ways" (45). During the 1980s and 1990s migration again increased but retained its two-way patterns.

There was also a greater dispersion of Puerto Ricans away from New York City because "economic restructuring in urban areas in the Northeast and the Midwest displaced Puerto Rican workers" (Whalen 37). Not surprisingly, Puerto Rican literature has emerged beyond the sensibilities of the Nuyorican movement in areas such as California and Hawaii with Puerto Rican enclaves that date back to the 1900s and rival early New York Puerto Rican communities. Edited by Aurora Levins Morales and Vanessa Pérez Rosario, the forthcoming anthology *OtheRicans: Voices of the Greater Puerto Rican Diaspora* brings together for the first time a body of literature that reflects the current geographic diversity of the Puerto Rican diaspora. While New York Puerto Ricans have defined themselves as U.S. people of color largely in relationship to African Americans, Hawai'ian Puerto Ricans fashioned their identities in very different conditions, in response to the Native Hawai'ians, Japanese, Chinese, Filipinos, and Portuguese among whom they settled at the turn of the last century, and in California, alliances and conflicts with the much larger Mexican population have been a defining characteristic of Calirican culture. This diversity can be noted in the literature written by Aurora Levins Morales, Judith Ortiz Cofer, Alba Ambert, and Rodney Morales. The study of this greater Puerto Rican diversity is also explored in *Writing Of(f) the Hyphen: New Perspectives on the Literature of the Puerto Rican Diaspora* edited by José L. Torres-Padilla and Carmen Haydée Rivera.[15]

In the twentieth century, Cuban literature written abroad followed a different course than that of Puerto Rican literature. The Spanish-Cuban-American War had different repercussions on the developing nation of Cuba. With the Treaty of Paris (December 1898), Spain granted independence to Cuba, and ceded Puerto Rico to the United States. A military government was established in Cuba by U.S. Congress to disarm insurgents and relieve malnutrition on the island. In 1900, elections were conducted and an assembly formed to write a constitution. Most representatives sought total independence, however, the McKinley administration was determined to protect U.S. property and investments on the island. This was done through the Platt Amendment that would ensure U.S. naval bases on the island, among other provisions. The Platt proposals were added by the Havana Constitutional Convention by 1901. Twentieth-century Cuba was ruled by a series of corrupt governments. To preserve order and protect U.S. interests, U.S. troops were sent to Cuba three times between 1906 and 1917, and again in 1922. Cuba enjoyed the highest standard of living in the region and the U.S. government agreed to purchase their exports and protect them from foreign powers. During World War I, Cuba prospered in unprecedented ways. However, when the price of sugar dropped Cuba's banks suffered greatly, depending once again on U.S. economic assistance.

The patterns and waves of Cuban exile and migration differed significantly from those in Puerto Rico. Cubans continued to flee the island as political exiles in the twentieth century. Alejo Carpentier and Lino Novás Calvo, two of Cuba's most important writers, left the island during the 1930s' Machado dictatorship.[16] Carpentier left for Paris and Calvo for Madrid. During this time, Nicolás Guillen also spent time traveling abroad. Batista's dictatorship, from 1952 to 1958 produced a small number of exile writers such as Roberto Fernández Retamar, Edmundo Desnoes, Pablo Armando Fernández, and Ambrosio Fornet. While many of these young writers did return after Fidel Castro came into power in 1959, the Cuban Revolution did produce the greatest wave of exiles to Miami, New York City, and San Juan. There are three distinct groups of exile writers post-1959 Revolution. The first group comprises those anti-Castro exile writers such as novelist Carlos Alberto Montaner who wrote *Perromundo* (1972) and Hilda Perera who wrote *El sitio de nadie* (1972). Other writers who left immediately following Castro's revolution include Lydia Cabrera who left in 1962, Carlos Montenegro in 1959, and Enrique Labrador Ruiz. The decade after the Revolution also saw the departure of important writers such as Guillermo Cabrera Infante, Matías Montes Huidobro, and José Sánchez-Boudy. In the 1980s, another group of exile writers emerged during the Mariel boatlift. Many established writers such as Heberto Padilla, José Triana, César Leante, Reinaldo Arenas, and Antonio Benítez Rojo sought asylum during this period. Compared to the literature these writers produced in Cuba, considerably less was published by them in exile. William Luis notes that "economic imperatives have forced them to devote themselves to other intellectual work, such as publishing and teaching" (14). Because these writers had already established themselves in Cuba prior to the 1959 Revolution, their writing tends to be anti-revolutionary, and a denunciation of the Castro regime that at times heavily censored their work and at other times persecuted them, as in the case of Reinaldo Arenas because of his sexual identity.

While these earlier generations of exile writers continued to write anti-Castro literature in Spanish, more recent writers started to write in English using Spanish in their writing as a marker of Hispanic identity. Earlier generations thought that their condition of exile and their stay abroad would be temporary; however, many have come to realize that their departure is permanent. Their themes encompass both island life and the experience of exile. They also explore questions of identity politics, cultural identity, and diaspora. Some of these writers include Zoé Valdés, Oscar Hijuelos, Achy Obejas, and Cristina García.

As with Puerto Rican and Cuban writers, Dominican writers have traveled to the United States throughout the twentieth century in greater numbers than in the previous century because of events on the island and increased U.S. involvement in Dominican affairs. In 1899, after President Heureaux's assassination, the Dominican Republic was left without a government and with an enormous debt it couldn't pay. Fearing intervention by European powers, U.S. President Roosevelt took over the collection of customs in 1905. Santo Domingo's finances remained under U.S. control until 1940, with U.S. marines occupying the nation from 1916 to 1924. During this time the United States restructured national finances, built schools, invested in infrastructure, and trained local police. Pedro Henríquez Ureña and his brothers arrived in New York after completing secondary school in Santo Domingo in 1901, sent by their father to attend Columbia University. Pedro Henríquez Ureña (1884–1946) was "the literary figure with by far the most international recognition" (Torres-Saillant *Before Diaspora* 261). Torres-Saillant argues the significance of New York in Pedro Henríquez Ureña's development as a professional writer and literary scholar: "one could contend that it was in the context of his New York experience that he, devoid of paternal supervision and protection made the serious decision to become a professional writer and literary scholar" (261). Ureña wrote regularly for the New York periodical *Las novedades* founded by Francisco José Peynado, Dominican intellectual and businessman. There was much anti-Trujillo activity in New York in the 1940s. Writers published in local Hispanic publications such as *Visión*, *La Prensa*, and *El Diario de Nueva York*.

While the Henríquez Ureña brothers, Pedro and Max, receive most of the literary and intellectual attention, their sister Salomé Camila Henríquez Ureña (1894–1973) remains in their shadow. She was born in Santo Domingo as the fourth child and only daughter of poet Salomé Ureña de Henríquez (1850–1897) and intellectual Francisco Henríquez y Carvajal (1857–1935). Her life of travel, as that of her brothers, began soon after her mother's death. She lived in various parts of the world, including Haiti, Santiago de Cuba, and Minnesota. She served on the faculty of Vassar College in the Department of Hispanic Studies from the years 1942–1959 and later retired in Cuba where she remained until her death in 1973. Her greatest contribution to the genre of the essay in the Hispanic Caribbean is her collection of essays on the contributions of women titled "Feminismo" (1939), "La mujer y la cultura" (1949), and "La carta como forma de expression literaria femenina" (1951) (Cocco de Filippis 2007).

Virginia de Peña de Bordas (1904–1948) is another important early Dominican woman writer who lived and studied in the United States during the 1920s. Most of her work was published posthumously by her husband. She is the author of *La princesa de los caballos platinados y la eracra de oro* (1978), the novel *Toeya* (1952) in the Indianist tradition and *Seis novelas cortas* (1978). Her experience abroad is reflected in her work as she often set her work in the United States and much of it was originally written in English. In her writing she raises important questions about the experiences of Caribbean women writers and their place in literary and cultural history (Cocco de Filippis 2002). Cocco de Filippis has noted the prevalence of foreign locations or settings in the novels of Dominican women writers before 1950s who tend to set their plots in faraway lands, preferring the "tourist's gaze" (2002, 53). Other writers who spent time abroad during this early period include José Bernard (1873–1954), Fabio Fiallo (1866–1942), and Manuel Florentino Cestero (1879–1926).

In 1930, Trujillo installed the longest and harshest dictatorship in the Dominican Republic of the twentieth century. Many fled the island and were exiled for political reasons. In 1965, U.S. troops once again occupied the island. In 1962, Juan Bosch briefly became president in a democratic election, but was later exiled to Puerto Rico in 1965 because of his communist sympathies. Joaquín Balaguer followed him in office in 1966 and again from 1970–1974. With U.S. aid, higher sugar prices, and growing investments the country seemed to prosper through the mid-1970s. However, the poor became poorer, unemployment increased, and sugar prices dropped. In 1979, two devastating hurricanes left many homeless. The economy of the Dominican Republic remained depressed during the 1980s, sugar prices remained low, and the population continued to grow. Tourism boomed and became the most important source of foreign income.

During the twentieth century Dominican literature has been particularly concerned with the Trujillo dictatorship. The dictatorship sent into exile Dominican writers such as Juan Isidro Jimenes Grullón, Juan Bosch, and Pedro Mir who continued to organize against Trujillo from abroad.

Dominican literature in the United States has remained greatly invisible among studies of American Literature. The development of literary magazines has been significant in promoting and publishing the work of Dominicans in the United States. These magazines include *Letras e imágenes* (1981–82), *Inquietudes* (1981–82), *Punto 7 Review* (1985–), and *Alcance*. A number of anthologies by Franklin Gutiérrez such as *Espiga del Siglo* (1984), *Niveles del imán* (1983), and *Voces del exilio* (1986) as well as an anthology by Daisy Cocco de Filippis titled *Poems of Exile and Other Concerns* (1988) have helped to render Dominican literature more visible and accessible in the United States. The success of writers such as Julia Alvarez and Junot Díaz has helped to bring more attention to Dominican literature.

Recent writers address themes that reflect life in the U.S., writing about their relationship to the past, loss of identity, the pressure to assimilate, and the search for the American dream. These writers also write about the experience of exile and their experience of racism within U.S. racial politics. Santiago Gutiérrez Campo (1956–) was born in the Dominican Republic and lived in New York for many years. He is the editor of *Universal Prensa* published in New York. He has published a collection of short stories *Los perros de la noche* (1993). His stories have appeared in magazines in the United States and the Dominican

Republic. José Carvajal (1961–) is a writer and journalist who was born in the Dominican Republic and has lived in New York since 1974. He has written for local papers and founded the cultural paper *Mambrú y cultura* that has helped to promote the literature written by Dominicans and other Latin Americans in metropolitan centers. He has also published the novel, *Por nada del mundo* (1991). Tomás Modesto Galán has lived in the United States since 1986 where he wrote the collection of stories *Los niños del Monte Edén* (1998) and the novel *Los cuentos de Mount Hope* (1995) where he explores the struggles faced by Latin American immigrants to the United States. One of the recent Dominican women writers in the United States is Marianela Medrano (1964–) who was born in the Dominican Republic and has lived in the United States since 1990. Her poetry has been published in various magazines including *Callaloo Magazine, Sister of Caliban: Contemporary Woman poets of the Caribbean and Central America, Letras Femeninas,* among others. Her collections of poetry include *Oficio de vivir* (1986), *Las alegres ojos de la tristeza* (1987), and *Curada de espantos* (2002). Yrene Santos López lives in New York and her work has been included in collections such as *Tertuliando/Hanging Out* (1997), *Conversación entre mujeres del Caribe Hispano* (1999), and she has also published the collections of poems titled *Desnudez del silencio* (1987), and *El incansable juego* (2003).

The literature written by Cuban, Puerto Rican, and Dominican writers abroad and their corresponding diasporas, challenge established cultural norms and expand our traditional notions of national literatures. These writers explore questions about identity such as, What does it mean to be Puerto Rican, Cuban, or Dominican? They raise questions about citizenship, residency, and community when they ask, How do we relate to traditions and customs? What are the boundaries of our community? They critique notions of race when they ask: How do we relate to our blackness and our African Heritage? They explore notions of gender and sexuality in questions such as: What are traditional gender roles? How do I express my sexuality? The essays included in *Hispanic Caribbean Literature of Migration: Narratives of Displacement* are organized around the four themes of migratory identities, origins and residency, gender and sexuality, and race.

The chapters included in *Migratory Identities* explore the literature of early Caribbean migrants José Martí, Juan Bosch, and Julia de Burgos. Active political writers, they championed hemispheric unity and solidarity against colonialism and imperialism. It is important to note that though they spent significant time abroad, their work is still incorporated into national literary canons in their countries of origins. We may note the importance of language choice by the author here. Because their work is almost exclusively in Spanish, it is incorporated into literary canons in their countries of origin, despite ideological rifts that existed between them and their contemporaries. In "The Unbreakable Voice in a Minor Language: Following José Martí's Migratory Routes," Laura Lomas establishes Martí as the initiator of a tradition of Latin American diasporic writing in the United States. She characterizes this literature as one where the author maintains uneasy relationships with both the host country and the homeland. In "*Mas que Cenizas*: An Analysis of Juan Bosch's Dissident Narration of *Dominicanidid* (Ausente)," Lorgia García Peña examines the relationship between literature, exile, and national identity. She credits Juan Bosch for initiating a revolutionary narrative project that transformed Dominican letters and expanded national boundaries to include the voices of the Dominican diaspora into the national dialogue. Her chapter offers a thoughtful look at the importance of exile and migration in the construction of a new under-standing of *dominicanidad*. Vanessa Pérez Rosario's chapter "Creating *Latinidad*: Julia de Burgos' Legacy in U.S. Latina Literature" focuses on Julia de Burgos' time in New York, situating her among other early New York Puerto Rican writers such as Jesús Colón and Bernardo Vega while highlighting her importance among Puerto Rican diaspora women writers of the late twentieth and early twenty-first centuries. These chapters recognize the ways that Martí, Bosch, and de Burgos expand traditional notions of national identity and anticipate the cultural expressions of later Caribbean Latino writers.

The chapters included in *Dislocated Narratives* explore questions of residency, citizenship, and belonging. In her chapter "Travel and Family in Julia Alvarez' Canon," Vivian Nun Halloran explores the importance of class on the experience of exile and diaspora in Julia Alvarez's work. Alvarez uses the trope of the family, Halloran argues, to demonstrate that the experience of exile has a lasting effect on the country the exiles leave behind as well as the home where they choose to settle. Ylce Irizarry contends that Junot Díaz performs several ethical interventions in his collection of short stories *Drown,* disrupting the dominant U.S. story of migration, acculturation, and belonging in her chapter "Making It Home: An New Ethics of Immigration in Dominican Literature" estab-lishing a *narrative of fracture* that challenges the dominant narratives of arrival. She questions how Latino/a writers narrate the Dominican immi-gration story to the United States if *arrival* is not the final goal. She notes that Díaz's narratives neither privilege nostalgia nor the idea of accultur-ation, arguing that the trope of arrival is not possible for working-class, dark-skinned people of the Caribbean. Carolyn Wolfenzon illustrates the way that the characters in Achy Obejas' novel *Days of Awe* resist accom-modation as subjects of multiple diasporas in her chapter "*Days of Awe* and the Jewish Experience of a Cuban Exile: The Case of Achy Obejas." She highlights the way the novel parallels the experience of living in exile to the Jewish Days of Awe—a time out of time—a state of permanent indeterminancy.

The chapters included in *Gender Crossings* explore the role of gender, homosexuality, and sexual orientation as causal factors for migration as revealed in Caribbean literature. The literature reveals that the social intolerance, discrimination, harassment, persecution, and other forms of violence experienced by LGBT characters leads to their exclusion from narrowly constructed national identities finding liberation through movement and migration. In "A Community in Transit: The Performative Gestures of Manuel Ramos Otero's Narrative Triptych," Mónica Lladó-Ortega traces Manuel Ramos Otero's development of a poetics of transit using autobiographical narrative strategies that also move between fiction and history, the collective and the individual. In this way he challenges Island's insular discourses on nationalism and rejects totalizing metaphors and fixed geographical boundaries. Ana Belén Martín Sevillano demonstrates in "A Revolution in Pink: Cuban Queer Literature Inside and Outside the Island" that exile became the territory where a queer and Cuban subject could be created in literature. She highlights the influence of exiled writers, Arenas and Sarduy, on a later generation of queer island-based writers Pedro de Jesús Lopez and Ena Lucía Portela and suggests that in this way these texts written from abroad form an integral part of the national literary canon, thus, ultimately confirming that exile is another territory of the nation. In "Gender Pirates of the Caribbean: Queering Caribbeanness in the Novels of Zoé Valdés and Christopher John Farley," Omise'eke Natasha Tinsley critiques contemporary U.S. media representations of the Caribbean as a site of backward sexual politics, for not simultaneously examining U.S. policies toward LGBT rights. Tinsley examines the novels *Lobas de mar* (2003) written by Cuban-born Zoé Valdés and *Kingston by Starlight* (2005) by Jamaican-born Christopher John Farley where these diasporic writers reverse the dominant discourse and imagine the Caribbean as a haven where northerners can travel to live out "fluid gender, sexual, racial, and class identities." Tinsley reveals the ways in which Valdés and Farley use fiction as a space to question the ways in which "sexual progress flows," imagining new possibilities and opening up a space for dialogue.

The collection closes with *Racial Migrations*, an exploration of the racializing process that many Caribbean Latinas/os experience as they migrate to the United States. In "Insular Interventions: Jesús Colón Unmasks Racial Harmonizing and Populist Uplift Discourses in Puerto Rico," Maritza Stanchich investigates the way that diasporic writer Jesús Colón exposes the incommensurability between racial discourses in the United States and on the island, destabilizing them both. She highlights how Jesús Colón's work anticipates the civil rights discourses of the 1960s and the Nuyorican movement of the 1970s. Yolanda Martinez-San

Miguel sheds light on the relationship between racism and colonialism in "Coloniality of Diasporas: Racialization of Negropolitans and Nuyoricans in Paris and New York," exposing the racializing process of colonial subjects who cross racial and cultural boundaries and become problematic members of metropolitan societies. She explores the limits of postcolonial discourse in two postcolonial Caribbean texts, Frantz Fanon's, *Black Skin, White Masks* and Piri Thomas' *Down These Mean Streets*, revealing the inherent contradictions in modern postcolonial state discourses. In the closing chapter "The Dominican Diaspora Strikes Back: Cultural Archive and Race in Junot Díaz's *The Brief Life of Oscar Wao*," Juanita Heredia draws on Paul Gilroy and Silvio Torres-Saillant's understanding of racial legacy in the multiple diasporas of the Dominican community in the United States. She reveals the way that Díaz's novel challenges gender and racial stereotypes critiquing race and gender master narratives in both the United States and the Dominican Republic.

This collection aims to illustrate the way that Puerto Rican, Cuban, and Dominican writers re-tell the experiences of multiple migrations, crossings, and movements between borders, languages, identities, and discourses. While their narratives at times appear to be displaced, the essays reveal that discourse is always placed, and Caribbean Latino writers speak and write from a particular place, and historical moment. The writers considered herein develop new forms of self-expression and representation that allow them to constitute "new kinds of subjects and thereby enable us to discover places from which to speak" (Hall 402).

Notes

1. Julio Ramos explores the way that José Martí distinguishes himself from the Latin American enlightened *letrados* such Andres Bello and Domingo Sarmiento, establishing a new kind of intellectual tradition in the Americas. See Julio Ramos' *Divergent Modernities: Culture and Politics in Nineteenth-Century Latin America* (Duke University Press, 2001).
2. The first Cuban exile press was founded by Father Felix Varela (1788–1853) in Philadelphia in 1824 with *El Habanero*, a Spanish-language paper which openly called for Cuban independence from Spain. Not long after, in 1828, other Cubans and Puerto Ricans would establish two newspapers in exile from New York, *El Mensajero Semanal* and *El Mercurio de Nueva York*. Varela was an intellectual who translated works by U.S. political leaders and thinkers of the time such as Paine and Jefferson and smuggled these translations into Latin America. In fact, Varela was considered the most popular writer in Cuba during the latter half of the twentieth century and his books were seen as the only bestsellers in Cuba, even though his name was banned on the island because of his outspokenness against the Spanish government (Fornet 73–74). Father Varela set the precedence among Puerto Ricans and Cubans for writing their political critiques from abroad and smuggling them

into their home countries and other parts of Latin America (Kanellos 10). It was not long before other Cuban and Puerto Ricans calling for independence followed in his footsteps and published papers abroad carrying their message for liberation.

3. Lazo notes that the "militant" and revolutionary language of this poetry is a consequence of "transnational conditions" and shows why *filibustero* poetry is a product of both Cuba and the United States in his study *Writing to Cuba: Filibustering and Cuban Exiles in the United States* (47). These writers are able to imagine an independent Cuba, because they write and publish from abroad creating what Lazo characterizes as "deterritorialized" writing because it simultaneously "provides a potential for liberation" and "a separation from the social structures" that these exiled writers struggle to change (55). He concludes that transnational writing is "always deterritorialized in the sense that to stop in one country is to be separated from the other. Transnational writing moves in and out of one nation and then another, meaning that it moves beyond and within the nation" (55).

4. For more on the emergence of a Cuban popular nationalism among exile Cuban communities during the nineteenth century and their contributions to *cubanidad* see Gerald Poyo's book '*With All, and for the Good of All': The Emergence of Popular Nationalism in the Cuban Communities in the United States, 1848-1898* (Duke University Press, 1989).

5. Another important Cuban nationalist writer who spent significant time abroad is Cirilio Villaverde (1812–1894). Villaverde is remembered for writing the great nineteenth-century Cuban *costumbrismo* novel, *Cecilia Valdez o La Loma del Angel* in 1882, however, it is often forgotten that *Cecilia Valdés*, the novel that has come to signify Cuban nationalism, was written in exile. Lazo notes that "the ideological interweaving of author, novel, and nation in studies of Villaverde has overshadowed decades of his work in the United States and his participation in a Cuban American writing community that emerged in New York in the late 1840s" (Lazo, *Action* 316). Cirilio Villaverde went into exile in 1849 in New York where he lived and worked as a political journalist and activist for forty-five years. He edited and contributed to several exile newspapers such as *La Verdad* (1852), *La Voz de America* (1865), *La Ilustración Americana* (1866), and *El Espejo* (1873) promoting militant Cuban independence from Spain. Villaverde's extended period in New York establishes him as important precursor to Martí although he is not often read or remembered in this way because he is mostly remembered for his novel *Cecilia Valdes* and not for his writings for the Cuban exile press (Lazo).

6. For more on Martí's ability to unite the Cuban exile communities in New York and Florida, see Gerald Poyo's book '*With All, and for the Good of All*'.

7. Flores notes that the writing by those political exiles in New York during the nineteenth century who fought for independence from Spain alongside Cubans such as "provide an invaluable antecedent perspective, a prelude of foreboding" of the literature and history of Puerto Ricans in New York (Flores 57). See Juan Flores, "Puerto Rican Literature in the United States: Stages and Perspectives." *Recovering the U.S. Hispanic Literary Heritage Vol. I.* Eds. Ramón Gutiérrez and Genaro Padilla (Houston: Arte Público Press, 1993, 53–67).

8. Early Dominican literature is absent from discussions of literature from the Spanish Caribbean. Examining the "political and cultural exchange between the two sovereignties, it becomes possible to trace the literary activity of Dominican in the United States back to the founding of the Dominican nation" (255).

9. For more on early Dominican writers in the United States see Silvio Torres-Saillant's essay "Before the Diaspora: Early Dominican Literature in the United States" and Daisy Cocco de Filippis and Franklin Gutierrez's collection *Literatura dominicana en los Estados Unidos: Presencia temprana 1900-1960*.

10. See Virginia Sanchez Korrol, *From Colonia to Community: The History of Puerto Ricans in New York* (Berkeley: University of California Press, 1994).

11. See Edna Acosta-Belen, "The Building of a Community." *Recovering the U.S. Hispanic Literary Heritage Vol. I*. Eds. Ramon Gutierrez and Genaro Padilla (Houston: Arte Publico Press, 1993, 179–195).

12. See *None of the Above: Puerto Ricans in the Global Era* edited by Frances Negrón Muntaner (Palgrave Macmillan 2007).

13. See *Divided Borders: Essays on Puerto Rican Identity* by Juan Flores (Houston: Arte Publico Press, 1993).

14. See Flores, *Divided Borders*.

15. José Torres-Padilla and Carmen Haydee Rivera. *Writing off the Hyphen: New Perspectives on the Literature of the Puerto Rican Diaspora* (Seattle: University of Washington, 2008).

16. See William Luis, *Dance Between Two Cultures*.

Works Cited

Acosta-Belén, Edna. "The Building of a Community: Puerto Rican Writers and Activists in New York City (1890s–1960s)." *Recovering the U.S. Hispanic Literary Heritage Vol. I*. Eds. Ramon Gutierrez and Genaro Padilla. Houston: Arte Publico Press, 1993. 179–195.

Anderson, Benedict. *Imagined Communities: Reflections on the Origin and Spread of Nationalism*. London: Verso, 2006.

Cocco de Filippis, Daisy. *Desde la diáspora: A Diaspora Position*. NY: Alcance, 2003.

———. "Una flor en la sombra: A Critical Edition of the Complete Works of Virginia de Peña de Bordas." *Recovering the U.S. Hispanic Literary Heritage Vol. IV*. Eds. José Aranda and Silvio Torres-Saillant. Houston: Arte Publico Press, 2002.

———. Hija de Camila: Camila's Line. Santo Domingo: Editorial Nacional, 2007.

Cocco de Filippis, Daisy and Franklin Gutierrez, eds. *Literatura domincana en los Estados Unidos: Presencia temprana 1900–1960*. Santo Domingo: Editora Búho, 2001.

Flores, Juan. *The Diaspora Strikes Back: Caribeño Tales of Learning and Turning*. NY: Routledge, 2009.

Flores, Juan. "Puerto Rican Literature in the United States: Stages and Perspectives." *Recovering the U.S. Hispanic Literary Heritage Vol. I*. Houston: Arte Publico Press, 1993. 55–68.

Gutiérrez, Franklin. *Voces de Ultramar: Literatura Dominicana de la diáspora*. Santo Domingo: Dirreción General de la Feria del Libro, 2005.

Hall, Stuart. "Cultural Identity and Diaspora." Colonial Discourse and Post-Colonial Theory: A Reader. Ed. Patrick Williams and Laura Chrisman. New York: Columbia University Press, 1994. 392-403.

Hoffnung-Garskof, Jesse. "The Migrations of Arturo Schomburg: On Being Antillano, Negro, and Puerto Rican in New York 1891–1938." *Journal of American Ethnic History* (Fall 2001): 3–49

Kanellos, Nicolas & Helvetia Martell. *Hispanic Periodicals in the United States Origins to 1960: A Brief History and Comprehensive Bibliography*. Houston: Arte Publico Press, 2000.

Lazo, Rodrigo. *Writing to Cuba: Filibustering and Cuban Exiles in the United States*. Chapel Hill: University of North Carolina Press, 2005.

———. " 'A Man of Action': Cirilo Villaverde as Trans-American Revolutionary Writer." *Recovering the U.S. Hispanic Literary Heritage Vol. III*. Eds. Virginia Sanchez Korrol and Maria Herrera Sobek. Houston: Arte Publico Press, 2000.

Lomas, Laura. *Translating Empire: José Martí, Migrant Latino Subjects, and American Modernities*. Durham: Duke University Press, 2008.

Luis, William. *Dance Between Two Cultures: Latino Caribbean Literature Written in the United States*. Nashville: Vanderbilt University Press, 1997.

Negrón-Muntaner, Frances, ed. *None of the Above: Puerto Ricans in the Global Era*. New York: Palgrave Macmillan, 2007.

Ramos, Julio. *Amor y anarquía: Los escritos de Luisa Capetillo*. Río Piedras: Ediciones Huracán. 1992.

———. *Divergent Modernities: Culture and Politics in Nineteenth-Century Latin America*. Trans. John D. Blanco. Durham: Duke University Press, 2001.

Said, Edward. "Reflections on Exile." *Reflections on Exile and Other Essays*. Cambridge, MA: Harvard University Press, 2003.

Sanchez Korrol, Virginia and Vicki Ruiz, eds. *Latina Legacies: Identity, Biography, and Community*. New York: Oxford University Press, 2005.

Torres-Padilla, José and Carmen Haydée Rivera, eds. *Writing Off the Hyphen: New Perspectives on the Literature of the Puerto Rican Diaspora*. Seattle: University of Washington Press, 2008.

Torres-Saillant, Silvio. "Before the Diaspora: Early Dominican Literature in the United States." *Recovering the U.S. Hispanic Literary Heritage Vol. III*. Eds. Virginia Sanchez Korrol and Maria Herrera Sobek. Houston: Arte Publico Press, 2000.

———. *El retorno de las yolas: Ensayos sobre diáspora, democracia y dominicanidad*. Santo Domingo: Editora Manatí, 1999.

I

Migratory Identities

The Unbreakable Voice in a Minor Language: Following José Martí's Migratory Routes

Laura Lomas

Pero no te voy a negar que Martí fue, inter alia, el primer gran escritor latino de Nueva York. Escribió sobre los anarquistas, los inmigrantes de Chicago, sobre Nueva York como sólo podía odiarla y quererla un boricua del Lower East Side.

—Julio Ramos (*Por si nos da el tiempo*, 2002)

*la que en tu voz herida viera herirse
la patria que en tus labios se le fuera.*

—Julia de Burgos ("Canto a Martí," 1996)

Following the circumlocutions of the double negation in the epigraph above, let us take as a point of departure Julio X. Ramos' comment to his interviewer in Julio Ramos' novella *Por si nos da el tiempo* (2002), in which the narrator announces José Martí as the first great writer in a tradition of Latino writing in New York.[1] In this novella, the principal narrator—an academic who recalls encounters of Latino and Latin American writers in transitory public spaces, while examining the City of San Francisco from behind bars—elliptically proposes the obvious: that the errancy, displacement, and deterritorialization of migration make possible the literature of the Latin American diaspora in the United States: "Todo, o casi todo, comenzó con un viaje" (9). Migration, which begins with a voyage, makes it possible for the narrator to tell the story, for it shapes the deterritorialized subject, who is marked by the juxtaposition of distinct cultural elements, idioms, and fragments, and by the self-conscious power of the Latino voice to remake colonial legacies. Migratory Hispanic Caribbean writers who claim José Martí as a forerunner in New York enable us to rethink the quintessential exiled writer also as a Latino migrant.[2]

How migration to New York City shapes Latino diasporic writing becomes clear as the reader imagines—and listens to—conversations in this mixture of criticism, oral history, and fiction. By Latino diasporic writing I refer to literature of Latin Americans living outside the region for economic or political reasons over an extended period. José Martí, for example, resided in New York for fourteen years before returning to Cuba to fight in the war for independence. An aesthetic and dialogic engagement with a minor language—in this case Spanish in the United States—rather than with a single place of origin—defines Latino literature, whether written in Spanish or English. Latino diasporic writing in Spanish maintains intimate and uneasy relations to both the host country's and homeland's literature. Over a century of Latino literary texts challenge our understanding of any literature's relationship to a single nation or a linguistic and ethnic subculture: it is not coincidental that we owe the crucial concept-metaphor of the border to Chicana/o and Latina/o Studies.[3] Thus, while the history of Latino writing in New York that José Martí launches may be a nationalist literature of exile, it also dialogues with and helps to remake the dominant, host culture of the Anglo-American metropole. Latino diasporic writing from Martí to the present evokes an evanescent, transgressive spoken word in a minor language as a means of cultural survival, affiliation, and collective protest against the isolation and disdain of the Anglo-dominant city.

Martí's poignant responses to life in New York—in poetry and prose—reveal both this cry of protest and a sense of possibility and wonder due not so much to making money or to upward mobility as to the potential of a politicized, culturally conscious, migrant community. Like earlier Mexican-American writer Francisco Ramirez or the early Cuban exile writer Félix Varela, who both criticized the denial of freedom to people of color in the United States and signaled the hypocrisy of slavery, Martí decried white racial bias.[4] Building on these precursors, Martí affirms his readership as "gente latina," by which he means a multiracial, and bilingual culture of Latin American origin that in New York is marked by processes of migration.[5] Observing a family strolling together outside New York's public library, Martí, who lived separated from his wife and son most of his years in New York, notes the despair of the migrant in the stranger's gait: "iba con ese paso lento con que se anda en las tierras extrañas" (OC 22: 253). To counteract this melancholy foreignness and longing to add to the archive of his *América*, Martí joined gatherings of artists, poets, intellectuals, and activists in creating a Latino subculture in New York. Common experiences shared by members of "la raza" mysteriously unifed displaced Latin Americans in New York: "La raza es vara de mago, rosa mística, calor en el invierno, pueblo inefable, y resurrección de la misma muerte en medio de la soledad: en tierra extraña se cae en brazos de un desconocido de nuestras propias tierras sollozando de júbilo, como se caería en brazos de un hermano."[6] Martí's lesser-known contemporaries such as Francisco Gonzalo "Pachín" Marín, Manuel Pichardo, Latin American essayists such as Rubén Darío and Gabriela Mistral, pioneer Latino memoirists such as Bernardo Vega, freelance journalists, poets, and political activists of the mid-twentieth century such as Julia de Burgos and Jesus Colón, and contemporary writers such as Julio Ramos and Francisco Goldman celebrate, remember, and invoke Martí. Together, these texts sketch the interconnections of Latino writing and migration, and reveal Martí's key role in this tradition. Shifting emphasis away from the monumentalizing busts and statues that have tended to cement Martí in his role as founding father of Cuba's national culture, Latina/o writers from the nineteenth-century to the present found in Martí's poetry and prose resonances that inspired their own literary work. Martí and subsequent writers underscore how contact among languages generatively can remake colonial and imperial linguistic legacies from the inside. These writings gesture to how the innovative practices of *la voz* and *la lengua* in and beyond the written word, enact a form of anti-colonial vengeance.

1.1   La Voz y La Lengua

These two terms—which I have reduced to the weak English equivalents of "voice" and "language" in my title—have complex, untranslatable multivalences in Spanish, which illuminate why Latino diasporic writing insistently refers to these terms to distinguish itself from other traditions that assume their linguistic medium to be unaffected by other languages. Interestingly, texts of this diaspora in Spanish use a formerly colonial language to express a minor subjectivity, so they give expression to the historicity and mutability of any language's position. Although certainly U.S. Latino texts written entirely or mostly in English also reveal the effects of linguistic difference, texts written in Spanish in the United States define their minority status from the very first word. While English-language Latino literature—such as in the Nuyorican tradition now performed at cafés around the United States—also evokes a distinct Latin American Spanish grammar and bilingual imaginary that transgresses the rules of Standard American English, Spanish-language texts in the United States problematize the notion of ready fungibility across languages.

The *Real Academia de la Lengua Española* attributes to the vocable *voz* several acceptions, which include the sound of air passing through the vocal chords, but also, a word or a vocable. *Voz* is also a grammatical classification that reveals activity or passivity in execution. It implies the faculty of speaking, but does not confer the right to vote. Like the Latina/o migrant who feels tied to the United States, who may love and hate the city where she or he makes a life, *la voz* evokes the persistent creativity and transformative influence of the millions who—because of their economic or juridical situation, or because of the economic under-development of Latin America—reside in a limbo where they are unable to leave the United States even though they enjoy neither citizenship rights nor full civil, labor, or human rights. Made up of a string of *voces*, *la lengua* connotes language—a culturally specific semiotic system and a sense of shared aesthetic criteria. It also suggests a site of desire, oral-ity, and intimacy perceived by the material density of a bodily organ, the tongue. *Lengua* connotes abstractly and concretely, refusing the clas-sic Manichean separation of the physical and metaphysical. The mul-tiple meanings of both terms in Spanish create a space for clandestine memory, merciless ridicule, wordplay, and secret uspeakable histories to which Latino diasporic writing sometimes alludes. These writers often have little choice but to make their critique of empire or of racism ironi-cally or in code. Their texts draw on the unbreakable cry, the solidarity of other voices, and the humor that flies under the radar of a dominant language to overcome the isolation and sense of not being heard that Latina/o migrants have all too often encountered in New York.[7] This essay begins by reading Martí during his sojourn in New York City, and then traces twentieth-century Latino diasporic writing that invokes Martí and invites us to imagine him in a migratory tradition.

1.2 José Martí and His Interlocutors: "Voces Americanas"

Why does language become a refuge, a weapon, and an object of struggle for Martí and others of this tradition? Language survives the anguish of *el destierro* and provides solace and joy despite separation from the home-land. Voice reclaims and remakes a linguistic inheritance and becomes a medium of creativity and expression in the wake of colonial and imperial dispossession. Between a violent uprooting from Cuba as a seventeen-year-old deportee and a magical reencounter with his native land as part of the invasion that launched the war of Cuban independence of 1895, José Martí lived mostly at a distance from his island. He penned his major essays, including "Nuestra América," his critical assessments of Ralph Waldo Emerson, Walt Whitman, Oscar Wilde, and José Antonio Pérez Bonalde, several volumes of *modernismo* poetry and thousands of pages of literary journalism or *crónicas* in the emerging American empire's belly. Martí's peripatetic course after two political exiles to Spain and a series of attempts at making a life in Mexico, Guatemala, and Venezuela culminated in a fourteen-year residence in New York. As he put it in his letter of April 22, 1886, to Manuel Mercado, "todo me ata a esta copa de veneno" (*Epistolario* 1; 332).

Language becomes a weapon of denunciation and secret warning in the midst of the racial violence of late-nineteenth century United States. Martí lived in New York in the wake of a failed Reconstruction that witnessed the rise of lynch law and Jim Crow. He noted in his chronicles the Chinese Exclusion Acts and the massacre of Chinese migrant workers in Rock Springs, Wyoming in 1885. He alludes to the final stages of Indian removal, the widespread practice of the Ghost Dance, and the massacre at Wounded Knee. As a former resident of Mexico, he wrote with horror about the continued U.S. plots to annex Mexico's mineral-rich Northern States. Even while working in the relatively privileged position of a freelance writer, a diplomat and a teacher, Martí came to identify with the assassinated anarchists of the Haymarket Affair and drew connections between the anti-immigrant and white supremacist violence of this period. By the late 1880s, he would warn his readers about the arrogance of U.S. travel writers who had become authoritative interpreters of culture and politics in Mexico and Argentina. To combat this misinformation, Martí called for a new mode of infiltrative translation by Latinas/os inside the United States, which might warn his *América* of the pernicious views their northern neighbors harbored.[8]

Martí lived in the United States as a migrant—without ever becoming a citizen. His journalism emphasized the liminal moments of arrival during the constant waves of arrivants during these years, which permits him to illustrate for his readers common vulnerabilities and aspirations among Latino migrants and other groups struggling with the lasting effects of conquest, enslavement, and xenophobia. José Martí compared Castle Garden, the point of entry for thousands of immigrants in the nineteenth century to a "maravilloso monstruo," the open door that he and others began to fear for its "fauce enorme" (OC 9: 290). His slightly younger contemporary, Francisco Gonzálo "Pachín" Marín, a Puerto Rican who died in the Cuban manigua after migrating through several Caribbean islands, echoed Martí's sentiments when he noted New York City's tendency to swallow migrants alive, as if it were "la boca de un horrible monstruo ocupado constantemente en tragar y vomitar a la vez seres humanos; y es en medio de estos grandes ruidos y de estos grandes centros donde con más frecuencia nuestra alma se ve atacada de esa horrorosa enfermedad que se llama tristeza y toma los caracteres sombríos del aislamiento y del silencio" (61). Both Martí and Marín note the monstrosity of a society that voraciously consumes the labor of millions of migrant workers yet arbitrarily devalues their culture and retains the right to eject them from one moment to the next. To the instability of migration, Latino migrant writing responds by representing the power of voice and language.

As the émigré community continued to grow in the wake of anti-colonial wars in Cuba and Puerto Rico, Spanish-language conversations in semi-public waystations of migrants and travelers, such as hotel lobbies, restaurants, or boarding houses began to transform the public space of the city. Martí revelled in what the New York Puerto Rican Guillermo Cotto-Thorner would later describe as the "tropics in Manhattan," as Latino migrants commenced the claiming and marking of their urban landscape as home to people from Latin America and the Caribbean, a process Frances Aparicio and Susan Chávez-Silverman have called "tropicalization."[9] On the occasion of the celebration of Bolívar's centenary, Martí describes the covering of the enormous dining room of Delmonico's in New York with tropical palms and the flags of his *América*. *Hispanoamericanos* cheered when Martí's Venezuelan friend, Pérez Bonalde, declared "del Bravo al Plata no hay más que un solo pueblo":

> notábese que en la fiesta nadie andaba solo, ni triste, ni encogido; parecía que se juntaban todos a la sombra de una bandera de paz, o que una inmensa ala amorosa, tendida allá en el cielo de la espalda que sustenta un mundo, cobijaba a los hombres alegres. Por los salones, llenos de flores, palmas y banderas, andaban en grupos, hermanando de súbito, hombres de opuestos climas, y unidos por la fama....Alegría es poco; era júbilo; júbilo cordial, expansivo, discreto.[10]

Whereas the dominant culture often aimed to atomize and divide the Latino community in the United States, the celebration of Bolívar illustrated to the attendees the power of coalition. The vision of a posh Latino Delmonicos filled Martí with jubilation.

Like the restaurant, the boarding house, the Pullman car, and the hotel lobby have offered a hybrid between home and public space for conversation in the urban Latina/o diasporic intellectual tradition from Martí's time to the present. Martí's brief advertisement for a Venezuelan boarding house in *La América* suggests his intimate knowledge of what the Latin American without a "casa propia" in a foreign country hopes to find in such temporary residences (OC 28: 530). The train also provided a privileged site for alternative forms of attachment. Félix de los Ríos, a Gallego to whom Martí so passionately described his revolutionary vision while riding together on a train, decided to take the first steps toward gambling his life in the service of Cuban independence. Martí recommended that de los Ríos stay at the Hotel América, at Irving Place and Fifteenth Street because its policy was to reserve the third floor for "latinos" (over the Hotel Central to which the *gallego* had been directed in still-colonial Havana).[11] These accounts of hotels and trains suggest the tropicalization of public spaces in the late nineteenth century. Martí called on de los Ríos in the parlor of this Hotel América three days later to follow up on his impassioned invitation to the young Spaniard to join the fight. Often these public spaces permitted fervent conspiratorial conversation and strategizing outside the bounds of home.[12]

In the struggle against colonialism and imperialism that Martí likened to David facing Goliath, language and voice proved to be indispensable tools. One of Martí's little-known manuscripts, a glossary of "voces" that records different Latin American cultures' invention of new meanings, illustrates Martí's sense of the power of *la voz* to remake and transform the colonial legacy of Spanish, as part of his broader ideological battle:

> No es mi objeto hacinar en cuerpo horrendo corruptelas insignificantes de voces españolas, porque valdría esto tanto como hacer en España diccionario especial para la lengua de los meracados y los barrios bajos y los pueblos andaluces; sino reunir las voces nacidas en América para denotar cosas propias de sus tierras, y señalar las acepciones nuevas en que se usen palabras que tienen otra consagrada y conocida. (OC 8: 119)

To make the case that new meanings of Spanish words have arisen in the New World, Martí compares these "voces americanas" to the class- and culturally marked dialects within Spain. While this passage reeks of a certain arrogance of the highly educated professional with respect to the language of the marketplace, poor neighborhoods, and of the darker Moorish regions of Spain, this claim also insists on the internal heterogeneity and mutability of the imperial language undergoing change within and along the periphery of Spain's former empire. By citing words like "cholo" to refer to the mestizo of Perú, "la caña" to refer to a great difficulty to be overcome in Santo Domingo, or "el guanaquismo" to refer to that which is proper to El Salvador, "Voces americanas" illustrate Martí's connection to a wide range of Latin American influenced Spanishes, all of which add to the decolonizing power of the voice. By breaking and remaking the existing rules that govern these words' meanings, his America had appropriated and reinvented the significance of a colonial language. This transformation of the language proved a useful tool for poetic invention also, as we shall see.

Although writing of the Latin American diaspora begins with a voyage, it differs from mainstream travel writing. Unlike the European and white North American travel writers' reactions to the flora and fauna of exotic landscapes in poorer and darker regions of the world, writing by Latin Americans in the United States that results from economic displacement reveals a canny sense of the way discourses about race in the nineteenth century serve the interests of the class at the helm of imperial expansion. Although Martí manages to pass himself off as a "Fresh Spaniard" when he writes in English about New York and reproduces a Europeanist bias in some of his early travel writing about Guatemala and Curaçao, he nonetheless becomes—in the course of a fourteen-year residence in New York—different from the European or North American explorers who assumed a disembodied transparency as they surveyed the land and the bodies they expected to soon possess.[13] The experience of living and working in New York during the intensely racialized period of the late nineteenth century leads Martí to challenge the European focus of the "exotic creoles" in his América (which had also been his own). In the United States, he began to define himself as writing for an integrated and multiracial, working-class intellectual readership, both Latina/o and Latin American, that extended from New York throughout the Americas. Martí's writing in the United States responds to both Spanish colonial scars on his teenaged back and to plans he saw taking shape in New York for economic exploitation of Latin America's resources. With his finger sensing the pulse of an inventive migrant subculture of Cubans, Puerto Ricans, and others, Martí learned to read the United States from the position of the racialized migrant, majority working-class and revolutionary-minded group for which he became known as a spokesperson.[14] For migrant writers the difficulty of displacement also can quicken the imagination and facilitate the critique of imposing and aggressive states.

1.3   La Lengua de Martí

A long history of writers celebrate Martí as a literary ancestor precisely because his texts exemplify the transformative effects of migration across national borders upon language and voice, and because of the extent to which Martí creatively transformed Spanish language poetics in the process. According to Rubén Darío, Martí created a new language for Americans who speak Spanish as he forged the weapons of war. For Darío, Martí's lasting and most victorious struggle is not on behalf of the "triste estrella, la estrella solitaria de la Isla, estrella engañosa" (195), but in his invention of his own language: "unos indios sioux [...] hablaban *en lengua de Martí* como el Manitu mismo le inspirase" (198, my emphasis). Darío's eulogy, published in *Los Raros* (1896), emphasizes Martí's use of language to evoke convincingly the sentiments of the Sioux after Wounded Knee. In the pages of his journalism, Martí invents "la lengua de Martí," and it gives voice to the peculiar agonies of postcolonial America. Martí's voice emerges from the mouths of the oppressed groups including his own. As a reporter Martí created a medium and form open enough to give expression to a wide range of cultures he encountered in the United States.

Martí's lasting effect upon a long arc of writing in America reverberates especially in New York–based Hispanic Caribbean writers. These writers give life to an errant, nomadic Martí, whom nationalist accounts tend to discount. Puerto Rican writers, such as Bernardo Vega, Julia de Burgos, Jesús Colón, and Julio Ramos provide evidence of Martí's spectral shaping of a Hispanic Caribbean tradition outside the islands. In a tradition replete with the talking books of the African-influenced tradition, the great Puerto Rican tobacco worker, activist, and historian Bernardo Vega alludes to the key role of animated talk among emigrants, including long transcriptions of oral accounts by his Uncle Antonio Vega, in shaping the community's history. In the opening pages of his *Memorias de Bernardo Vega* (1977), his interlocutors plot an imminent return to Puerto Rico while still aboard the *Coamo* that is transporting them to the United States. A lingering tension takes shape in the space between departure and arrival into the jaws of the "dragón de hierro" New York City (Vega 21). Writing that emerges through migration attenuates the nation's various disciplinary apparatuses, contaminates the fictions of national language and culture, and demands that a migrant's roots become portable.[15]

The process of migration directly impinges on the Latino writer's representation of time. The creation of a fiction while traveling may create a detour whereby the narrator serendipitously regains a chunk of time—a stolen past, a way into the future, and a means to its elaboration. Alternatively, the traumatic experience of cultural displacement frequently creates a desperate sense of having no time. In the Puerto Rican Francisco Gonzálo "Pachín" Márin's sketch, "Nueva York por Dentro," the narrator complains that his brusque initiation into New York life consists of learning that time is crystallized value, so millions walk with such agitation and speed that they trample each other, and continue on their way as if nothing has happened. A few decades later, in a gesture that marks his self-mocking initiation into life in New York, the young Bernardo Vega throws his watch into the sea before docking in front of the Statue of Liberty. Forming part of the chapter's title, the act suggests an unmooring from or rejection of time's surveillance under Fordist capitalism; it also conveys his apprehension of a North American colonial discourse about Puerto Rico as a "vació en el tiempo" (*Memorias* 63). In the socialist Jesús Colón's *A Puerto Rican in New York and Other Sketches* (1961), the captured teenaged stowaway from Cayey could not stop working long enough to see if his "sweaty dirty face would truly be reflected in the plate" that he had cleaned, washed, and shined (23). The absence of his reflection in the products of his labor becomes a figure for the vacuum of knowledge about working class Puerto Ricans' contributions to the economic and cultural advancement of the Western hemisphere. A lack of time that creates a silence stands in contrast to the "clear, strong voice" of the *lector* in the cigar factory of his youth in the opening vignette of the book. In a tradition that emerged in the Hispanic Caribbean, *tabaqueros*, or artesans who rolled cigars, listened to a *lector*, who read novels and Spanish-language newspapers aloud in the workshop. *Tabaqueros* paid the salary and democratically selected the works to be read aloud. This tradition helped to create a highly educated and well-organized working-class among Latino communities along the Eastern seaboard.[16] Along with earlier writers like Marín, the *Sketches* compiled from Colón's contributions to the working-class press, and Vega's collected and collective memories, recapture lost time and recount a Hispanic Caribbean diasporic history of New York before and after the U.S. occupation and colonization of Puerto Rico.

Even as Latina/o narrators and poetic subjects document the desperation and loneliness of life in New York, they also insist on the lasting, yet, still under-recognized contributions of the products of their physical and imaginative cultural labor to the U.S. culture. Vega's astute editor, César Andreu Iglesias, culls from the memoir several of Vega's comments that show how Puerto Rican migrants' combative persistence, political commitments, and creativity have enriched the culture of the United States, from their origins to the present. As emissaries of a post-slavery Caribbean society, *boricuas* practiced what Vega calls a "racial open-mindedness" that, while not itself devoid of racism, European and other working-class immigrant groups never managed to achieve.[17] Working-class multiracial Hispanic Caribbean communities have tended not to collect the wages of whiteness that other light-skinned immigrants have reaped by entering the white-dominant racial system of the United States. Rather, African-influenced Caribbean music and the Hispanic Caribbean Spanish and Spanglish of the urban center have built unbreakable bridges among black and Latina/o groups and have enlivened North American culture. Because of the sharing of compact space in an urban center such as New York, the Hispanic Caribbean community marshalled an effective response to the racializing Anglo stereotype of Cuba and Puerto Rico as "two islands inhabited by savages whom the Americans had beneficently saved from the clutches of the Iberian lion" (xiv). Vega is right to emphasize how the urban location of Puerto Ricans ignited and facilitated what became the broad cultural impact of Latina/o writers. Vega concludes that the political astuteness—exemplified by the *tabaqueros*—helped to amplify the sound of Hispanic Caribbean voices over time.

Another Puerto Rican poet who migrated, Julia de Burgos, launched a powerful cry from Welfare Island, a place at which she did not imagine arriving and which threatened to engulf her in its monstrous jaws. Burgos' "cry" on that island breaks a desperate silence and isolation in the midst of a temporary forgetting. Her voice is "forgotten but unbreakable / among comrades of silence" (*Song of the Simple Truth* 356). In Burgos' two poems addressed in their titles to Martí, "A José Martí" (364) and "Canto a Martí" (386), the poet's wounded voice becomes the medium by which the colony of Puerto Rico reactivates its claim to Martí's legacy and redefines the significance of that legacy. In calling upon Martí to awaken from the dead, both poems define his future significance in terms of Puerto Rico's unfinished liberation. This brilliant move to reconnect Martí to his "isla menor" simultaneously revises misrepresentations of Martí as a pathological dreamer or as pragmatically willing to submit to the inevitable course of annexation.

With humility about her groundbreaking contribution, the poet describes her voice as unfinished or barely made. The poet and the island's voice take on the qualities of Martí's voice:

> La que en tu sangre vio rodar su sangre/ Cuando hundiste en Dos Ríos tu primavera;/ la que en tu voz herida viera herirse/ la patria que en tus labios se le fuera. (386)

Standing for both the seemingly contradictory referents of "la patria" and "la voz," the "la" that repeats in this section of the second stanza binds the two wings of the bird that in Lola Rodríguez de Tío's famous phrase constituted the union of Cuba and Puerto Rico. In the voice of the poet, the wounds of one become the wounds of the other. In Julia de Burgos' lifetime, the *patria* that we would presume Martí to have founded, that is the Cuba of Machado and of Batista, actually becomes evanescent and morphs on the poet's lips: the motherland becomes instead what escaped being spoken by unjust leaders (*se le fuera*). It becomes the silence of "*destierro*" from which the poet shouts, not in weeping, but in a cry of rebellion. Julia de Burgos' "Canto" restages Martí's own transformation of the heroic statuary into living, breathing, avenging men in the *Versos sencillos*. Here, instead of the youthful soldier's terrified touching of the cold statue, the poet's song, the poet's words, the poet's kiss all call upon him to awaken. The voice and tongue have more power than the sword. It awakens Martí so that our memory of him can no longer sleep in the face of the "dolor más grande de América"(288), which now includes not only the islands but also a global empire.

1.4   Martí Nuyorkino: Julio Ramos' *Por si nos da el Tiempo*

In defining a Martí *nuyorkino* or *boricua* as a point of departure for Latino writing in New York, Julio X. Ramos—the fictional character—describes the uprooting of migration as an agonizing but necessary element of the intellectual tradition of a colonized territory. Conjuring the distant homeland and a distinct future through bitter, intimate knowledge of the metropolis, voices in transit transform displacement and loss into a counter-memory of empire in Hispanic Caribbean writings of the diaspora. Ramos' fictional persona suggests that deterritorialization exposes the illusory quality of the continuity and coherence of the subject, in the sense of an individual person, a literary tradition, or a monovocal national culture.

Ramos' novella draws on the groundbreaking scholarship of his influential book—*Desencuentros de la modernidad en América Latina* (1989)—and explores in fiction the implications of his insight that migratory routes are indispensable for Latin American diasporic writing. Calling attention to the limits of academic prose, Ramos makes the centerpiece of his novel a conversation in the lobby of the hotel *Habana Libre* between a professor who shares the author's name and profession and a Chilean graduate student and freelance writer. The conversation exists for the reader as an event in the narrative and as an unpublished manuscript that was to have been published in a projected collection of essays entitled *Los mas raros todavía*, styled after Rubén Darío's volume *Los Raros* (1896). The humorous and self-deprecatory irony of the inclusion of the university professor and authoritative critic among a new generation of "raros"—thus updating Rubén Darío's own 1896 volume, which included Martí alongside Paul Verlaine, Edgar Allan Poe, and others—points to silenced and in some cases unspeakable histories that national and moral imperatives push to the margins in accounts of intellectual and aesthetic accomplishments: the novel returns the reader to "aquello que acaso nunca logrará decir" (102), by enacting a way of writing "como si el futuro ya te hubiera donado un pedazo de tiempo" (47). Despite acknowledging the impossibility of fully recounting this memory, the novella insistently reconstructs overlapping historical narratives in order to illuminate the conditions of Latino diasporic writing, especially as it originates like shimmering sparks in marginal and transitory spaces.

The novella points to the transgressive or effusive forms of a tradition that constantly responds to the overwhelming chill of capitalist modernity. The novella reconstructs Martí's articulations of the difference between himself and the world around him, as someone from the tropics who awakens to a snowy city morning, "como lobo encerrado en las paredes fosforescentes de una vasta sepultura" (OC 9: 243). While the joyful and sometimes obscene consumption of the holidays transpired around him, Martí struggled to find ways to write down his thoughts so as to calm their howling inside the glowing, tomb-like walls of his adopted city. Ramos' fictional Martí elaborates on footnotes in the academic work to find in unpublished poetry, fragments, diaries, letters, prologues, an occasional aside, or oblique image, such as this "enclosed wolf," which reveals the submerged tensions and desires with which the Latino diasporic writer responded to the intense pressures of an artificial urban paradise.

Much as Bernardo Vega and Jesus Colón speak into a void of silenced history and supplement the record with the legends and anecdotes obtained in conversation with lost relatives, Julio Ramos' fictional account of his critical *corpus* reinserts the oral histories of his uncle Pepón Arroyo to reveal the historical and personal conditions that shaped the writing of *Desencuetros*. Construing the published, official, national, or academic narrative as a doubly woven, two-sided text, the novella reveals the knotted reverse side of the tapestry. As a figure of impossible translation that records the opaque poetics that cannot find full expression or transcription, *Por si nos da el tiempo* records, for example, the fictional interview between Ramos and Santiago Lavoe in the lobby of a post–Special Period *Habana Libre*. Here, the traffic of gestures and messages exist outside yet shape the literary history. Literary allusions to a rich and diverse Latin American intellectual tradition and gaps in the conversation point to silenced histories that demand fictive or poetic representation.

Ramos' novella introduces anecdotal histories that explain the urgency of his critical *corpus*. In the novella, the publication of Ramos' work on the relations of aesthetics and politics in Latin America's nineteenth-century coincided with the death in 1989 of his uncle Pepón Arroyo, and he notes his (unachieved) desire to dedicate the book to this long-lost uncle. Arroyo supposedly fled the United States for Ecuador for reasons that while impossible to determine, seem connected to the threat of political imprisonment or worse in the wake of his involvement in preparations for the 1954 attack by four Puerto Rican nationalists on the U.S. Congress. Stories circulated in the family about his pursuit of *una mala mujer*, a woman from the Afro-Ecuadorean city of Esmeralda, and of his Hotel Puerto Rico located in the impoverished colonial section of Quito. This fictional account ultimately upholds the mysterious "golden-armed" hotelier's—and the interviewed critic's—right to obscurity.[18]

Writers in the Hispanic Caribbean tradition articulate responses to the threat of the violent imposition of U.S. culture, but as Ramos' novel reveals, these reactions rarely appear in straightforward or transparent forms. An irretrievable immediacy, the voice—in the context of conversations in front of the sea, in hotel lobby interviews, in discussions of revolutionary projects in a minor language—permits the necessary clandestinity of insurgency. In the novella, the active or former guerrilla organizer or collaborators, congregants in lobbies and semi-clandestine intellectuals all live with constant surveillance and threat of criminalization that has become a hallmark of capitalist modernity. For example, Ramos' character confidentially comments on the various lives of the

North American modernist William Carlos Williams—who spent several days drinking Jamaican rum in Rutherford, New Jersey, with the same Pepón Arroyo—and of Casey Calvert, the Baltimore, Maryland-born Cuban writer whose suicide in Rome raised critical suspicions about his intense desire for an impossible return to Cuba. What must remain illegible or, worse, a caricature of pathology, may become in fiction a reasonable rebellion in order to bring about a seemingly impossible liberation. Fiction enables a rethinking of these nomadic figures from outside of the pathologizing gaze of the state. The dangerous supplement of silenced histories appears as an echo of the irretrievable voice, the minor language, and the radical political organization that must take place on the margins of the nation, the established literature, the major language, and the legitimate history. Ramos suggests in this novella that these opacities give life to writing of Latino migrants who loved and hated New York as only a *boricua* could.[19]

Notes

1. According to the *Oxford English Dictionary*, "Latino" refers to "a Latin-American inhabitant of the United States," but I want to note the long-standing and well-known critique of the overarching and homogenizing effects of this term. As opposed to "Hispanic," "Latino" refers to a postcolonial position.
2. I am grateful to interlocuters at the U.S. Hispanic Recovery Project in Houston and the Cuban Heritage Collection in Miami, and to Nicolás Kanellos, David Luis-Brown and George Yúdice in particular, for comments and questions in response to presentations that have enriched my thinking in this essay.
3. Aparicio, "Latino Cultural Studies," 20; Flores, "Latino Studies," 198.
4. See "Editorials," published by Francisco P. Ramírez in *El Clamor Público*, July 13, 1855 and August 28, 1855; rpt. *Herencia*, 110-111; and Félix Varela's "Essay on Slavery,"f.p. 1822; rpt. *Herencia*, 523-428.
5. Martí a Manuel Mercado, *Epistolario 1*, 299.
6. "Biblioteca Americana," *La América*, Enero 1884; rpt. *Obras Completas*, 8:313.
7. By identifying *la voz* and *la lengua* in this preliminary way as practices of a Latin American diaspora, I do not propose that they supplant the effect of constant racializing of skin pigment in the United States: *la voz* and *la lengua* supplement and complicate the color schemes and visual regimes that have dominated the discourse of race in the United States.
8. See my discussion of Martí's response to Charles Dudley Warner, who reported on South America for *Harper's* in 1887 in "José Martí between Nation and Empire."
9. Aparicio, Frances R. and Susana Chávez-Silverman, eds. *Tropicalizations*, 1–17.
10. "El Centenario de Bolívar," *La América*, New York, agosto de 1883; rpt. *Obras Completas* 8: 178–179.

11. De los Ríos, Félix, "El Tren de Martí," 152. De los Ríos clarifies that the differentiation did not reflect the usual discrepancies of standards that accompanied racial segregation of public space during the period: "no había diferencia en cuanto a los servicios interiores de cada piso y un solo elevador les servía a todos" (152).

12. See for example, the intensely erotic fragment from note 29, p. 217 of *Divergent Modernities* which Ramos' novel transforms into a poem of enjambed eight syllable lines within the typical endacasílabos of his *Versos libres*, in *Por si nos da el tiempo*, 61.

13. See Frank Martinus Arion's critique of Martí's response to the papamiento of Curaçao in some of his early travel writing, for example.

14. I assume here that the writing launched by Martí differs in terms of its cultural location—i.e. amongst mostly working class, migrants of color and identified with a minor language and against U.S. expansionism—from preemancipation often pro-annexation writers such as the contributors to *El Laud del Destierro* (1858). Martí notes the danger of staying too long in the United States. Living without interruption in the United States posed a danger for some poets of Cuban origin, such as Francisco Sellén, whose poetry occults his pain and proclaims a problematically vague faith that reflects his lack of a sense of agency (OC 5:190).

15. Ramos first makes this point in his essay on Martí and Tato Laviera, "Migratories," first published as "Migratorias" in *Las culturas del fin de siglo en América Latina*, 52–64 and published in English as a chapter of *Divergent Modernities*.

16. See Araceli Tinajero's important cultural history of the *tabaqueros*.

17. Quoted in César Andreu Iglesias, "Introduction," xiii.

18. Edourd Glissant asserts this right in *Caribbean Discourse*, 2.

19. Ramos, *Por si nos da el tiempo*, 101.

Works Cited

Aparicio, Frances. "Latino Cultural Studies." In Juan Poblete, ed. Critical Latin American and Latino Studies. Minnesota: University of Minnesota Press, 2003. 3–31.

Aparicio, Frances R. & Susana Chávez-Silverman, eds. *Tropicalizations: Transcultural Representations of Latinidad*. Hanover, NH: University Press of New England, 1997.

Burgos, Julia de. *Song of the Simple Truth: Obra poética completa/the complete poems of Julia de Burgos*. Trans. and Compiled by Jack Agüeros. Willimantic: Curbstone Press, 1997.

Colón, Jesús. *A Puerto Rican in New York and Other Sketches*. New York: Monthly Review Press, 1982.

Flores, Juan. "Latino Studies: New Contexts, New Concepts." *Critical Latin American and Latino Studies*. Ed. Juan Poblete. Minneapolis: University of Minnesota Press, 2003. 191–205.

Glissant, Edouard. *Caribbean Discourse: Selected Essays*. Trans. J. Michael Dash. Charlottesville: University Press of Virginia, 1989.

Iglesias, César Andreu. "Introduction." *Memoirs of Bernardo Vega: A Contribution to the History of the Puerto Rican Community in New York.* Ed. César Andreu Iglesias. Trans. Juan Flores. New York: Monthly Review Press, 1984. xiii–xix.

Kanellos, Nicolás, et al., Eds. *Herencia: The Anthology of Hispanic Literature of the United States.* New York: Oxford University Press, 2002.

Lomas, Laura. *Translating Empire: José Martí, Migrant Latino Subjects and American Modernities.* Durham: Duke University Press, 2008.

———. "José Martí Between Nation and Empire: Latino Cultural Critique at the Intersection of the Americas." *The Cuban Republic and José Martí: Reception and Use of a National Symbol.* Eds. Mauricio A. Font and Alfonso W. Quiroz. New York: Lexington Books, 2006. 115–127.

Marín, Francisco Gonzalo. "Nueva York Por Dentro: Una faz de su vida bohemia." *Cinco Narraciones de Francisco Gonzalo Marín.* Prólogo de Cesareo Rosa-Nieves, Glosas de Patria Figueroa de Cifredo. San Juan de Puerto Rico: S.N., 1972.

Martí, José. *Obras Completas. 28 tomos.* La Habana: Editorial de Ciencias Sociales, 1973.

———. *Epistolario, 5 tomos.* Compilación, ordenación cronológica y notas de Luis García Pascual y Enrique H. Moreno Pla. La Habana: Editorial de Ciencias Sociales, 1993.

Martinus Arion, Frank. "The Great Curassow, or the Road to Caribbeanness." *Calalloo* 21.3 (1998): 447–452.

Pratt, Mary Louise. *Imperial Eyes: Travel Writing and Transculturation.* New York: Routledge, 1992.

Ramos, Julio. *Desencuentros de la modernidad: literatura y política en América Latina.* México: Fondo de Cultura Económica, 1989.

———. *Divergent Modernities: Culture and Politics in Nineteenth-Century Latin America.* Durham: Duke University Press, 2001.

———. *Por sí nos da el tiempo.* Rosario, Argentina: Beatriz Viterbo Editora, 2002.

Ríos, Félix de los. "El Tren de Martí: Memorias de un Gallego Mambí, en el 140 aniversario del natalicio de José Martí." *Yo Conocí a Martí.* Ed. Carmen Suarez Léon. Villa Clara: Ediciones Capiro, 1998.

Tinajero, Araceli. *El lector de tabaquería: Historia de una tradición cubana.* Madrid: Editorial Verbum, 2007.

Vega, Bernardo. *Memorias de Bernardo Vega: Contribución a la historia de la comunidad puertorriqueña de Nueva York.* Edición de César Andreu Iglesias. Río Piedras: Ediciones Huracán, 1977.

2

Más que Cenizas: An Analysis of Juan Bosch's Dissident Narration of *Dominicanidad* (Ausente)

Lorgia García Peña

The first time I heard Juan Bosch speak I was eight years old. I was playing jacks on the floor of my grandfather's living room with one of my cousins while my grandfather and my uncle Claudio were watching one of those incredibly boring morning shows on Dominican television where two men sit across each other and argue until one of them gets red-faced and loses his temper. I remember because I had advanced to the highest level of *canasta*, when, despite my cousin's impatience and disapproval, I stopped bouncing the ball so I could listen to the man talking on television. Something about the tone of his voice seemed different to me, *hablaba lindo*. I looked up and asked my uncle who that man on television was. He told me it was Juan Bosch. I had heard that name before; it had been the cause of many fights among the men in the family because lately, some of the very faithful *perredeísta* uncles had decided to switch to the purple party, and embrace what apparently was the anti-Christ preaching of Bosch, who my grandmother said was an atheist.[1] Not totally convinced, I then asked him where Bosch was from. Claudio chuckled and responded, "What kind of question is that? Why, he is Dominican, of course, and from El Cibao, La Vega, to be exact." I paused for a moment, and then said: "Well, he does not sound Dominican to me." And went right back to my game.

My reaction to Bosch's speech at such an early age was the recognition of a sense of foreignness that I somehow could not name but could perceive. It was the same mark of *dominicanidad ausente* that many years down the line would be bestowed upon me during my many failed attempts to return home with that incredible ability to read one's foreignness (*lo de afuera*) that only Dominicans who have never left the island possess, and which I lost many years ago.[2] Fortunately, at the time of Bosch's return to the Dominican Republic in the 1960s, the national discourse had not yet deemed *dominicanos ausentes*, and more specifically *Domincanyorks*, as the "sole cause of our society's moral corruption" (Torres-Saillant, *El retorno de las yolas* 18).[3]

This chapter examines the relationship between literature, exile, and some notions of nationality through an analysis of the intellectual production of Juan Bosch. A writer, thinker, and the founder of two of the three dominant political parties in the country, the Partido de la Revolución Dominicana (PRD) and the Partido de la Liberación Dominicana (PLD), Bosch became one of the most influential political figures in twentieth-century Dominican Republic. His short stories and essays, as well as his political thought, influenced Dominican letters, creating a distinctive style that sought to challenge the margins of the nation and the rhetoric of oppression imposed by the various U.S. military occupations of the twentieth century and the Trujillo regime. Yet, most of Bosch's influence in Dominican culture and politics was exercised from exile where he spent a large part of his productive life. Inspired by the ideals of solidarity and unity that Eugenio María de Hostos and José Martí had dreamt of in the nineteenth century, Juan Bosch was able to become, during his long and multiple absences (1938–1962, 1963–1970), one of the first thinkers to articulate and promote the creation of a transnational *dominicanidad* that could exist outside the geographical borders of the nation. He did this by believing in the possibility of a community alliance of Dominicans living abroad and despite the challenges of communication that existed in his time. Bosch's inclusive rhetoric was the basis for the articulation of a revolutionary narrative project that transformed Dominican letters and culture by allowing the voices from the diaspora to insert themselves in the national dialogue, interpellating history and complicating the notion of national frontiers.

My reflection seeks to examine the significance of exile in the construction of Bosch's rhetoric of (trans) *dominicanidad* while demonstrating its incidence in the solidification of a transnational (literary) community. For this purpose, my work will engage Pedro Vergés's text *Sólo cenizas hallarás, (bolero)* (1980), a novel that examines the anxiety that emerged among Dominican youth during the last months leading to Bosch's election as the first democratic president of the Republic in 1962, as well as the general disillusion that followed after the *coup d'état* that sent him back to exile in 1963. These two events, which Vergés also examines from a distance as he resided in Spain while writing this novel, end up making Bosch throughout the second half of the twentieth century both an emblem of dissidence and a reminder of a failed national democracy project. Through an analysis of Bosch's life and intellectual production, I hope to propose a thoughtful look at the significance of exile and migration in the construction of a new version of *dominicanidad.*

2.1 *La Dominicanidad Ausente*: Juan Bosch's Discourse, from Exile

Emigra quien no puede quedarse... Nuestra emigración es una expatriación

—*Silvio Torres-Saillant ("Confesiones de un Dominican-york")*

Caribbean literature has traditionally played an important role in documenting significant historical moments, particularly in reference to the dictatorships, colonialism, imperialism, and migration. Antillean writers have often claimed or been granted by subsequent generations of *letrados* historical authority.[4] This is further complicated by the presence of authors such as José Martí and Máximo Gómez, who in addition to being writers were actors and subjects in the history of their nations. This Caribbean complexity has produced a rich variety of narratives in which the lines between genres are many times blurred because, as Pedro San Miguel argues, fictional texts have often been able to reconstruct social reality in moments of censorship or strict government control when history has served the purpose of the state (28).

When examining Bosch's life, most scholars seem to concentrate on either his political work or his creative writing. My purpose here however is to look at Bosch's literature and politics as he saw them—two complementary passions that cannot be separated from each other. Despite the fact that it was through his participation in Dominican politics that Bosch was known amongst all segments of the population, it is important to remember that writing was Bosch's first political act as he himself expressed in a 1965 interview with journalist Mateo Morrison: "Yo empecé a escribir porque había que decir cosas del pueblo dominicano. No sabía bien qué cosas eran, eso no lo podía determinar aún [...] Por eso los proyectos literarios como tal no me interesaban [...] Para mi la literatura por definición debía servir un propósito social" (62). Bosch was unwilling to accept literature and other forms of art that did not reflect the social reality of his nation, a fact that marked his political path while earning him the aversion of the right-wing faction of Dominican military and of the U.S. government, two organizations that frowned upon the democratic policies he wanted to implement during his tenure as president. This resulted in a *coup d'état*, a civil war, and the second military intervention of the United States in twentieth-century Dominican soil.[5]

Knowing that Trujillo wanted to buy him off with a position in Congress, Bosch managed to leave the country in January of 1938, settling in Puerto Rico. There, Adolfo Hostos, the son of Puerto Rican thinker, educator, and independence leader Eugenio Maria de Hostos, welcomed him and gave him work (Kury 31). A year later, Adolfo asked Bosch to oversee the edition and publication of his father's complete works in Havana, Cuba. There, following the ideals of the *confederación antillana*,[6] the writer's desire for social justice matured into a strong political thought, inspired by the principles of solidarity and freedom that Hostos had envisioned at the end of the nineteenth century:

> Si mi vida llegara a ser tan importante que se justificara algún día escribir sobre ella, habría que empezar diciendo: Nació en La Vega, República Dominicana el 30 de junio del 1909, y volvió a nacer en San Juan de Puerto Rico, a principios de 1938, cuando la lectura de los originales de Eugenio María de Hosots le permitió conocer qué fuerzas mueven y cómo la mueven, el alma de un hombre al servicio de los demás. (35)

With the support of Enrique Cotubanamá Henríquez (Pedro Henríquez Ureña's brother), Juan Isidro Jimenes Grullón, and many other important Dominican and Latin American thinkers, Bosch took on the difficult task of organizing the very disperse Dominican exiles into a transnational unified community in order to create a revolutionary party that would potentially fight the Trujillo regime and return peace and democracy to the country: "Yo no aceptaba posponer la tarea de proceder a organizar a los dominicanos exiliados [...] Me dediqué a pensar en la manera de solucionar el problema causado por la dispersión geográfica de los llamados a ser miembros de la fuerza política que el pueblo dominicano quería para librarse de la sanguinaria tiranía que los oprimía" (Kury 47). This is how the Dominican Revolutionary Party (PRD) was created in 1942.[7] Traveling to the various countries where Dominicans had gone during the regime, Bosch was able to form small sections of *perredeísta* supporters under the leadership of local *juntas*; a method that would later become the basis for the Dominican party system. New York and Cuba became the two most important enclaves of dissidence for PRD members, while the technology of writing, the use of writing as a mobilizing machine, functioned as the medium for the creation of this transnational community and for the drafting of a unique narrative of social justice.

Upon his arrival in Puerto Rico in 1938, Bosch realized that he was known as a writer because some of his short stories had been circulating in literary magazines. Through the process of reading his short stories many readers, including important writers and thinkers, befriended Bosch:

> Cuando llegamos a Puerto Rico tenía solo 90 dólares pero encontré que allí me conocían; por lo menos me conocían en los círculos literarios y a los pocos días tenía amigos que hicieron todo por ayudarme, antes del mes estaba trabajando en la trascripción de todo, casi todo lo que había escrito Hostos, y puedo afirmar que Hostos fue para mí una revelación, algo así como si hubiera vuelto a nacer. Es curiosos que un maestro pueda seguir siendo maestro 33 o 34 años después de muerto, pero en el caso mío, Hostos hizo su obra de formador de conciencia un tercio de siglo después de su muerte. (Kury 105)

Much like the closeness that Bosch developed with Hostos while working on the edition of his works, through the literary circles of the Caribbean many people had also embraced Bosch and his ideals and so he soon found himself part of a much larger community and greater social project. The writer had left his homeland in search of freedom to write because he recognized that "lo que primero tuve no fue conciencia de lo que quería decir, sino la angustia de no poder decir lo que debía decir..." (Piña Contreras 36) and while in exile, this search became the basis for his revolutionary project. With the anxiety of censorship gone, Bosch was able to conciliate, in exile, his memories of the Dominican Republic with his desire for a democratic future. While many of his stories were inspired by the life that Bosch lived in La Vega as a young man, it was not until later "in Cuba, during long and multiple exiles" (Piña-Contreras 49) that he was able to externalize these experiences into a coherent narrative of social justice that was later linked to the democratic rhetoric of his political party.

One of Juan Bosch's most articulate examples of his socially committed narrative written while in exile can be located in his collection of short stories *Cuentos escritos en el exilio* (1962). The title he chose to give his collections later on in life alludes to the geographical distance of the writer at the moment of conceiving each of these narratives, as well as to a sense of legitimacy through the implicit forced displacement of the narrator from his homeland.[8] It is important to note, however, that most of the stories that appear in this collection had already been published as individual texts or as shorter compilations under different titles. The latter decision to employ the narrative of exile in the compilation, however, alludes to Bosch's awareness of the significance of his condition of *ausente*. In addition, it functions as a performative act that seeks to deal with the contradictions that led the author to write about the Dominican reality from a distance, making him both an agent and a subject of history.[9] Bosch insisted on the legitimacy of his narration of *dominicanidad ausente* as a form of resistance and of patriotism, because as Torres-Saillant has argued "se va quien no puede quedarse" (*El retorno de las yolas* 18). In the case of Bosch's particular experience, his absence from the national territory is presumed, in the titles of his books, as a necessity, an involuntary circumstance caused by the persecution of a dictatorial regime. His discourse, however, could also be read in the present as a premonitory legitimation of the diasporic Dominican voices of the late twentieth and early twenty-first centuries; voices of those who have also left their homeland in search of democracy and progress once the project embodied in Bosch had been destroyed. Like Bosch, these *dominicanos ausentes* of the present have embraced the possibility of writing about their nation from the outside in hopes to do in the diaspora what they are not allowed to do back home. Exile provided Bosch with a new freedom to voice (and publish) all his concerns and to propose a new way of representing the subaltern of Dominican society—the poor, the black, the Haitian immigrant—as part of the nation-building project.

I would like to dwell on the analysis of one of Bosch's most important short stories "Luis Pié"(1943), which I believe exemplifies his ideals of Caribbean solidarity as it demonstrates Bosch's attempt to portray the marginal subjects: the poor, the weak, the immigrant, as possessing the true inner goodness needed for the strengthening of the Dominican nation; an idea that directly contradicted the existing official narrative of the nation which excluded precisely those subjects that Bosch sought to place at the center of *dominicanidad*.

The construction of the dominant Dominican national discourse that Bosch sought to change had its basis in the language of the early Republic (1844–1890), which promoted the idea of Dominicans as a hybrid, non-black race defined in direct opposition to the neighboring Haitians, who were often depicted as black, evil, and savages.[10] This was in part because after its independence from Haiti, Dominican elites had an increasing desire to mark the difference between the two island nations in order to ultimately justify Dominican independence from Haiti. They attempted to do so by claiming Hispanic heritage and civility for Dominicans while deeming the neighbors as black brutes; a narrative that becomes evident in the works of early Republic intellectuals and writers such as Manuel de Jesús Galván, and Félix María del Monte, to mention only a couple. Although influential in shaping Dominican politics and public opinion, the works of early intellectuals did not translate into a tangible re-definition of national identities among the peasantry and the borderland population because borders, both geographical and psychological, continued to be fluid for the two nations sharing the island of Hispaniola as people, particularly those who lived in the borderlands often found common interests that united them. It was not until the Trujillo Era (1930–1961) that these ideologies introduced by the founding fathers and early intellectuals of the Dominican Republic were translated into tangible actions that reinforced clear national, territorial, and psychological borders through law, force, and violence when anti-Haitian rhetoric was appropriated, widely disseminated, and manipulated by the Trujillo dictatorship in order to serve the goals of the nation-state (namely Trujillo himself) thus resulting in the imposition of a Haitian-Dominican border that was built on xenophobia, intolerance, and ultimately, the massacre of more than 20,000 ethnic Haitians in the Dominican borderlands.[11] Inspired by this particular concern, Bosch wrote "Luis Pié."

"Luis Pié" was written shortly after the massacre,[12] and constitutes one of the earliest examples of what Marcio Veloz-Maggiolo has called "the literature of compassion" (23) and a clear demonstration of Bosch's awareness of the intricacies of Dominican social reality notwithstanding his geographical distance. Despite being exiled, or perhaps because of it, Bosch was able to maintain an impressive closeness with his homeland, a task he admitted was difficult yet rewarding: "Los efectos del exilio en un escritor pueden ser muy malos; desarraigan al escritor. Lo que ocurre es que yo no me desarraigué [...] Es decir, iba viviendo, minuto a minuto, la vida de la República Dominicana" (44). This closeness becomes evident in his rendering of "Luis Pié" as Bosch introduces his reader to the discourse of unity that he, like Martí and Hostos,[13] believed should be at the heart of the construction of a national identity. Knowing the stigma that the Haitian figure carried in Dominican society, Bosch suggests that solidarity should start with the neighboring country as he attempts to describe the possibility of reconciliation through acts of forgiveness and compassion. Creating a social consciousness on his potential Dominican reader while condemning anti-Haitianism and xenophobia, Bosch's "Luis Pié," embodies the Caribbean Solidarity through a formulation of the Haitian-Dominican experience.

A widower and father of three little children, Pié, the main character of Bosch's story, left his homeland of Haiti to find work in the neighboring country's prominent sugar cane plantations. One day at work Pié suffers a horrible accident, which makes it difficult for him to walk the several kilometers from the sugar cane field to his shack in the *batey*. Bosch's narrative takes place during the excruciating hours in which Pie crawls through the ravines while begging God for strength so he can make it home to feed his little children: "Ah…Pití mishé tá esperan a mué-dijo con amargura Luis Pié. Temía no llegar en toda la noche y en ese caso, los tres hijitos le esperaría junto a la hoguera…sin comer" (53). Throughout the story, the reader sees the character of Luis Pié through the eyes of an omniscient narrator who attempts to enter the heart and mind of Luis in order to offer the reader glimpses of this man's painful ordeal. The story continues with a depiction of Pié's attempt to crawl home to his children, which is interrupted when a rich plantation manager accidentally causes a huge fire after throwing his lit cigarette out the window of his fancy car. Dominican overseers and the military immediately go looking for the person responsible for this fire and upon finding Pié, who had coincidentally lit a match to look at the state of his wound, accuse him of arson and tie him up dragging him across the *batey* in a macabre procession that the reader perceives will end with his execution: "Inmediatamente aparecieron diez o doce hombres, muchos de ellos a pie y la mayoría armados de mochas. Todos gritaban insultos y se lanzaban sobre Luis Pié" (57). Confused by the sudden aggression and not knowing what he was being accused of, Pié prayed to the God of the Dominicans to save him from what seemed like his imminent death:

> Luis, con su herida y su fiebre delirante, había quedado atrapado dentro de un incendio que por descuido causó su patrón en el cañaveral, hecho por el que luego sería culpado. En momento de desesperación, Luis clama a Bonyé [Good God], al dios de los cristianos que según sus cavilaciones debe ser tan bueno como los 'dominiquen bom' que le han dado la oportunidad de trabajar en su tierra. (56)

But the Dominican God did not listen to this Haitian man, and the story ends with the image of Pié's little children watching as their father is slowly murdered by an angry mob of Dominicans who seem completely blind to this poor man's suffering.

Luis Pié is ultimately recreated in Bosch's narrative as a martyr in an effort to recast a narrative tradition that has persistently portrayed Haitians as inhumane, violent, and dangerous.[14] Through the use of various rhetorical steps, Bosch attempts to deconstruct the established perception of the Haitian as an evil savage: first, the author shows us Dominicanized Pie through the insertion of recognizable Dominican popular values such as the relationship to the land, to family, and to a Christian God; then, Pié is presented as the victim of two systems of oppression: the sugar cane plantation economy and institutionalized racism; finally, at the end of the story, Pié is rendered as a hero and a martyr. Bosch's story succeeds in provoking a critique on the U.S. imperial socioeconomic systems that reproduced poverty and oppression in many Latin American countries throughout the twentieth and twenty-first centuries as exemplified in the sugar plantation, but fails to analyze the role of cultural production and narration in shaping popular ideas that ultimately served to perpetuate racism and oppression in the nation. In that sense, "Luis Pié" battles with the need to attack anti-Haitianism and the author's political desire to maintain the psychological borders of the Dominican nation-state. This contradiction can be seen throughout

Bosch's literary career and will be reflected in Dominican literary production of the second half of the twentieth century.[15]

Just as Luis Pié's only way to freedom appears to be death due to the oppression and xenophobia that dominated the Dominican Republic at the time, exile is also rendered in Bosch's narrative project (as evidenced in his book titles) as the only possible alternative for reaching intellectual and political freedom. The network of friends and allies that welcomed him in Puerto Rico, Cuba, Costa Rica, and Venezuela provided Bosch with the nurture and support he needed to develop into the passionate political figure that those who knew him in the mid-twentieth century remember him as. In exile Bosch recognized the possibility of literature as a political act, and therefore persisted in writing about that which he knew constituted the main goal of his life "the well-being of the Dominican people" (Piña Contreras 69). The writing and publication of "Luis Pié" in the middle of an international crisis caused by the Haitian massacre of 1937 became a clear defiance against the regime and against the accepted national anti-Haitian rhetoric. Perhaps Bosch would have written this and many other stories even if he had chosen to stay and join the regime in 1938. However, it seems evident to me that these stories would not have translated into a powerful sociopolitical proposal had it not been for the support and solidarity that Bosch found during his "second birth" in Puerto Rico during the first year of his long exile.

2.2 *Más que Cenizas*: Remembering the Trauma of 1965

On April 28, 1965 the U.S. military landed in Santo Domingo with the excuse of protecting American investment in the island during the civil revolt. The revolt had begun a few days earlier with the purpose of restoring the democratically elected president, Juan Bosch, now in exile. A little over a year prior to the intervention, Bosch had been elected President of the Republic by an overwhelming majority vote, only to be overthrown seven months later, on September 25, 1963, by a military *coup* headed by Colonel Elías Wessin y Wessin.[16] A triumvirate was established shortly after, but dissidence and the desire for democracy created a series of social upheavals that ultimately gained the support of the liberal faction of the military that favored the return to the Constitution and that of the elected President Juan Bosch. After three days of battle, however, the United States invaded the island siding with the *coup* leaders and keeping Juan Bosch from occupying the presidential position that he had earned during the 1962 elections. The presence of the Marines created a sense of frustration among Dominicans, who found themselves with nothing but their anger and their fists to fight a giant and powerful force. The events of 1965 ultimately destroyed the democratic dreams of an entire nation embodied in the figure of Juan Bosch.

Demoralized by their loss and with the country in the hands of the right-wing *Trujillistas* once again, many Dominicans began to look at migration as their only alternative to repression and hunger. Soon it became clear to the people, as well as to Bosch, that the ideals of freedom and democracy that he embodied would never be materialized in his country as long as the United States continued to intervene in the matters of the nation: "Creo que en la República Dominicana Latinoamérica ha recibido una lección [...] que no es posible establecer democracia con la ayuda de los Estados Unidos, y que tampoco es posible establecer democracia contra los Estados Unidos" (Piña-Contreras 187). The intervention and the ultimate trauma of 1965 led Bosch to a different type of exile than his first one in 1938: he stopped writing, became disillusioned, lost faith in his party, and ultimately became much more radical in his political views. Never again would he be president of his country. Ironically, for many of his followers, this dissolution marked the beginning of a massive migration to the United States, which has lasted over four decades.

In her book *Tears of Hispaniola,* Lucía Suárez proposes literary writing as a form of remembering trauma and violence, therefore challenging the politics of silence imposed by national discourses and the official history (15). Pedro Vergés in his 1980 novel *Sólo cenizas hallarás* examines this topic by unpacking the complexity of the trauma caused by the failure of democracy as embodied in the historical figure of Juan Bosch and the subsequent massive emigration of Dominicans to the United States and Europe that resulted from this. Utilizing the seductiveness of *bolero*, Vergés looks at the impossibility of democracy in a nation fractured by the rhetoric of progress, political corruption, and a long history of oppression. Despite the hopes embodied in Juan Bosch after the death of the dictator, the characters in Vergés's novel find themselves disheartened because they begin to understand the fatality of history that will somehow keep them from enjoying a democratic government. As a result, migration is rendered as an alternative for reaching national consciousness and freedom, and as the only potential way to change the nation (from the outside).

The title of the novel denotes two significant narrative goals: first, it attempts to make the reader aware of *bolero* as alternative medium from which the individual as well as the collective trauma of the characters can be narrated. In a nation where the forces of history (Vergés 32) keep the majority of the people from gaining any form of political representation, *bolero* functions as an allegory of the official narration of historical invisibility (Trouillot xix). Second, this particular *bolero* by Wello Rivas, entitled *Cenizas* alludes to the collective national trauma caused by the long dictatorship of Trujillo while becoming, in a sense, a premonition to the future ruins and emptiness that will remain after the 1965 defeat. The rhythm of *bolero* inserts itself within the plot as a seductive, political voice that invites the people to dream about finding love. A type of love, however, that is mediated by the rhetoric of progress and success that can now be envisioned as part of the democratic capitalist process. However, at the end of the novel all forms of love are rendered unattainable, and like in a *bolero*, the characters are left with nothing, not even the memory of that which could have been. Historical amnesia is suggested in the narrative as a force that emerges after 1965 in those who stay allowing for men such as Joaquín Balaguer, Trujillo's right hand man, to gain control of the nation.[17] Migration, as seen in some of the characters, is presented as the only way of retaining historical consciousness, because those who leave, as Torres-Saillant argues, never forget (*El retorno de las yolas* 34).

Lucila, one of the main characters in the novel is the first to introduce the readers to this romantic and seductive *bolero* of history. A representative of the farmer class who now finds herself free to wander into the city in search of the new "progress" that promises to emerge in the post-Trujillo nation, Lucila finds a job as a maid in the home of some powerful UCN (Unión Cívica Nacional) allies after being seduced by the national *bolero*:[18] "Ella vivía feliz en el patio, haciendo la comida, planchando la ropa, lavando y escuchando el radito de pilas que ponía unos boleros chéveres de Vicentico, de Daniel y de Lucho [...] En eso demostraban las doñas que buenas eran, en cuanto ella llegó le dijeron toma este radito para que te entretengas y se lo pusieron encima de la mesa" (43). The ladies of the house, who represent the emerging Dominican bourgeoisie, give Lucila (the peasant) a radio to entertain her with the national *bolero*. Lucila, seduced by the new possibilities presented by this discourse, lets herself be entertained and falls in the arms of the UCN against her consciousness that told her Bosch was really the best candidate: "que gane la UCN, y ya se veía en el futuro la señorita Lucila, encargada de tal o cual, con un sueldito chévere" (Vergés 108). Lucila is very interested in national politics. However, for her this interest represents a particular way to attain social mobility and to escape the stagnation that her family had been forced to endure during the Trujillo regime. Therefore, Lucila's dream was not the creation of a collective, freer country, but rather the assurance that she would move forward and progress, either by marrying up or by making sure that her presidential candidate won, granting her the opportunity to become somebody. Ultimately, when all those plans fail and she finds herself back in the *campo* poor, pregnant and disillusioned, she imagines herself flying to New York and searching there for her dreams of having a better life. However, this possibility does not seem to materialize and the reader can visualize Lucila finding herself a maid again being seduced once more by the rhythm of yet another *bolero*.

The main character of *Sólo cenizas hallarás*, Freddy Nogueras, also struggles with his dreams for progress and the uncertainty that emerges after the death of Trujillo and before the 1962 elections. An idealist and a dissident during the last years of the regime, Freddy loses all hopes in the democratic project after realizing that his beloved father had not been assassinated by the regime like he believed, but had been killed in a drunken brawl. This ideological parricide leaves a huge void in Freddy's life. But at the end, the uncertain political climate and the evidence of continuous corruption makes Freddy decide to migrate to New York in hopes of a new way to imagine his national identity: "Yo creo que me fuera de todas formas, con muertos o sin muertos. Yo creo que uno no entiende este país hasta que no se aleja de él [...] Lo malo, contestó Wilson, es que después lo comprede tan bien que ya no hay quien te haga regresar" (260). Freddy's awareness of the forces of history makes him predict that Bosch will not last long in power, that democracy will not succeed, and that he will never be able to simply be within the oppressing walls of the nation:

> En los últimos días, en efecto, Freddy había tenido en todo momento la sensación de que...la Historia, los demás, lo que estaba más allá de sí mismo- acabaría agarrando por los pelos y arrastrando por toda la ciudad con los ojos abiertos y asombrados...sabía de sobre que nunca sería hoy, que jamás surgiría semejante oportunidad y que los que eran como él no tenían más remedio que largarse o joderse o pegarse un plomazo en la cabeza. (15)

In the midst of his exasperation, Freddy finds comfort in the possibility of exile from which he hopes he will eventually return with a deeper understanding of his own country. But the reader imagines that it will be many years before Freddy will be able to come back and as predicted by his friends, it will never be to stay. Like Bosch in 1938, Freddy recognizes that he cannot do anymore from within the nation. He becomes aware of the possibility of being Dominican from the outside. Unlike Bosch, however, Freddy's absence ends up being marked by forces of history that over time turn him into a *Domincanyork*, an unwanted element in late-twentieth-century official Dominican narration.

The lives of the two characters—the fictitious Freddy and the historical Bosch—intersect in Vergés's text, through a narrative of disillusion that ultimately separates both men from their homeland and their political dreams. As predicted by Freddy, the same historical forces that attacked him, end up destroying Bosch's possibility of governing the nation, sending the writer and revolutionary back to exile and condemning the country to what seems like an eternal crisis of democratic values. In *El retorno de la yolas*, Silvio Torres-Saillant argues that Dominican emigrants did not choose to leave their homeland, but rather, were forced to by a country that could not secure the basic needs for its citizens (Torres-Saillant 19). According to this argument Freddy became an exile, a person who left his homeland against his own will because "los que se van, aunque sus recursos analíticos no siempre les permitan discernir las fuerzas que moldean su decision de partir...son expulsados" (Torres-Saillant 19).

The inclusive discourse of solidarity that Bosch drafted between 1938 and 1961 has served as the basis for the creation of "fronteras intranacionales" (Martínez-San Miguel 12) from which a dissident discourse of *Dominicanidad* has continued to emerge through the diasporic voices of those deemed *ausentes*. In the last ten years, U.S. and European media have published numerous articles examining the question of Dominican identity and the controversial issues surrounding Haitian-Dominican border relations. The coronation of Denny Méndez, a black Dominican immigrant, as Miss Italy in 1996,[19] and the subsequent electoral triumph of another Dominican woman, Mercedes Frías, as a deputy of the Italian parliament in 2006, added another dimension to a dialogue that had mostly existed between the island and the U.S. diaspora. As a result, a series of controversial discussions have emerged among Dominican thinkers in the island and abroad regarding the legitimacy of *dominicanidad* narrated by *dominicanos ausentes*. It appears that the *return of the yolas*, to borrow Torres-Saillant's term, has succeeded in blurring the lines between *here* and *there*, questioning the official version of Dominican national identity.

My examination of Bosch's political and narrative project produced while in exile (1938–1962) illustrates how the discussion of what constitutes *Dominicanness* has been a project of diasporic transcendence for nearly a century, and that the transnational quality of Dominican politics and culture has been and continues to be a significant element in the ongoing discussion of *dominicanidad*. The emergence of a strong Dominican diasporic narrative in the last two decades, as evidenced in the works of Josefina Báez, Junot Díaz, and Nelly Rosario, to mention only a few, has allowed for the interpellation of history and the questioning of the dominant rhetoric of *dominicanidad*.

Bosch's narrative of exile created the opportunity for framing a new form of *dominicanidad* rooted in democratic ideas and in the possibility of Caribbean solidarity. In the middle of the growing democratic crisis of the current Dominican state, as depicted in the photo that appears in the next page, this chapter hopes to remind readers of the legacy of Bosch's narrative project that insisted on questioning the *forces of history* from within and from without the national space, ultimately rendering literature as an antidote to historical amnesia.

Figure 2.1 *Más poesía, Menos Policía*, John Paul Gallagher

Source: This photograph was taken in el Malecón, Santo Domingo, December 2006. Reproduced with permission from John Paul Gallagher.

Notes

1. *Perredeistas* is a Dominican term used to name followers of the PRD (Partido Revolucionario Dominicano) one of the dominant political parties, founded by Juan Bosch while in exile in 1942.
2. *Dominicanos ausentes* is a term used to refer to Dominicans in the diaspora. See Silvio Torres-Saillant's *El retorno de las yolas* (1999) and *An Intellectual History of the Caribbean* (2006).
3. Dominicanyork was a derogatory term used to describe Dominican people who reside in New York City.
4. See Angel Rama. *La ciudad Letrada*.
5. During his presidency, Bosch promoted a socio-economic restructuring of the State. On April 29, for instance, he promulgated a new constitution, wherein for the first time there was a declaration of specific labor rights, rights for pregnant women, for the homeless, and for the children. See Roberto Cassá *Capitalismo y dictadura* (1982) for a more detailed depiction of Bosch's state restructuring.
6. The *Confederación Antillana* is an idea introduced by Puerto Rican thinker Ramón Emeterio Betances that promoted the need for natives of the Spanish

Greater Antilles to unite into a regional entity that would seek to preserve the sovereignty and well-being of Cuba, the Dominican Republic, and Puerto Rico.

7. According to Farid Kury, Bosch was asked by Henríquez to organize the Dominican exiles into a cohesive force that would ideologically combat the regime (45). However, in the early 1940s the Dominican diaspora was small and had not yet concentrated in one geographical area. This became an extraordinary task for Bosch who had to travel constantly to New York, San Juan, and Caracas among other places, to meet with the exiles who resided there. The fact that he was a known writer, who had often published in the local papers of these cities allowed him to gain the trust and solidarity of many exiles and of the local Latin American leaders.

8. It is important to note that Bosch's short stories, including, "Luis Pie," which I analyze in this chapter were published at various moments under different titles or as sole publications in journals and newspapers. Therefore, the publication dates for the anthologies does not correspond to the actual date in which the stories therein included were written and/or first made available to readers.

9. Bosch's short stories appeared in various collections entitled: *Cuentos escritos en el exilio* (1962), *Más cuentos escritos en el exilio* (1962), and *Cuentos escritos antes del exilio* (1975).

10. See Teresita Martínez-Vergne and Pedro San Miguel.

11. Eugenio Matibag explores this phenomenon in detail looking at the intricacies of the rhetoric and its reproduction in twentieth-century literature.

12. In 1937 following an order by Dominican President Rafael Trujillo, more than 20,000 ethnic Haitians were assassinated in the northwestern border of the Dominican Republic. The massacre also known as "el corte" was the climax of a xenophobic campaign that attempted to "protect" the territorial borders of the Dominican nation from the "silent invasion" of Haitians. See Richard Turits *Foundations of Despotism* (2003) and Eugenio Matibag *Haitian-Dominican Counterpoint* (2003).

13. José Martí had imagined in the nineteenth century a Caribbean community based on fraternity among all peoples of all races and classes. In his diaries, essays and poems, Martí articulates this community through a faith in the (innate) solidarity of all men of the Caribbean (and Latin America). Martí's discourse has influenced twentieth-century Caribbean intellectuals who have reconstructed Martí's community through what Benítez Rojo would call "coincidencias político-sociales en la historia del archipiélago" (12) that is, through the histories of colonization, imperialism, sugar plantation, racial identities, and migrations that have defined the history of modernity in the region.

14. Soon after the massacre and all through the decade of the 1940s, many Dominican intellectuals took on the task of justifying the genocide through an aggressive anti-Haitian campaign that reclaimed the history of the Haitian occupation (1822–1844) and the various colonial border conflicts. This was in part due to increased attention in the international media and diplomatic pressures from the United States. The decade that followed *el corte* resulted in a series of texts that minimized the transcendence of the events

in order to justify them. These nationalist writings presented the events as a conflict between Dominican peasants and Haitian immigrants; the latter were being often accused of trying to take over the land while stealing cattle from Dominican borderland ranches. In this context, the 1937 conflict was presented to the international community as a necessary action taken by civilians in order to protect the borders of the nation from the tyrannical, neighboring enemy.

15. In a narrative of contradiction that was greatly inspired by Duarte, late nineteenth- and early twentieth-century Dominican intellectuals sought to assert their national identity as culturally Hispanic, racially mixed, and above all different from Haiti and therefore other than black. From its declaration of independence, Haiti had been constructed (and perceived by the outside world) as a black nation (Heiln 338). So in order to imagine a separate nation within the same island the notion of blackness, which was equated with Haitian, had to be erased from the discourse of the emerging Dominican state.

16. On April 28, 1965 the United States intervened in the civil war and dispatched 42,000 troops to the island. President Lyndon Johnson justified the invasion based on his belief that the PRD was full of communists. See Piero Gliejeses' *The Dominican Crisis* (1978).

17. One of Trujillo's main advisors, Joaquín Balaguer, became an influential figure during and after the regime. He even served the role of Trujillo's puppet president. After the assassination of the dictator in 1961, Balaguer sought the presidency of the Republic, and gained it with U.S. support in 1966. He ruled uninterrupted for twelve years (1966–1978) and then again from 1986 to 1996.

18. The UCN was the party that opposed Bosch during the 1962 elections.

19. On September 7, 1996, Denny Méndez was elected Miss Italy at the age of eighteen. This event caused a major scandal throughout Italy and other parts of the world because it was the first time that a woman of non-Italian ancestry was elected to represent the country in an international beauty pageant. See *Jet Magazine*, September 23, 1996.

Works Cited

"First Black Miss Italy Picked amidst Two Judges' Disapproval" *Jet Magazine*. September 23, 1996. Farmington Hills, MI: Johnson Publishing.

Benítez-Rojo, Antonio. *La isla que se repite: el Caribe y la perspectiva posmoderna*. Hanover, NH: Ediciones del Norte, 1989.

———. *Cuentos escritos en el exilio y apuntes sobre cómo escribir un cuento*. Santo Domingo: Póstigo, 1968.

Gallagher, John Paul. "Más poesía, menos policía" *El Malecón: A Wall of Shame*. New York: John Paul Gallagher Photo, 2007.

Kury, Farid. Juan Bosch. *Entre el exilio y el golpe de estado*. Santo Domingo: Editora Búho, 2000.

Martínez-San Miguel, Yolanda. *Caribe Two Ways: cultura de la migración en el Caribe insular hispánico*. San Juan: Ediciones Callejón, 2003.

Morrison, Mateo and Jóvine Bermúdez. "Encuentro con Juan Bosch" *La Noticia.* Santo Domingo, August 10, 1965 (2–5).

Piña-Contreras, Guillermo. *En primera persona. Entrevistas con Juan Bosch.* Santo Domingo: Editoras Feriadelibro, 2000.

San Miguel, Pedro Luís. *La isla imaginada: historia, identidad y utopía en La Española.* 1st. ed. San Juan; Santo Domingo: Isla Negra; La Trinitaria, 1997.

Suárez, Lucía. *The Tears of Hispaniola: Haitian and Dominican Diaspora Memory.* Gainesville: Florida University Press, 2006.

Torres-Saillant, Silvio. *El retorno de las yolas: Ensayos sobre diáspora, democracia y dominicanidad.* Santo Domingo: Trinitaria, 1999.

Trouillot, Michel-Rolph. *Silencing the Past: Power and the Production of History.* Boston, MA: Beacon, 1995.

Vergés, Pedro. *Sólo cenizas hallarás. Bolero.* Barcelona: Destino, 1980.

3

Creating *Latinidad*: Julia de Burgos' Legacy on U.S. Latina Literature

Vanessa Pérez Rosario

When Julia de Burgos embarked on a journey to New York from Puerto Rico in January 1940, she was twenty-five and an aspiring poet. She had already written three collections of poetry and published two. She had been married and divorced. The repressive island culture of the 1930s had stigmatized her divorce, so she left the island on that day in January with no plans to return; "I want to be universal," she claimed in a letter to her sister, Consuelo, shortly after her arrival in New York. In New York, de Burgos struggled to make a living off of her writing. She published her work in local Spanish-language newspapers, and worked as the Art and Culture Editor of *Pueblos Hispanos*. De Burgos' writings for these New York newspapers reveal her commitment to Puerto Rican national affairs, as they simultaneously demonstrate her concern for the lives of Puerto Ricans and others of Latin American descent in New York. Thus, de Burgos forms part of a transitional generation that helps to bridge the historical divide between Puerto Rican nationalist writers of the 1930s and the Nuyorican writers of the 1970s. Julia de Burgos' struggle to establish herself as a writer, and her Pan-American and Afro-Antillean ideas enable us to read her as a precursor to later women writers of the Puerto Rican diaspora. While it is rare for a poet to become a cultural icon, Julia de Burgos has evoked feelings of bonding and national identification in Puerto Ricans and Latinos in the United States for over half a century. Her experience of migration, dissidence in relation to the nation island, and her fight for survival resonate with these communities.

In recent years, scholars of Puerto Rican literature and studies have attempted to bridge the historical divide between Puerto Ricans living in the States and on the island. Julia de Burgos is an early figure at the center of these debates as a nationalist writer who left the island in 1940 to Cuba, and later New York where she settled and lived until her death in 1953. Intellectuals on the island who embraced a homogenizing image of Puerto Rican identity based on Antonio Pedreira's *Insularismo* (1934), rejected the writings of Puerto Ricans in the United States because this literature challenged the narrowly defined nation conceived by the *Generación del treinta* writers. This Puerto Rican identity was based on the myth of the *jíbaro* described as a white farmer of European descent and traditional values of fraternity and brotherly love that was racist in practice and denied the specter of disease and poverty that plagued the working class on the island at the time.[1] During the 1930s, de Burgos actively partici- pated in the Nationalist Movement led by Pedro Albizu Campos and her early writing is often allied with the *Generación del treinta*.[2] Although she actively associated with both of these groups, a close critical reading of her poetry reveals ideological differences, often overlooked by scholars on the island, that distinguish her from both of these groups in important ways.[3] While the Nationalist Movement and the writers of the *Generación del treinta* articulate a narrowly constructed identity, de Burgos always speaks for the oppressed sector of the population that is not written into the national identity of the time; an identity that in so many ways persists as the dominant Puerto Rican identity today. In her early poetry she calls for social justice, denounces U.S. imperialism on the island, and calls for Puerto Rican independence without ever romanticizing the lives of the peasant farmers. She also expresses her frustration with the institution of marriage and limiting gender roles for women in Puerto Rico in poems such as "A Julia de Burgos" and "Pentacromia."

Much of the myth of de Burgos grew out of her love affair with Dominican intellectual, Juan Isidro Jimenes Grullón, and her tragic death on the streets of Harlem on July 6, 1953. Early that morning two police officers found de Burgos unconscious on the street corner of 105th Street and Fifth Avenue. She died on her way to the hospital. Because she had no identification on her, she was buried in an unmarked New York City grave. Her friends and relatives searched for her for a month. Her body was later exhumed and returned to the island. She is often read as a martyr for the Puerto Rican cause who died tragically on the streets of New York.[4] A critical reading of her work challenges the notion and romanticized myth that Julia de Burgos was a victim of her lover, Jimenes Grullón, and the idea that this is what led her to leave the island. The island's limiting and repressive gender roles coupled with her strong desire to establish herself as a serious poet and writer of interna- tional acclaim were important factors that informed her decision to leave and never return. While she certainly suffered isolation, loneliness and despair in exile, her travel abroad also allowed her to grow as a writer. During her time abroad, she expanded her political perspective. In Cuba and New York, she developed a Pan-American and Pan-Latino identity modeled after Cuban revolutionary poet José Martí's concept of "nuestra América." Many Puerto Rican writers in New York take up the themes that de Burgos addressed in her later work, although it would be left to a later generation to express a Nuyorican sense of identity.

Interest in de Burgos' life and work resurfaced in the political climate of the 1960s.[5] Yvette Jiménez de Baez published the first book-length study of de Burgos' life and work in Puerto Rico in 1966 entitled *Julia de Burgos: vida y poesía*. Because de Burgos lived on the verge of the U.S. women's movement of the 1960s and the Puerto Rican movement of the 1970s, her life story captured the imagination of Puerto Ricans and was used as a reminder of the importance of community and solidarity in popular culture. A psychological approach to understanding the way that de Burgos has become a cultural icon among Puerto Ricans (and specifically Puerto Rican women artists) is explored by Iris Zavala-Martínez in her essay "A Critical Inquiry into the Life and Work of Julia de Burgos." De Burgos' experience of migration, Zavala-Martínez argues, "forecasted the struggle for survival, identity, and legitimation that future generations of Puerto Rican migrants would live in the United States" (18). She notes that de Burgos' death generated a "community of solidarity" among future generations of Puerto Ricans (25) and her poetry "bonds many women's experiences" energizing and legitimizing the "collective emancipatory striving of many Puerto Ricans" (25).

Julia de Burgos moved to New York at the end of the first wave of Puerto Rican migration to New York City, and therefore, her work shares much in common with both the *pioneros* (1920–1950), as well as with those who migrated during the second wave (1950–1970).[6] De Burgos' writing for the Spanish-language newspapers in New York is autobiographical and journalistic in style like the work of other *pioneros*. She wrote short sketches and vignettes in Spanish where she explored the themes of migration, Pan-Latino solidarity, and the way that Latinos disrupt the U.S. black/white racial binary.[7] The *pioneros*, Jesús Colón, and Bernardo Vega, are remembered as visionaries for anticipating the importance of recording the development of the New York Puerto Rican community for future generations. However, Julia de Burgos' contributions to the development of the Puerto Rican/Latina/o community in New York are often overlooked. I would like to briefly explore some parallels in style and theme between Julia de Burgos' writing, and Jesús Colon's, who also wrote for *Pueblos Hispanos*.[8] Both write about the experience of migration, they often write short vignettes or sketches rather than fully developed short stories and they explore themes of race, as we will see below. And finally, just as Jesús Colón wrote in English in his later years because he knew that the Puerto Rican community in New York would not be able to read his work in Spanish, de Burgos wrote her final

poems in English anticipating the language shift of the Puerto Rican/
Latina/o community in New York.

However, unlike the *pioneros*, Julia de Burgos was an established
writer when she left the island. She continued to write poetry from abroad
demonstrating the literary sophistication of the writers of the second
wave of migration (1950–1970) such as Pedro Juan Soto, René Marqués,
and José Luis González. De Burgos' life, poetry, and journalistic contributions to the Spanish-language weeklies in New York should be read
in the context of these early Puerto Rican migrants to New York. Her
story is an invaluable contribution as it offers a gendered perspective of
the migration experience prior to the Great Migration of the 1950s. We
can see her influence on the women writers of the Nuyorican movement
of the 1970s; a movement that emerges as the first Puerto Rican literary
movement in the States. It distinguishes itself from earlier writing by this
community as it is an urban literature that reflects the language of the
community with frequent code-switching in English and Spanish.

In de Burgos' writing from New York, she articulates the concerns of
Puerto Ricans on the island while simultaneously advocating for the rights
of Puerto Rican/Latina/os in New York. Although Puerto Ricans arrived
in New York as U.S. citizens, they experienced racial and linguistic discrimination.[9] De Burgos was astute in understanding the challenges that
Puerto Ricans faced in the 1940s and in anticipating how those tribulations would become more acute and evolve over time. She set out to tackle
these trials by featuring important historical and literary figures of Puerto
Rico and the Spanish-speaking world in her writing, understanding the
importance of having positive role models and developing a sense of history. Over time, de Burgos emerges as part of the tradition of resistance
on the island, and a champion for civil rights in the States.

Julia de Burgos was the Art and Culture Editor of *Pueblos Hispanos*,
a leftist Spanish-language newspaper first published in New York in
1943, founded by her former colleague and Puerto Rican nationalist leader, Juan Antonio Corretjer and his wife, Consuelo Lee y Tapia.
Pueblos Hispanos continued the mission of the Puerto Rican Nationalist
Movement from New York. Although the paper demanded independence
for Puerto Rico, it is important to note that it had a much broader mission. It was committed to furthering José Martí's mission of hemispheric
unity as the paper's title suggests, while simultaneously promoting the
rights of Puerto Ricans and other Latina/os in the States. In her essay
"Cultura en Función Social," published in the April 1, 1944 issue of the
paper, de Burgos lays out the objectives of the paper and of the Art and
Culture section specifically:

> Si hoy nos encontramos lado a lado en la elaboración del programa
> de PUEBLOS HISPANOS, es por coincidencia de principios y de

posiciones frente a la batalla general entre las fuerzas reaccionarias y la justicia humana, y frente a la lucha específica que sostienen los pueblos hispanos en Nueva York por su supervivencia y superación. (*Periodista*, 36)

She acknowledges the struggle for survival and the challenges of prejudice and discrimination that Puerto Ricans and other Latina/os face in the United States. She then highlights the purpose of the paper, and the way they plan to achieve their goals of defining, preserving, and promoting the cultures of Hispanic America in the United States:

Uno de los propósitos cardinales de PUEBLOS HISPANOS es el de mejorar las relaciones entre las Américas mediante las difusión de las "culturas hispánicas." [...] Si por cultura entendemos una proyección o manifestación directa del espíritu de una colectividad, llegamos a la conclusión de que en América Hispana el mestizaje ha sido la fuente máxima de nuestra expresión autóctona. Por razones de colonización la cultura, refrescada y enriquecida en la virginidad americana, aportó elementos determinantes en la estructuración de nuevas formas de cultura. (*Periodista* 36)

She recognizes Latin American *mestizaje* as a strength and notes that while the cultures of Latin America have evolved into distinct cultures, they have a shared history of colonialism and slavery.

She argues in this April 1 essay that the arts precede the development of a national and international culture and contends that many countries in Latin America have yet to evolve into synthesized national cultures. The paper was created with the intention of promoting Hispanic cultures in the United States through rigorous self critique, analysis, and study. They planned to establish a publishing house, a bookstore, and hold conferences on Latin American history and culture. She notes that the paper's first objective is:

Antes que nada, afrontar, con mente abierta y espíritu crítico, todos nuestros problemas; analizarlos, sin olvidarnos del marco limitado donde se presentan, con mente universal; someterlos desnudos al pueblo para concienzudo estudio, y fijarle causas auténticas y soluciones permanentes. [...] (*Periodista*, 36)

De Burgos is aware of the need to continue to educate those of Latin American descent living in New York about their history and proposes concrete steps to achieve this goal. She understands that knowledge of the community's history is central to a sense of identity and anticipates the consequences of cultural alienation and oppression. While critics would argue that in later years de Burgos abandoned her concerns for social justice and her struggle for the oppressed, her writings for *Pueblos Hispanos* and for *Semanario Hispano* attest that she remained true to the mission of social justice, which was revealed in her early poetry.[10] De Burgos expanded her struggle against oppression to include those of Hispanic descent in the United States. Her writing also reveals an awareness of the problems that a cultural group faces when colonialist and imperialist intervention separate a people from their traditions, culture, and rituals; problems that we see the Nuyorican artists address thirty years later in their work as they express a new understanding of what it means to be Puerto Rican, (and American), as we will see below.

Although it is not clear that de Burgos participated in establishing a publishing press or a bookstore during her time in New York, she did promote hemispheric solidarity, and Latin American and Caribbean cultures in the United States through interviews with various artists from across the Americas who were visiting New York, such as Puerto Rican musician Noro Morales and Cuban actress and *declamadora* Eusebia Cosme. She also interviewed artists who had permanently migrated to New York as children or were born in the city but were of Caribbean descent, such as Puerto Rican painter Esteban Soriano and Haitian dancer Josephine Premice. Her conversation with Puerto-Rican-born painter Esteban Soriano demonstrates how the nostalgia for the homeland and the island continued to influence the artist's work even though he had lived most of his adult life in New York. De Burgos recognizes Soriano as a Puerto Rican artist who promotes his culture in the United States: "es Soriano exponente reconocido e indiscutible de nuestra vida nacional, viva para siempre en sus cuadros" (*Periodista*, 38). De Burgos' vignettes and interviews for *Pueblos Hispanos* disrupt the dominant story of migration highlighting the many ways that Latinos who migrate remain intimately connected to their source countries. Their cultural production emphasizes the difference between minority cultures and mainstream dominant cultural trends.

De Burgos further explores the complexities around cultural expression, identity, gender, and migration in an interview with Josephine Premice, a young woman of Haitian descent who studies Vodun dance traditions and rituals (*Periodista* 59–60). Establishing that Premice was born in Port-au-Prince, but had moved to New York with her family as an infant, de Burgos notes Premice's ability to beautifully express Haitian Vodun ritual and dance:

En ella la nación cuna no ha dejado de ser, a pesar de su alejamiento del solar nativo. En ella la nación de la raíz social que la engendró en la tierra, no ha dejado de definirse, a pesar de estar su mente enfocada hacia la socialización universal. Es que ella parte, por necesidad histórica de reajuste mundial, desde el punto de partida de todo ser verdaderamente libre: desde el encuentro y el respeto de uno mismo para mejor encontrar y comprender y luchar por el hombre en toda la tierra. (*Periodista* 59)

Premice's story challenges all the dominant notions of migration and emphasizes the cultural alliances between people of Caribbean descent, and Black Americans in New York.

In her vignette, "Perfiles Mexicanos," de Burgos explores the way Latinos disrupt the black/white racial binary in the United States. She describes an encounter with Mexican workers who were brought temporarily to the States to work in factories making military equipment. De Burgos opens the article with a poetic portrayal of the train station that highlights the racism that exists in the United States and how it is reflected in the economic structure of the country. She writes: "Rostros negros. Rostros negros de hermosas mujeres que barren el camino de los blancos. Rostros agitados de prisa y de cansancio en un vaivén de vueltas que choca por su uniformidad" (*Periodista*, 41). She illustrates how the monotonous repetition of the train station is shocking in the way that it dehumanizes the scene. It is an attraction to the familiar and the recognizable that stands out in this monotonous crowd: "De pronto, una mancha distinta del tono blanco y negro atrae mis ojos. Es una mancha India, sola y quieta, que en un rincón disuelve la monotonía de la estación de Pennsylvania" (41). In this description we can read her desire to identify with and humanize this crowd, which appears before her eyes as estranged and unfamiliar.

For de Burgos, the independence of Puerto Rico was critical to self-determination and the development of its national culture. Her 1945 essay "Ser o no ser es la divisa," on the political status of Puerto Rico published in New York in *Semanario Hispano*, received the *Ateneo Puertorriqueño* essay prize. At the time, Luis Muñoz Marín's political party set out to improve the economic conditions on the island, with little concern for how this goal was achieved. The economic development plan, Operation Bootstrap, implemented during Muñoz Marin's administration led to the overdevelopment of the island and a massive migration of Puerto Rico's working class to New York City. The question of Puerto Rico's political status is one that has consumed Puerto Ricans in the twentieth century and remains unresolved.[11] Although de Burgos recognized the importance of the economic development of the island, she adamantly believed that the only way to attain and sustain economic mobility was through independence. She saw the solution offered by the United States of making Puerto Rico a Free Associated State as one that would provide only temporary relief, and she felt strongly that in the long term the consequences of continued dependence would be devastating to the island and its people. De Burgos' essay is a response to Muñoz Marín's position and to the political question facing the island in 1945. She writes:

> No hay otro camino para el hombre de ahora, que situarse en una de estas dos alternativas: o se sitúa al lado de las fuerzas reaccionarias, o escoge el camino del progreso, que siempre es un camino de libertad, por más que quiera ser desvirtuado por demagogos al servicio de las fuerzas retrogradas de siempre. (*Periodista*, 77)

She argues that man must choose to be either in favor of progress and freedom or against it. She adds that refusing to take a decided stand for liberty is to automatically side against it, as she sees no room for an intermediary position. Indifference and passivity, she adds, is a choice against freedom. Her essay makes a direct connection between Puerto Rico's government and the contemporary dictators notorious for repressive governments in other Caribbean and Central American countries such as Trujillo in the Dominican Republic, Somoza in Nicaragua, and Carias in Honduras, and argues "o levantamos los americanos nuestra voz y nuestro esfuerzo para ayudar a destruírlos, o nos colocamos automáticamente, por indiferencia o simpatía al lado de sus gobiernos criminales" (*Periodista*, 77).

Although de Burgos wrote essays and vignettes in New York, she continued to develop her craft as a poet exploring themes similar to those addressed in her journalistic writing. For example, de Burgos' position on the status of Puerto Rico is clear and uncompromising. This sentiment is echoed in her poem "Puerto Rico está en tí": "La voz de Independencia que contigo segiumos/ Los que vivos de honor limosna rechazan/De un Puerto Rico 'estado asociado y ridículo'" (500). This poem reiterates her position on the national question. In her estimation, voting to make Puerto Rico into a Free Associated State will prolong dependence of the island and make it appear ridiculous before other nations. This option is nothing more than a "limosna" that will only ensure the continued dependency of the island and prolong the colonial relationship.

In both of Julia de Burgos' poems, "23 de septiembre" and "A José Martí," the poet recalls pivotal moments in Puerto Rico's history of resistance. September 23, 1868, marks the date of the *Grito de Lares* [Lares Revolt], the day when Puerto Rican revolutionaries fought for independence from Spain: "vivo en el gran desfile de todos los patriotas/ que murieron de ira y de ira despiertan"(400). She remembers all who fought for independence from Spain, many of them were organizing from New York. She closes her poem aligning herself with all who fight for social justice: "vivo en el hombre nuevo que pelea en cada frente/ libertades de pan y justicia de ideas" (400). In the poem "A José Martí," she recalls the incomplete struggle for independence led by Cuban revolutionary poet José Martí, who promised to liberate Spain's oldest colonies in the Caribbean, Puerto Rico, and Cuba: "Yo vengo de la tierna mitad de tu destino; / Del sendero amputado al rumbo de tu estrella; /El último destello del resplandor andino, /Que se extravió en la sombra, perdido de tu huella" (364). In de Burgos' writing from New York, we can trace a genealogy for the later Puerto Rican/Latina/o writers who follow her, and we can also see how de Burgos becomes an important figure of resistance in the history of Puerto Rico, both on the island and in the States.

De Burgos' final poems "Farewell in Welfare Island" and "The Sun in Welfare Island" (1953), written in English, express a deep sense of desolation and isolation. Welfare Island, today Roosevelt Island, was home to numerous hospitals, asylums, and correctional institutions. She spent weeks and at times months, in the facilities at Goldwater Memorial Hospital between the years of 1950–1953 because of her advanced state of cirrhosis of the liver due to her alcoholism. The loneliness and despondency that she felt while in exile away from her homeland, family, and friends, was magnified while she was in the hospital, as we can note from these poems: "Where is the voice of freedom,/ freedom to laugh,/ to move /without the heavy phantom of despair?" (356). De Burgos wrote her final poems in English in 1953 because she was aware of the linguistic ruptures and discontinuities of future generations of Puerto Ricans and Latinos in the United States. The dream of freedom, which is symbolized by the United States, and especially New York City which has served as an entry point for numerous immigrants over the years, is occluded by the sense of despair and hopelessness expressed in these poems. One must also read the repeated line in this poem "It has to be from here," as a reference to geographic location, from the United States. To return to Puerto Rico in her deteriorated condition would be to acknowledge defeat. In "The Sun in Welfare Island," which is believed to be her final poem, she reveals her desire for solitude and death through contrasting images of life that threaten to disturb the peace she longs for. Throughout the poem, she continues to evoke strong images of life such as the birds, hymns, daisies, sweetness, liberty, rivers, dancing, and the sun which threaten her solitude: "My eyes are full of /Solitude/And all of me is loneliness/ In a rebellious heart" (358). Although her segregation, dejection, and misery are conveyed in both of these poems, the life that continues to thrive within her is revealed in the closing lines of both poems. Her heart is still "rebellious" and she remains "unshaken" (358).

De Burgos' rebellious spirit and her determination to establish herself as a writer are what led her to leave the island in 1940. Although de Burgos believed in the independence of Puerto Rico, her dissonance in relation to the nationalist leaders of the time, her divorce, her lifestyle, and her humble background created unbridgeable rifts between her and the intellectual elite on the island. Although she has captured the imaginations of Puerto Ricans both on and off the island, her presence is especially felt in the work of contemporary Puerto Rican women writers who grapple with her influence in their work, as we will note below.

Rosario Ferré dedicates her collection of essays entitled *Sitio a eros*, to women writers such as Virginia Wolf, Sylvia Plath, and Julia de Burgos who inspire her because, despite their tragic deaths, they were able to overcome mortality through passion and imagination (7). In "Carta a Julia de Burgos," included in this collection, she provides a short biographical summary of the poet's life, where she contrasts de Burgos' life with her work, underscoring the contradictions between them. Her anger at de Burgos is palpable in this letter. Ferré reprimands her for assuming a submissive role before the men in her life and not living up to the standards she set for herself in poems such as "A Julia de Burgos" and "Yo misma fui mi ruta." In the end, she recognizes that de Burgos was a woman who lived ahead of her time. She closes her letter to de Burgos in reconciliation with de Burgos' life and who she was:

> Porque tú lograste superar la situación opresiva de la mujer, su humillación de siglos. Y al ver que no podías cambiarla, utilizaste esa situación, la empleaste, a pesar de que se te desgarraban las entretelas del alma, para ser lo que en verdad fuiste: ni mujer, ni hombre, sino simple y sencillamente, poeta. (151)

She closes these lines referring to de Burgos as "poet" which is above all what de Burgos struggled to become. It was her vocation and the life she chose for herself at a time, and in a society that made it almost impossible for her to establish herself simultaneously as a woman, an intellectual, a poet, a journalist, and an activist.

Almost fifty years after de Burgos wrote "Ser o no ser es la divisa" warning against Puerto Rico becoming a Free Associated State, contemporary Puerto Rican writer Esmeralda Santiago, published "Island of Lost Causes," in *The New York Times* exploring the political status of the island in 1992 on the day that the plebiscite on the island would take place to determine its status. The echoes of de Burgos' essay "Ser o no Ser es la Divisa" are haunting. Esmeralda Santiago is best known for her memoir *Cuando era puertorriqueña,* where she explores the complexities of Puerto Rican identity on the island due to the history of colonialism, slavery, and imperialism; complexities that are exacerbated by migration to the mainland. In "Island of Lost Causes," she explores the consequences of commonwealth status on the island such as an unclear sense of identity and an attitude of resignation before the struggle for independence. She notes, however, that since she now lives in the New York she is "not eligible to vote on these questions" (23). She claims that the "plebiscite gives Puerto Ricans only the illusion of self-determination—an illusion that deflects attention from the basic problems on the island"(23), such as the high unemployment rate, the exploitation of the land, and of the workers on the island by American companies who go there for the tax breaks provided as incentives by the government, a plan for economic development that dates back to Luis Muñoz Marín. Santiago states that the ninety-five years of Puerto Rican political affiliation with, and dependence on the United States have destroyed and confused Puerto Ricans' sense of national identity. She underscores, "In our hearts, we want to believe independence is the right choice, but our history forces us to see it as a lost cause" (Santiago 24). She argues, like de Burgos, that "a vote for commonwealth insures that we don't have to commit one way or the other" (22). She concludes the article with words that echo de Burgos' 1945 essay, "We need to look at ourselves hard and to stop hiding behind the status quo. It is not a choice. It is a refusal to choose" (24). It is striking that de Burgos was able to clearly see the way the current problems created by the dependency of the island would continue to evolve and preclude the island from achieving independence and a sense of national identity in the future.

Julia de Burgos' writing reveals her insight into the challenges Puerto Rican people would face if their history of resistance and the fight for independence on the island were forgotten. These are ideas that are further explored forty years later by Sandra María Esteves, in her poem "It is Raining Today." Esteves is one of the important contemporary Nuyorican voices who writes of her bicultural identity and her impoverished knowledge of her past as a woman of Puerto Rican descent growing up in New York City. Esteves recalls the violent history of the Caribbean in general and Puerto Rico in particular as she longs for a deeper understanding of her heritage. Notable also is the choice of writing in English and Spanish in this poem. If rain is history, her understanding of her history is nothing but mist. In the poem she attempts to claim her past when she writes: "I pray to the rain/ Give me back my rituals/ Give back truth/ Return the remnants of my identity/ Bathe me in self-discovered knowledge… / Speak to me of rain" (Esteves, *Boricuas*, 19–20). She understands that knowledge of her history, past, and traditions is critical to developing a sense of identity and self-worth.

In Esteves' poems the history of Puerto Rican resistance is traced first to the indigenous people of the island and later to the African peoples brought to the island in the transatlantic slave trade. Juan Flores notes that the omission of the cultures and struggles of pre-Colombian times in the history of resistance of the island and "the dimunition of their enduring cultural significance are earmarks of a colonialist frame of thinking" (20). The overdevelopment of the island under programs such as Operation Bootstrap and the massive migration of working class Puerto Ricans to the States are the central historical developments that separate the writers of the *Generación del treinta* and Pedreira from the present time. In his essay, Flores argues that the cultural production of Puerto Ricans in New York such as the works of Sandra María Esteves, Tato Laviera, and Eddie Palmieri "escape interpretation within the cramped intellectual horizon of *Insularismo*" (15).

In Sandra María Esteves' poem "A Julia y a Mí," dedicated to Julia de Burgos, Esteves reproaches de Burgos for giving into the sorrow, despair, and isolation which she felt as an outcast in New York City. She reproaches her as Ferré did: "You let life cut your sorrow from wrinkles young/ You let the wine mellow your hatred/ Dissolving the fuel that nourished your fires of wisdom" (*Yerba*, 50). She notes that what young Latina/o children need are not images of despair, but rather images of hope that will sustain them through the challenges they will face in New York City. Esteves contrasts herself with de Burgos. While de Burgos numbed and anesthetized her pain with alcohol which slowly killed her, Esteves found an alternative way to confront the pain of life as noted in the final stanza of this poem: "my fist is my soul/ it cuts into the blood of dragons/ and marks time with the beat /of an afrocuban drum" (*Yerba*, 51).

It is important to note the ways that Esteves and de Burgos use language differently. While de Burgos did write in Spanish most of her life, and later switched to English because she witnessed the language shift taking place among Latina/os in the United States, Esteves uses both languages in a way that reflects the language of the community at the time. In her work, there is also a celebration of the African presence as source of strength.

I would like to close this study of de Burgos and her legacy in Puerto Rican women's writing by looking at a later generation Nuyorican writer, Mariposa. It is compelling to hear Mariposa speak of her coming into poetry. In her various performances, she notes that she first recognized the power of poetry in the words of African American women poets, Ntozake Change and Gwendolyn Brooks. Through these poets, she then came to Sandra María Esteves who introduced her to the work of Julia de Burgos. In her poem, "Ode to the DiaspoRican" written in English and Spanish, she claims her Puerto Rican heritage, learned in the streets of New York: "some people think that I'm not bonafide/cause my playground was a concrete jungle/cause my Río Grande de Loíza was the Bronx River/ cause my Fajardo was City Island/my Luquillo, Orchard Beach/and summer nights were filled with city noises/instead of coquis." Her free verse carries the same intense language, full of passion and imagination that resembles de Burgos. It is in poetry that de Burgos found freedom; in a similar confessional tone, Mariposa claims in "Boricua Butterfly": "The reborn/The living phoenix/Rising up out of the ashes/of my conquered people/ . . . /Not fragmented but whole/Not colonized but Free."

De Burgos' legacy is felt and remembered by poets and writers such as Esmeralda Santiago and Puerto Rican women writers Rosario Ferré and Sandra María Esteves. The latter two acknowledge the debt that they owe to Julia de Burgos who paved a path before them as a professional woman writer and intellectual who faced discrimination and prejudice because of her ethnicity, gender, humble background, language, and culture. Against all odds, she continued to struggle for human dignity, social justice, and the rights of the oppressed. It was her work, along with the work of those other early migrants that opened doors for those Puerto Ricans who came to New York as part of the Great Migration of the 1950s. Her writing, along with the work of other early migrants, set the stage for the cultural expressions from the diaspora that were born of the Civil Rights and Women's Movements in the 1960s, and the Puerto Rican Movement in the 1970s.

Notes

1. The nationalist writers of the 1930s embraced a homogenizing image of Puerto Rican identity based on Antonio Pedreira's essay *Insularismo* that silenced the various voices of the nation based on language, gender, class, and racial difference. In his study *The Puerto Rican Nation on the Move: Identities on the Island and in the Diaspora,* Jorge Duany clearly outlines the problems and tensions between the Puerto Rican communities on the island and in the United States when he acknowledges that "most nationalists have not fully acknowledged the implications of spatial dispersion and cultural fragmentalization, perhaps because, following political doctrines prevailing since the nineteenth century, they have typically defined national sovereignty and identity within strictly territorial boundaries" (20).
2. Juan Gelpí notes in *Literatura y paternalismo* that she is the only woman who is associated with this movement although she remains marginal.
3. One exception to this take on de Burgos is found in the article written by Juan Gelpí, "The nomadic subject in the poetry of Julia de Burgos," published in *The Cultures of the Hispanic Caribbean,* edited by Conrad James and John Perivolaris (37–49, London: Macmillan, 2000).
4. In fact in the only biography written of this important figure, *Julia en blanco y negro,* Juan Antonio Rodríguez Pagán only briefly mentions de Burgos' life in New York, claiming that during this time she was no longer productive as a writer because of her alcoholism and illness.
5. The first book-length study of de Burgos was a MA thesis written by Yvette Jiménez Baez, a student at the University of Puerto Rico. Her study raised much interest in de Burgos as she recounts many of the sensational aspects of her life, her divorce, her affair with a prominent Dominican politician and intellectual whose name is never revealed in the study to protect him and his

family. He is mysteriously referred to as *el Señor X*, only raising greater interest and speculation about her story. All of this greatly added to the myth of Julia de Burgos. Her writing for newspapers in New York is not mentioned as this predates the Puerto Rican Movement of the 1970s. These stories remained buried in archives at that time.

6. Twentieth-century Puerto Rican literature in the United States followed the three waves of Puerto Rican migration: the *pioneros* (1920–1950), the writers of the Great Migration (1950–1970), and the Nuyorican writers (1970–). For more on the stages of twentieth-century Puerto Rican literature in the United States see Juan Flores' essay "Puerto Rican Literature in The United States: Stages and Perspectives" published in *Divided Borders*.

7. See the introduction by Edna Acosta Belén and Virginia Sánchez Korrol of *The Way It Was and Other Writings* by Jesús Colón; and *Memoirs of Bernardo Vega: A Contribution to the History of the Puerto Rican Community in New York,* edited by Cesar Andreu Iglesias and translated by Juan Flores. Julia de Burgos' work was yet to be collected and translated into English. De Burgos also wrote multiple vignettes with two fictional characters, Iris y Paloma. These vignettes have yet to be seriously considered.

8. In addition to Jesús Colón's and Julia de Burgos' contributions to the newspaper, Puerto Rican poets Clemente Soto Vélez, Luis Llorens Torres, and Luis Palés Matos also wrote for *Pueblos Hispanos*. In addition to important Puerto Rican writers of the time, other notable writers from Latin America published in *Pueblos Hispanos* such as Pablo Neruda, Juan Marinello, Juan Bosch, and Raul Roa—all writers who Julia de Burgos had met during her stay in Havana, Cuba between the years of 1940–1942.

9. See Virginia Sanchez Korrol's *From Colonia to Community: The History of Puerto Ricans in New York City,* Bernardo Vega's *Memoirs of Bernardo Vega,* and Joaquín Colón López's *Pioneros puertorriqueños en Nueva York 1917–1947.*

10. See Juan Antonio Rodríguez Pagán's, *Julia en blanco y negro.*

11. See *None of the Above* edited by Frances Negrón Muntaner (New York: Palgrave Macmillan 2007).

Works Cited

De Burgos, Julia. *Julia de Burgos: periodista en Nueva York*. Ed. Juan Antonio Rodríguez Pagán. San Juan, PR: Ateneo Puertorriqueño, 1992.

———. *Song of the Simple Truth: The Complete Poems*. Ed. and Trans. Jack Agüeros. Connecticut: Curbstone Press, 1997.

Duany, Jorge. *The Puerto Rican Nation on the Move: Identities on the Island and in the United States*. Chapel Hill: University of North Carolina Press, 2002.

Esteves, Sandra María. "It Is Raining Today." *Boricuas: Influential Puerto Rican Writings*. Ed. Roberto Santiago. New York: Random House, 1995.

———. *Yerba Buena*. NY: Greenfield Review Press, 1980.

Ferré, Rosario. *Sitio a eros: quince ensayos literarios*. México: J. Moritz, 1986.

Flores, Juan. *Divided Borders: Essays on Puerto Rican Identity*. Houston: Arte Público Press, 1993.

Kanellos, Nicolás and Helvetia Martell, eds. *Hispanic Periodicals in the United States, Origins to 1960: A Brief History and a Comprehensive Bibliography*. Houston: Arte Público Press, 2000.

Mariposa (aka Maria Teresa Fernandez). "Ode to the Diasporican" *Boricua Poetry*. http://www.virtualboricua.org/Docs/poem_mtf.htm. Downloaded on July 22, 2009.

Santiago, Esmeralda. "Island of Lost Causes." *Boricuas: Influential Puerto Rican Writings-An Anthology*. Ed. Roberto Santiago. New York: Random House, 1995.

Zavala-Martínez, Iris. "A Critical Inquiry into the Life and Work of Julia de Burgos." *The Psychosocial Development of Puerto Rican Women*. Eds. Cynthia T. García Coll and María de Lourdes Mattei. New York: Praeger, 1989. 1–30.

II

Dislocated Narratives

4

Travel and Family in Julia Alvarez's Canon

Vivian Nun Halloran

Literary critics have praised Julia Alvarez's imaginative reconstruction of the Trujillo dictatorship and the reign of terror he inflicted upon both his countrymen and on Haitian civilians in works such as *How the García Girls Lost Their Accents, In the Time of the Butterflies, Something to Declare,* and *Before We Were Free.*[1] Her literary canon depicts the lives, loves, and troubles of a set of economically and culturally privileged characters of Dominican origin, many of whom immigrate to the United States to escape the political persecution of the Trujillo regime. Although they occasionally come into contact with members of the oppressed classes in the island—both the working poor and the unemployed—the wealthy protagonists of Alvarez's novels, poems, and life writings enjoy privileges unavailable to most of the population of the Dominican Republic. As Alvarez recalls in her collection of autobiographical essays, *Something to Declare*: "In the Dominican Republic no one could travel without papers, and the dictatorship rarely granted anyone this special permission" (13). Despite these autocratic travel restrictions, the Alvarez family and most of the wealthy Dominican protagonists of Julia Alvarez's novels manage to obtain access to legal documents which let them travel abroad to further their education or enhance their career prospects, receive medical treatment or, even, get safely away from the oppressive political regime.[2] Although these real and imagined families have both wealth and political connections, the elite Dominican characters in Alvarez's *oeuvre* rarely spend their money on leisure travel to far-off vacation destinations. Before they are exiled, these Dominican families leave their homes in the city to spend summer vacations together in a family compound in the countryside. After they migrate to the United States, these same families rake up frequent-flyer miles, shuttling back and forth between the island

and the mainland to stay connected to members of their extended family. Although their base of operation changes due to the political persecution of the *trujillato*, the Dominican elites who figure in most of Alvarez's fiction prize family togetherness above solitary luxury.

Travel matters to these characters as a means to an end rather than as an end in itself—the older family members travel out of nostalgia, in order to preserve their ties to Dominican culture and the Spanish language, while the younger generation is more idealistic and wants to be involved in shaping the social and economic development of future generations in the Dominican Republic. Alvarez's depiction of this intergenerational struggle in her fiction and life writings is set against the background of the long and troubled history of American military intervention in the island's politics as well as the totalitarian paternalism with which Trujillo ruled his people; she is aware that the ongoing involvement of exiled Dominicans and Dominican Americans in the internal affairs of this sovereign nation raises the specter of cultural imperialism. Both the author and her protagonists recognize that the frequency with which the U. S.-based families visit the island heightens the likelihood that the generations' different ideologies will come into conflict but, at the same time, their regular contact with the branches of the extended family who never left the island reminds young and old alike that they are no longer citizens or residents of, but merely visitors to, the Dominican Republic.

In his landmark treatise on travel practices, *Routes: Travel and Translation in the Late Twentieth Century*, James Clifford analyzes the relationship that links travel, geography, and the spatial dimension of dwelling as he considers how people perceive their lives and their role in society according to the relationships they establish with others around them. Clifford contrasts diasporic and exilic cultural forms and explains their relationships to travel:

> Diaspora is different from travel (though it works through travel practices) in that it is not temporary. It involves dwelling, maintaining communities, having collective homes away from home (and in this it is different from exile, with its frequently individualist focus). Diaspora discourse articulates, or bends together, both roots *and* routes to construct what Gilroy (1987) describes as alternate public spheres, forms of community consciousness and solidarity that maintain identifications outside the national time/space in order to live inside, with a difference. (251)

Julia Alvarez depicts both the exilic and the diasporic outlooks in her canon. The older characters in Alvarez's earliest novels actively harbor the idea of return to the motherland and, thus, consider themselves exiles. The longer Alvarez has written, the more she has incorporated into her novels a myriad of outlooks, historical as well as personal, about the condition of displacement from the homeland. Alvarez prizes her regular trips to the Dominican Republic as an important way to remember her roots, and better understand the routes she has carved out for herself through time and experience, as she announces in *Something to Declare*: "To know who I am, I have to know where I come from. So I keep coming back to the Island. And for fuerza, I go back to this thought: it really is in my Caribbean roots, in my island genes to be a pan-American, a gringa dominicana, a synthesizing consciousness" (175). As I read them in both her fiction and memoir, these journeys back and forth across time, language, and geography are proof of Alvarez's diasporic outlook, which is not always shared by her fictional characters.

While wealthy Dominican characters in Alvarez's canon do have "collective homes away from home," and "maintain identifications outside the national time/space in order to live inside, with a difference," they do so only in the context of the specific family unit, and not within a larger "community" of other exiles. These characters experience exile as individual family units, not as solitary travelers as Clifford's distinction would seem to imply. In Alvarez's canon, Dominican characters who legally immigrate to the United States settle down either in rural settings, like Vermont or New Hampshire, or else in exclusive suburbs of major metropolitan areas. None of Alvarez's novels depict the protagonists' families residing within an identifiable Dominican diasporic community. Alvarez's protagonists rarely encounter other Latinos, much less other Dominicans, in their daily lives.[3] Only those secondary characters in Alvarez's works who reside in urban areas can be said to participate in a diasporic community made up of other Dominicans and Latino immigrants: in *Something to Declare*, Dr. Alvarez sees Latino patients in his practice and hires nurses from Puerto Rico and the Dominican Republic; the elder Guzmáns in *How Tía Lola Came to ~~Visit~~ Stay* live in New York City and run a *bodega*; Alma Rodríguez's parents in *Saving the World*, Mamacita and Papote, retire to Miami. However, these examples are few and far between in Alvarez's canon; they are the exception, rather than the rule.

Most of the Dominican families Alvarez depicts in her fiction arrive in the United States as a direct result of political persecution during the time when General Rafael Leónidas Trujillo was in power in the island, directly or behind the scenes, from 1930 until his assassination in 1961.[4] In Alvarez's fiction, poetry, and life writing, the older generation of wealthy Dominican characters define themselves primarily through their immigration experience as political exiles in the United States; this label identifies them as unwilling immigrants whose departure from the island constituted an emotional hardship on their part. The trauma of their involuntary departure from the land of their birth still haunts Dominican characters persecuted for their beliefs or political activities and forced to seek refuge in American shores; the parents and grandparents who survived Trujillo feel a lasting emotional connection to the *patria*, or homeland, and continue to regard themselves as authentically Dominican despite remaining in the United States after the death of the dictator. However, their experience of life in the Dominican Republic is in itself exclusionary; even when they live on the island, these characters interact only with other Dominicans from a similar economic background. Thus, their remembered Dominican identity is predicated as much on their class status as it is on their national identity.

The wealthy Dominican families' seeming nostalgia and idealization of a past way of life is a political act in Alvarez's works, and not merely a sign of the dotage of old age. Their frequent trips back to the island allow these characters to maintain an ongoing relationship with the "imagined community" of people, in Benedict Anderson's terms, who perform and affirm a common Dominican cultural identity in each other. The shared ties of language and culture that bind Alvarez's exiled Dominicans to their compatriots who remain on the island also include class status, as I mentioned previously. As they hold steadfastly to their cultural and national identity even as they live out their lives in the United States, the heads of the Alvarez, García, and Rodríguez families described in *Something to Declare, How the García Girls Lost Their Accents* and *¡Yo!*, and *Saving the World*, respectively, try to undo the negative effects of their exilic voyages. After the dictator's death, the family travel circuit between the United States and the Dominican Republic allows this older generation to reclaim some semblance of the normalcy and autonomy they had to give up when Trujillo took power and conflated patriotism with a cult of personality. The older generation's choice not to repatriate to their island, however, acknowledges that the break they made with their past way of life is permanent, and that their children have made a life for themselves in the new country.

The post-*trujillato* Dominican-Americans have no personal recollection of the family's original departure from the *patria*; instead, they remember all the subsequent voyages their family made "back" to the island to see relatives and continue making the trip "home" a part of their adult lives. As self-supporting adults, the Dominican-American characters in Alvarez's fiction continue to benefit from their parents' privileged economic status, although they eventually challenge or reject their parents' rules, cultural expectations, and economic elitism. In *Something to Declare*, Julia Alvarez remembers that even when she was broke as an adult, her New York-based parents continued to fund her regular trips to the island: "Every year, my parents offered me a trip 'home' to see the family, the one handout I always took" (182). While she considers this transaction a "handout" tantamount to charity, and knows that her parents' hope is that she will fall in love and marry a "real" Dominican man and have his children, the prospect of the trip itself holds enough attraction to Alvarez that she swallows her pride and takes advantage of it. Yolanda García, Alvarez's alter ego, visits her Dominican relatives with her family, with her American friends, and on her own even after both branches of the extended family feels she has betrayed them by including inaccurate or twisted versions of their private affairs in her published fiction. In *Saving the World*, Alma Rodríguez, another of Alvarez's alter egos, publishes under the pseudonym, *Fulana de Tal*, which translates roughly into Ms. So and So, at her own family's request; they want to avoid embarrassment and political repercussions for her extended family which remains in the Dominican Republic.

> Why couldn't Alma use her real name? And she was frank, explaining how her family had requested that she not use "their" name; how, yes, she resented their petty reasons—their fear of social embarrassment (Latina girls enjoying sex before marriage; enjoying sex period; having breakdowns, divorcing—just like spoiled gringa girls)—but she also understood their terror, the deep scars after years in a dictatorship, the possibility they cited of political repercussions to the extended familia who had stayed back home. (21)

While Alma's side of the family has permanently settled in the United States and is safe from any retaliatory violence from agents of the government in the Dominican Republic, the rest of her extended family primarily resides on the island. In order to continue visiting her relatives whenever she goes to the island with her American husband and his kids, Alma agrees to this small act of deception or hiding.[5]

Each set of immigrants within the family unit wants to impose its national values and cultural beliefs upon someone else: the older generation sees its assimilated children as innocents who can be 'properly' brought up to observe traditional Dominican values, while the young people want to disseminate their American ideas among the poor, illiterate natives of their parents' homeland. The frequent trips the older generation takes to the island with its children are designed to reinforce the superiority of traditional Dominican moral values, language, and culture over American ones. The Dominican-Americans who immigrated as children or were born in the U. S. mainland perceive the island as their parents' domain; despite residing within the family compound surrounded by people they know and to whom they are related, members of the younger generation feel somewhat displaced when they visit the island as children or young adults. They feel they have no real peers within the extended family because their cousins who grew up on the island share their parent's sense of class status as the main part of their Dominican identity.

This pattern of exilic immigration and self-imposed isolation from other Latinos means that wealthy Dominican families in the Alvarez canon exist as insular pockets of cultural and linguistic "otherness" within a larger, predominantly white, Anglo majority in the United States. In her book-length analysis of Julia Alvarez's fiction, Kelli Lyon Johnson argues that "Alvarez, in fact, constructs throughout her writings a gendered map of exile, one in which the trajectories are neither linear nor solitary. Alvarez's novels in particular reveal multiple trajectories, apexes, and voyages, each approaching one another without merging into hybridity" (29). Johnson correctly points out that Alvarez's depictions of exile are always collective. I want to go further than that and argue that not only is exile not a "solitary" experience in novels like *How the García Girls Lost their Accents*, *¡Yo!*, and *In the Name of Salomé*, but it is a familial experience. These novels all feature families who leave the island together and in her collection of autobiographical essays, *Something to Declare*, Julia Alvarez describes exile not only in terms of separation from her homeland, but more personally, as a tearing apart of a large family unit: "When my parents and sisters and I came to this country, we left behind the protection and patronage of the larger *familia*. We were on our own. In this country, we had only ourselves to count on" (119–120). By illustrating how the departure of those exiles affected the lives of those members of the extended family who remained in the island in *¡Yo!*, *Before We Were Free*, *In the Name of Salomé*, and *Saving the World*, Alvarez uses the trope of family to demonstrate that the experience of exile has a lasting effect as much on the country the exiles leave behind as well as on the place where they settle down.

Johnson's claim that Alvarez's textual mapping of exile is "gendered," however, is more problematic because of its ambiguity. Male characters are generally those facing severe punishment or incarceration from Trujillo and his secret police in *How the García Girls Lost their Accents*, *Something to Declare*, *¡Yo!*, and *Before We Were Free*; however, the very fact that most of these men leave the island accompanied by their families means that, whether or not they were directly involved in plotting against the dictator's life, female and child characters also experience exile when they leave the land of their birth.[6] Alvarez's fiction and life writings describe the experience of exile from both male and female points of view. The fragmented nature of Alvarez's narrative structure in novels such as *How the García Girls Lost their Accents*, *¡Yo!*, and *In the Name of Salomé*, as well as the self-contained autobiographical essays of *Something to Declare* mean that there is no unified, overarching, gendered perspective on any one event; different characters have the opportunity to narrate their lives and feelings through the lens of their own, gendered experience. Since most of Alvarez's privileged Dominican characters define themselves relationally, according to the role they play within the extended Dominican family unit to which they belong, I contend that it is more productive for us to consider how the different generations within a given family experience and describe the separation they feel from their homeland in Alvarez's fiction and life writings than to note the gender of each character forced to leave his or her island.

The only contact Alvarez's characters have with other immigrants takes place within the very patriarchal family household model they preserve in the Dominican Republic and have recreated in the United States: members of an extended family live together with their domestic servants in a common family compound but continue to observe a strict set of social and economic hierarchies. While the exiled nuclear family may have left the Dominican Republic out of political necessity, in their commitment to maintain the social status and way of life they practiced in the island, these privileged families helped spur a secondary wave of economic immigration to the United States. By only hiring the relatives of people who were domestic servants to their extended family back "home" instead of American-born maids, the Alvarez and García families broaden the economic and educational horizons of a small percentage of the Dominican population who would otherwise not have had any access to legal immigration and/or international travel. Because their maid wears a uniform to work, she becomes the outward sign of privilege and difference that distinguishes the García household from others in their Bronx neighborhood. In ¡Yo! Alvarez demonstrates how public perceptions of the maid's daughter's immigration status and ethnic identity are shaped by her mother's clothing, as much as by her daughter's skin tone: "Stories spread at school. I was fairly light-skinned and rather pretty—all the García girls said so. In fact, most people guessed I was Italian or Greek. I had a fancy address on my report card. Kids on the bus reported that a maid in a uniform waited for me—on rainy days she carried an umbrella" (61). Even though Sara and her mother, Primi, lived in the García home, their neighbors and acquaintances did not recognize that mother and daughter shared their employer's ethnicity or national identity. Primi's darker skin pigment was read as a sign of her economic inferiority to her lighter-skinned daughter, whose own nationality was misread as darkly European.

Despite maintaining this outward sign of difference from American nuclear family units, the Dominican families in Alvarez's canon who settle down in the United States fully participate in American society. They form ties of friendship and community with their neighbors, regardless of their race, gender, or ethnicity. The most explicit example of this tendency toward community-building in Alvarez's canon takes place in *How Tía Lola Came to ~~Visit~~ Stay*. Not only does the eponymous Lola, Miguel Guzmán's mother's colorful *tía*, come to reacquaint him and his sister with the Spanish language and Dominican cultural traditions that are his family's legacy, but she shares her cooking, dancing, and love of color with their new neighbors in Vermont. This Spanish-speaking woman transcends the barriers of language and brings the whole small town together in support of the Little League team and in order to celebrate her niece's first birthday alone since her traumatic divorce. As the sun sets on her birthday, Miguel can tell that his mother, Linda, finally feels at home in her new surroundings: "Mami, too, is thinking that she is so lucky. Although she no longer lives on a beautiful island with her large *familia*, she has found a new home with her children and favorite aunt among a warm *familia* of friends in Vermont" (128). Because of Lola's unabashed introduction of her culture, language, and enthusiasm into this New England college town, the Guzmán family has developed a syncretistic definition of *familia* by incorporating friends and kin within a large social and emotional support group.

The author and her fictional alter egos further cement this alliance between Dominican characters and their neighbors when they marry American men—the real Julia Alvarez married Bill Eichner, a doctor and farmer she met in Vermont; Yolanda García marries Douglas Manley in ¡Yo!; Alma Rodríguez marries Richard Huebner in *Saving the World*, and *How Tía Lola Came to ~~Visit~~ Stay* raises the possibility that the eponymous character has found a nice, widowed American suitor of her own. Of course, these exogamous romantic alliances result in further trips to the Dominican Republic to visit the extended family compound. Thus, a travel cycle develops within the Dominican household dynamic: the more people who join the family, whether through birth or marriage, the more reasons characters have to fly back and forth between the island and the mainland and strengthen the ties of kinship that link all of them together.[7]

Since they are more fully integrated into American life than their parents, the members of both the 1.5 and second generations of Dominican immigrants regard the United States as their home country, and the Dominican Republic as their sentimental *patria*, or inherited homeland, in the various texts.[8] When they visit the island, Julia Alvarez and her assorted alter egos—Yolanda García, the *gringa dominicana* writer from *In the Time of the Butterflies*, Camila Henríquez Ureña, and Alma Rodríguez—face constant challenges from their extended family to their claims to authenticity: no one regards them as real *dominicanas* because of their behavior. In *Something to Declare*, Alvarez recounts how the elders in the Dominican side of the family "tried unsuccessfully to stem the tide of our Americanization," by asking the young people to speak more Spanish: " 'Tienen que hablar en español,' they commanded" (64). On the island, the Alvarez girls and their fictional counterparts are expected to dress or behave in accordance to local cultural norms, in which women are primarily defined through marriage and motherhood, whereas a man's worth is determined by his chosen occupation. For her part, Alvarez and her fictional alter egos reject the idea that they have to measure up to standards of "Dominican" cultural and linguistic authenticity when they are on the island. Even a sympathetic female friend defends the young Julia from criticism by pointing to her nationality, as Alvarez recounts in her memoir: "When the matrons in town complained about our miniskirts or about our driving around with boys and no chaperones, Mamacán threw up her hands and said, '¡Pero si son americanas! They're American girls!' " (66–67). While they consider themselves "Dominican-Americans," embracing the hyphenated identity as a sign of doubleness and cultural multiplicity, rather than a marker or mediocrity, Dominicans do not embrace the hybridity of that term. To them, Alvarez's and her sisters' lifestyle and behavior on the island mark them as permanent outsiders.

The rebellious flaunting of cultural and moral Dominican traditions— Alvarez's and her alter-egos' failed marriages and childlessness—can also be read as political acts; their defiance of their respective families' expectations demonstrates a desire to remain involved in Dominican cultural, political and economic life through change and innovation instead of by mimicking their elders' automatic veneration for some past golden era. The younger generation has higher moral expectations of itself than do their parents; they not only want to become involved with a broader segment of the Dominican population than the narrow social circle among whom their parents socialize, but they also want to spearhead and participate in the Dominican Republic's entry into modernity. This post-Trujillo generation rejects the older group's impulse toward nostalgia and tradition, but they nonetheless enjoy the wealth and privileges they have inherited from their elders and which mark them out as different from the poor people they try to help. As her characters grow up, mature, and start earning their own keep, however, Alvarez shows them developing a moral consciousness distinct from that of their progenitors; she considers the class status that comes from her inherited wealth her "golden handcuffs" and explains how this privilege prevents the elites from being true to themselves: "those positions of privilege that often trap us women into denying our bodies, our desires, our selves—and what is worse or just as bad, into denying the souls of others" (*Something to Declare* 156). While they never forfeit their relational identity as members of a given family household, the post-Trujillo Dominican-American characters view their travels back "home" to the island as opportunities to carry out their ideological convictions about social justice and feminism.

Instead of fraternizing with other well-heeled young socialites like their cousins when they visit the island, the scions of the Alvarez, García, and Rodríguez families reach out to segments of the local population with whom their parents would rather not associate. However, these "hyphenated person[s]" (66), as Alvarez calls herself in *Something to Declare*, do not travel alone; characters like Yolanda García, the *gringa dominicana* from the second novel, and Alma Rodríguez often bring their American boyfriends or husbands with them to the family compound and involve them in their schemes to help the kind of poor, uneducated Dominican people that their elders view only as potential domestic workers. These idealistic young men and women regard the Dominican Republic as a large scale, social engineering laboratory where they introduce educational, agricultural, and economic innovations to the natives, as the teenage Alvarez did on a trip to the island during the 1960s: "I arrived with my DO-YOUR-OWN THING!!! T-shirt and bell-bottom pants and several novels by Herman Hesse, ready to spread the seeds of the sixties revolution raging in the States" (*Something to Declare* 65). These interactions between rich "Dominican-Americans" and poor "dominicanos," however well-intentioned, are not without their risks, as the plot lines of the novels discussed below illustrate.

In both *Something to Declare* and the short parable she published in 2001, *A Cafecito Story*, Julia Alvarez discusses how she and her husband, Bill Eichner, decided to purchase land in the Dominican Republic and run an environmentally sound, fair trade coffee plantation with an accompanying literacy center.[9] The project is a success; it exports coffee and sells it through various websites in the United States and welcomes eco-tourists who pay a small fee and volunteer at either the farm or the literacy center. However, the literacy part of the project was developed from the top down; no one from the vicinity asked Alvarez to supplement the educational system in place in the Dominican Republic. Instead, the novelist sought to use her (cultural and economic) capital to remedy a situation—rampant illiteracy—she found intolerable. Alvarez's alterego, Yolanda García, and her third husband contemplate following a similar path to their real-life counterparts in *¡Yo!*. In both instances, the male American characters come up with the idea of owning a piece of the island with which the Dominican characters identify emotionally. Yolanda García's husband, Doug, finds the idea of farming in the Dominican Republic so comforting that he daydreams about working on the land he has yet to purchase: "He is on the island on a mountain farm in an upper field by a roaring river. They are planting the yucca in long even rows. He is helping another man whose face he does not see, or maybe the other man is helping him" (*¡Yo!* 276). Part of what makes this imagined interaction so satisfying to Doug is the prospect of working closely alongside a native farmer, José, to whom he could pay "a good salary" (275) so he could support his large family with dignity. Alvarez describes Doug's desire to have a positive impact in his wife's native country in terms of mental dislocation, or "mind travel" (276), which poses none of the legal or economic impediments that physical journeys do for potential travelers.

A more disturbing instance of "mind travel" takes place in *Saving the World*, where Alma's husband, Richard Huebner, feels consumed by a deep desire to help the locals by using his own agricultural skills, like Doug. He goes to the Dominican Republic as a representative of Help International, a non-profit non-governmental agency in charge of setting up an eco-friendly agricultural center and literacy school, as well as a health clinic which would carry out research into AIDS vaccines. In an ironic twist of fate, Richard finds himself in a precarious political situation on the island precisely because his Dominican wife decided *not* to travel with him, choosing to remain at home in Vermont so she could write uninterrupted. Young, illiterate Dominican would-be terrorists take over Richard's "green center" and hold the workers hostage in exchange for valid travel documents so they can move to and work in the United States. Like Doug in ¡Yo!, the naïve Dominican kidnappers feel they, too, have "another, simultaneous life going on long distance" (¡Yo! 276). The main difference between these two instances of "mind travel" is that whereas the American doctor has the means to turn his fantasy into a reality, the young men from the poor village in the Dominican Republic have neither the money, the education, nor the employment possibilities which would allow them to realize their dream of emmigrating to the United States and make a better life for themselves.

Because the kidnappers got the idea for their scheme from watching news reports of terrorist attacks on cable TV, Alvarez reminds us in *Saving the World* that both information and goods travel along international, commodity exchange circuits as much as people move from one place to another. The young men's access to television broadcasts from around the world exposed them to the idea of using violence against civilians to obtain their goals; however, this same exposure to mass media, with its constantly changing headlines and endless promotion of costly goods through paid advertisements, made them impatient to see the benefits of immigration immediately instead of waiting to profit from the more slow-moving agricultural and medical innovations that were set in motion in their village.

In the final narrative flourish that closes the novel ¡Yo!, Alvarez redeems the idea of this mass transit of ideas and stories through the trope of the parental blessing. Thinking back to the moment under the *trujillato* when his young daughter's extravagant bragging about his illegal gun almost cost him and his family their lives, an aged Dr. García contemplates the enormous price he has paid through his long sojourn in the United States. Following the adult Yolanda's example, he chooses to alter the course of remembered history by changing the ending of that traumatic episode in the family's life. Rather than reacting violently by spanking his daughter, García now imagines himself congratulating her tenderly: "I lift the belt, but then as I said, forty years pass, and my hand comes down gently on my child's graying head" (308). In this new version of the past, he lifts the "injunction of silence" (307) and secrecy he had imposed upon her previously and instead, urges her to use her voice in print to undo the effects of cultural amnesia that he fears will be his grandchildren's only legacy: "Ours is now an orphan family. My grandchildren and great grandchildren will not know the way back unless they have a story. Tell them of our journey"(309). Through his own imaginative reconstruction of the past, Dr. García communicates with his Americanized daughter, Yolanda, his desire to bequeath to future generations the ability to travel mentally back in time, as well as to remain so interested in their inherited homeland as to physically see it someday. Dr. García, Yolanda, and Alvarez all value travel, actual as well as mental, as a means of maintaining kinship ties and owning one's family's history.

Travel facilitates the continued survival of the household as an organizing structure even when divorce or other outside forces threaten the fragmentation of the family unit in the Alvarez canon. *How Tía Lola Came to ~~Visit~~ Stay* is a case in point. This novel for young adults emphasizes the importance of assimilation to the culture and language of the country in which one's family "home" or household is located. Despite the youth of its target readership, this novel presents more complex travel dynamics than almost all of Alvarez's other fiction with the exception of *In the Name of Salomé* and *Saving the World*.[10] While she is a maternal relation, Tía Lola demonstrates her commitment to the idea of family togetherness by learning enough English to effectively chaperone Nita and Miguel as they travel to New York City to spend time with their father. Tía Lola also teaches the kids enough Spanish so that they can interact with their Dominican cousins during the Christmas trip they take together to the island. The third-person narrator points out the somewhat negative side of the reciprocity of this arrangement, remarking: "Now that Miguel and Juanita have learned so much Spanish, Tía Lola cannot speak in Spanish if she doesn't want them to understand. Vague, whispery sounds drift to the back seat as their aunt plans the next surprise treat for the family" (129). One larger implication within this passage is that once a family shares a common language(s), the elders can no longer summarily impose a linguistic hierarchy that gives them power over their younger charges.

The Dominican Republic and the United States are the two main hubs for legal immigration in Alvarez's fiction, and therefore become the de facto headquarters for different branches of the same family unit. Whether the events she narrates take place in the United States or in the Dominican Republic, the one constant feature in all of Alvarez's writings is the presence of a well-established household, made up of an extended family and its domestic and agricultural servants living and working together. The primary branch of any given family in the Alvarez canon resides within a large ancestral seat or family compound in the Dominican Republic: everyone from Alvarez's own clan described in

Homecoming, Something to Declare, and *The Other Side* to the Garcías in *How the García Girls Lost Their Accents* and *¡Yo!,* the Mirabals in *In the Time of the Butterflies,* the Henríquez Ureñas in *In the Name of Salomé,* to Miguel Guzmán's maternal grandparents in *How Tía Lola Came to* ~~Visit~~ *Stay,* and the persecuted de la Torres in *Before We Were Free* and the Rodríguez family in *Saving the World* know that there is at least one place in the island where they can feel at home, even if they have never been there. The secondary households in the United States house not only those family members who have immigrated in hopes of escaping political persecution, but also the children or relatives of their servants back home. Rather than participating in the free-market economy favored by Americans, exiled or immigrant middle class Dominican families in Alvarez's texts continue to honor the ties of kinship that bind them not only to their own blood relatives, but also to their village communities.

Notes

1. In 2005, Kelli Lyon Johnson published the first full-length critical analysis of Julia Alvarez's works, *Julia Alvarez: Writing a New Place on the Map.* Johnson emphasizes Alvarez's linguistic achievement, her domestication of English so it is the proper language to reflect her hyphenated identity, but her book imposes the Latino or Chicano paradigm of "borderlands" as a theoretical lens through which to interpret Alvarez's works. Johnson does not dedicate much space to discussing Alvarez's and her characters' travel practices and the geographic routes of their journeys.
2. In *Something to Declare,* Julia Alvarez explains that within her extended family alone, her grandparents, widowed godmother, and her own father all obtained legal documents to travel to the United States. Alvarez also mentions that her mother's family, the de la Torres, had a tradition of sending both their sons and daughters to study in the United States, even during the *trujillato.*
3. Because of the isolation of Alvarez's elite Dominican characters from other Latinos, I disagree with Lucía M. Suárez's contention that, "Alvarez undergoes a process of self-invention through writing that situates her in the center of Latina literature and defines her as a Dominican and diaspora writer par excellence" (117).
4. The major exceptions to this pattern are the García's maid, Primi, and her daughter, Sara, in *How the García Girls Lost Their Accents* and *¡Yo!.* The Garcías sponsored Primi's immigration so she could continue working for the family as a domestic servant, and they later helped her bring Sara so she could be educated in the United States. Alvarez depicts this pattern of hiring from the island in both her collection of autobiographical essays, *Something to Declare* and in the later chapters of *¡Yo!.* In the chapter entitled "The maid's daughter," the first-person narrator, Sara, explains: "I was eight years old when my mother left me in the *campo* with my grandmother to go off to the United States to work as the maid for the García family" (54).

5. Despite this cautionary action, Alma's own nuclear family gets hurt in political violence in the island; despite further obfuscating her identity by impersonating a journalist in order to infiltrate a hostage situation and be near her husband, Richard, he is killed in the crossfire with police.

6. Alvarez also portrays female Dominican characters who actively work to undermine the ruthless authority of their country's corrupt political leadership in *In the Time of the Butterflies* and *In the Name of Salomé*. The activist female protagonists of these novels never leave the Dominican Republic, however.

7. The novel that best exemplifies this ongoing travel circuit is Alvarez's first work for young adult readers, *How Tía Lola Came to ~~Visit~~ Stay*.

8. The term 1.5 generation refers to people who immigrated to a new country as teenagers or younger.

9. Eichner contributed the autobiographical Afterword that accompanies the story.

10. Camila Henríquez Ureña spends time living in the United States, Cuba, and the Dominican Republic, while her mother, Salomé Ureña, who suffers from tuberculosis, moves around from one end of the Dominican Republic to another in search of a more healthy environment in *In the Name of Salomé*. *Saving the World* features an international voyage to bring the smallpox vaccine to several countries.

Works Cited

Alvarez, Julia. *A Cafecito Story*. Whiteriver Junction, VT: Chelsea Green, 2001.

———. *Before We Were Free*. New York: Knopf, 2002.

———. *Homecoming*. New York: Plume, 1996.

———. *How the García Girls Lost Their Accents*. New York: Plume, 1992.

———. *In the Name of Salomé*. New York: Plume, 2001.

———. *How Tía Lola Came to ~~Visit~~ Stay*. New York: Alfred A. Knopf, 2001.

———. *In the Time of the Butterflies*. New York: Plume, 1994.

———. *Saving the World*. Chapel Hill: Algonquin Books of Chapel Hill, 2007.

———. *Something to Declare*. Chapel Hill: Algonquin Books of Chapel Hill, 1998.

———. *The Other Side/El Otro Lado*. New York: Dutton, 1995.

———. *¡Yo!* New York: Plume, 1997.

Anderson, Benedict. *Imagined Communities*. New York: Verso, 1991.

Clifford, James. *Routes: Travel and Translation in the Late Twentieth Century*. Cambridge, Mass.: Harvard University Press, 1997.

Johnson, Kelli Lynn. *Julia Alvarez: Writing a New Place on the Map*. Albuquerque: University of New Mexico Press, 2005.

Suárez, Lucía M. "Julia Alvarez and the Anxiety of Latina Representation." *Meridians: Feminism, Race, Transnationalism* 5.1 (2004): 117–145.

Making It Home: A New Ethics of Immigration in Dominican Literature

Ylce Irizarry

5.1 After Arrival: The Ethics of Immigration

Despite the media omnipresence of celebrities of Hispanic descent such as Reggaeton star Daddy Yankee, entertainer Jennifer Lopez, actress America Ferrera, and athlete Sammy Sosa, the ordinary people whom Spanish Caribbean writers depict remain a marginalized portion of U.S. society.[1] This essay discusses how the contemporary immigration narratives of Dominican American writer Junot Díaz are distinct not only from modernist European immigrant literatures that privilege acculturation but also from Spanish Caribbean exile narratives that privilege nostalgia. Díaz's fiction theorizes Dominican migration and the migrants' experiences of poverty, disillusion, and non-belonging in Latina/o America.[2]

The 2008 winner of the Pulitzer Prize in Fiction, Díaz's novel, *The Brief Wondrous Life of Oscar Wao*, explores the cyclical migrations of the Cabral family, problematizing the Dominican exile community's sense of identity, social status, and decline. This novel, though, follows the broader analysis of migration first depicted in his collection of short stories, *Drown* (1996). Both texts depict characters that migrate cyclically, reject oppositional conceptions of acculturation, and negotiate racial constructs present in both the Dominican Republic and the United States. Díaz's work engages various immigrant literature tropes but ultimately privileges the rejection of most of them, especially the trope associated with acculturation in a Caribbean Latina/o context, the trope of *arrival*.[3]

For early twentieth-century European immigrants groups such as the Irish, Italians, or Germans, *arrival* meant social mobility.[4] For Spanish

Caribbean immigrants, *arrival* has meant socioeconomic empower-ment without the loss of cultural specificity. *Arrival*, thus defined, has been largely impossible for Spanish Caribbean people. Individuals who are dark-skinned, working class, recently migrated, or who retain their original linguistic and cultural practices, face barriers to such accultura-tion. This rejection is particularly visible in narratives about the non-exilic immigrations of Dominicans and Cubans in the 1980s, as well as immigrations of Puerto Ricans following the island's designation as "Free Associated State" in 1952. These immigrations were spurred in the context of U.S. neo-colonialism; they reflect economic, rather than political, immigration and ought to be considered involuntary. This illu-minates the complexity of such migration and its distinction from exile: characters do not leave their country for temporary political refuge or to "make it big"; rather, they migrate to the United States so that they can earn enough money to survive in their nations of origin.

The rejection of *arrival* creates immigrant experiences for which Spanish Caribbean authors are developing new literary tropes. Elsewhere, I have called Diaz's collection a *narrative of fracture*, which addresses issues of acculturation within greater Latin America and displays several characteristics.[5] These characteristics undermine early twentieth-century conceptions of immigrant experience such as the notion that accultura-tion is desirable. The narratives also function within the discourse com-munity of Caribbean Latina/o America, not within the broader discourse community of Anglo America. Finally, they are consistent with post-modern narrative, utilizing shorter prose, ambiguity, and shifts in voice. In *Drown*, such craft gives the collection a fragmented rhythm, which contrasts early twentieth-century European immigrant narratives pat-terned on Aristotelian dramaturgy: rising action, crisis, dénouement, and resolution.[6]

Díaz's characters face a literal immigration problem: unending physical migration. In a critical way, this undermines modern depictions of immi-gration suggesting immigration ends when acculturation is complete. His characters experience continual physical migration compounded with psycho-cultural migration as they interact with new immigrants and reassess their place within the Spanish Caribbean diaspora. This process leaves such characters in a cultural stasis, in a third, always "becoming" cultural space, where they never fully become "American."[7] Dominican immigrants are often perceived as not truly "Dominican" either, because they did not grow into adulthood on the island, did not rise to elite social status on it, or have somehow lost their innate *Dominicanidad*.[8]

Bhabha describes "becoming" as an intermediate cultural space, between a past and a future cultural space. This is the most complex and interesting space because individuals and nations consistently make choices to define themselves against a past or articulate an as-yet inaccessible future.[9] The characters living in the 1980s and 1990s in *Drown* are constantly "becoming": they move within a new space of immigration, outside both exile and *arrival*. They are not political exiles, nor are they willing immigrants. The dreams associated with *arrival*—material successes, freedom of movement, cultural retention—have already been abandoned. The characters do not look at immigration as a path to empowerment; it is a temporary, expected solution to poverty. They have declared *arrival* inaccessible and they find themselves drowning in the wake of its impossibility.

As *narratives of fracture,* the primary function of Díaz's stories is to expose the ideologies about immigration created within the diaspora or projected onto Spanish Caribbean migrants. Díaz challenges readers to question long-held assumptions about the American dream, the diversity among Spanish Caribbean people, and the interaction within minority communities, particularly in racial and gendered contexts.[10] Because of this shift in Spanish Caribbean narrative, I have found theories used most often in the criticism of Caribbean Latina/o literature—Border Theory, Feminism, and Postcolonialism—unable to fully articulate these aesthetics.[11] I draw my approach from Narrative Ethics and focus on the cultural obligations and expected reciprocity among characters. What can narrative ethics offer to the study of Spanish Caribbean immigrant fictions that these other forms of analysis have not?

In his "Ethics" entry for *Critical Terms for Literary Study*, Geoffrey Galt Harpham offers several useful definitions for ethics in relation to literature.[12] Initially, he defines ethics as "the arena in which the claims of otherness—the moral law, the human other, cultural norms, the Good-in-itself, etc—are articulated and negotiated" (394). Harpham articulates what I see Díaz performing in his collection: "Literature contributes to 'ethical' understanding by showing motivations, revealing the ends of action, holding the mirror up to the community and the individual so they can judge for themselves, promoting explanatory models that help make sense of the diversity of life, and imagining the unit that might be desirable in human life" (400). Díaz creates a new ethics of Spanish Caribbean immigration literature by structuring the problems of the Dominican diaspora. He creates a nexus of relationships among the author, narrator, characters, and reader. He performs several ethical interventions: textual ruptures of accepted ideology about migration, acculturation, and belonging in Caribbean Latina/o America.

By defining Dominicans' and Dominican Americans' immigration experiences, Díaz challenges readers to reconsider their own ontology about immigration. As the narratives move away from *arrival* as a narrative end, he highlights how Dominican immigration is distinct from other Spanish Caribbean immigrations. Once *arrival* loses its cultural currency, how does one narrate Spanish Caribbean immigration?

5.2   The *Barrio* as Whirlpool in Junot Díaz's *Drown*

Dominicans are rapidly becoming the largest Hispanic immigrant population in cities like New York, Patterson, and Miami.[13] Unlike Puerto Ricans and Cubans, Dominicans have not significantly benefited from the United States' neo-colonialism.[14] The title of Díaz's collection, *Drown*, is the dominant metaphor for the struggle of the characters. They drown—economically and culturally—and are well aware of their failure to *arrive*. Most of the characters remain itinerant and emotionally resigned. Yunior and his family must *make it home*—learn how to survive and access power in each new locale—wherever they find themselves, because they have no permanent physical home. Thus, the characters within *Drown* are challenged to choose not so much where home is, but how home is.

The stories "Ysrael," "*Aguantando*," "Drown," and "How to Date a Brown Girl, a Black Girl, A White Girl or a Halfie," reveal how contemporary Dominican immigration creates a diaspora that actually begins with an ever-growing distance between classes on the island. Together, the stories depict immigration's psychological movements: "Ysrael" and "*Aguantando*" illustrate how children are disillusioned with immigration, as they try to reconcile abandonment and expectation. "Drown" delineates the struggle for characters to become Dominican *and* American. Finally, "How to Date a Brown Girl, a Black Girl, A White Girl or a Halfie" reveals how characters continually negotiate racial and gender identities.

"Ysrael" depicts an intra-national pattern of migration between two arenas of Dominican life: urban poverty and rural poverty. Nowhere are there descriptions of an island paradise: even for the older generations, matter-of-fact assessments of a sustained, but not luxurious, past replaces nostalgia. For example, the narrator, Yunior, recalls his grandfather bemoaning a time when "a man could still make a living from his *finca*, when the United States wasn't something folks planned on" (73). In contrast to European and Asian immigrant perceptions of the United States in the late nineteenth and early twentieth centuries, Spanish Caribbean immigrants of the late twentieth century do not view the United States as a land of milk and honey or of golden opportunity. Rather, it is a source of temporary employment, allowing the rural poor to relocate to the capital city of their nation of origin or to retire in less severe poverty.[15]

"Ysrael" depicts two brothers' contrasting experiences of this internal migration. For Yunior's brother Rafa, rural Ocoa is a nightmare: "In the *campo* there was nothing to do, no one to see. You didn't get television or electricity, and Rafa who was older and expected more, woke up every morning pissy and dissatisfied" (4). Yunior eventually grows re-accustomed to the conditions and boredoms of rural poverty asserting, "I didn't mind these summers, wouldn't forget them the way Rafa would" (5). Rural Ocoa offers Yunior a sense of importance as a city boy and as his brother's pal that he is denied in Santo Domingo: "In the capital Rafa and I fought so much, neighbors took to smashing broomsticks over us to break it up, but in the *campo* it wasn't like that. In the *campo* we were friends" (5).

This is strongly contrasted in the capital, where Rafa asserts his superiority by using slurs that reveal Dominican racism toward Haitians: "Most of [the routines] had to do with my complexion, my hair, the size of my lips. It's the Haitian, he'd say to his buddies" (6). These taunts join childlike behavior with a racism intended to distinguish Dominicans from Haitians. They powerfully re-inscribe attitudes about "the proper place" of Haitians—at work for, but not at home in, the country—encouraged by Trujillo.[16]

Yunior describes his life in each locale, giving the reader a sense of the disparities in and disillusionment with the United States—generally referred to as North America—that get conjured in the minds of the boys well before they even immigrate. Perhaps because so few Dominicans had "made it" in the United States by the 1970s, Yunior and those around him are very suspicious of anything connected to America. *Nueva* York becomes a taunting imaginary: the children simultaneously desire what it offers and loathe the offering. Objects from *Nueva* York mark those who possess them as traitorous. For example, Ysrael, the mutilated child in Ocoa, is doubly marked. His face is horrifically disfigured; because he is a friendless victim of bullying, his father buys him clothes and toys from New York, marking him, again, as an outsider in his own community.

These gifts provide Yunior a reason to hate, not just taunt, him: "Ysrael's sandals were of stiff leather and his clothes were North American. I looked over at Rafa, but my brother seemed unperturbed" (15). While Rafa isn't bothered by the boy's material possessions like his kite, he is bothered by Ysrael's belief in America, because it reminds him of his own disjointed relationship to it: " 'Where did you get that?' I asked. '*Nueva* York, he said. 'From my father.' 'No shit! Our father's there too!' I shouted. I looked at Rafa, who for an instant, frowned. Our father only sent us letters and an occasional shirt or pair of jeans at Christmas" (16). Thus, *Nueva* York offers material comfort to very few. Rafa and Yunior's father's occasional letters and gifts revive their expectations and subsequent resignation about *Nueva* York. When Ysrael asserts American doctors are going to help him, Rafa attempts to dash the younger boy's hopes: "They're lying to you. They probably just felt sorry" (17). Rafa's unwillingness to believe in *Nueva* York is not merely a thinly veiled hatred for his father. Rather, *Nueva* York's indifference to Dominicans prevents his father from *making it home* and Ysrael from being healed.

This is one of Díaz's most significant ethical interventions. He challenges the notion that the United States is a highly desirable place for migration. The perceptions of the United States by the wave of Dominicans immigrating in the years following Trujillo's 1961 assassination were very different from those of Puerto Ricans and Cubans immigrating during the same era.[17] Here, Díaz engages the reader's and characters' (Yunior and Ysrael) beliefs about migration. This intervention is significant: even though Dominicans immigrate, they do not articulate the sense of hope about the United States that Puerto Ricans often do, nor the nostalgia for "old" Havana that Cubans do. Their expectation is to immigrate several times for the explicit purpose of surviving financially on the island.

"*Aguantando*" means bearing or standing, in the sense of "putting up with" some situation. In this story, the narrator Yunior juxtaposes several kinds of *aguantando*: what his mother had to bear with a husband absent for five years, what he had to bear as a son waiting almost endlessly for his father's return, what they all had to bear as an impoverished urban family in New Jersey. Linguistically, the word is a nice play on the collection's title: non-Spanish speakers might recognize the word "agua" and suppose it had something to do with water and/or drowning, echoing the collection's title. It evokes the principal mode of immigration for Dominicans: travel by boat and swimming, which often lead to the drowning and/ or shark attack deaths of migrants.

The story offers an analysis of the internalization of migration discourse: rather than drowning in cultural difference, characters drown in expectations of escaping poverty and of reuniting as a nuclear family. As Yunior asserts, their poverty is so comprehensive, few are worse off: "We lived south of the *Cemetario Nacional* in a wood frame house with three rooms. We were poor. The only way we could have been poorer was to live in the campo or to be Haitian and Mami regularly offered these as brutal consolation" (70). This story focuses on the family's expectations for the father to send for them or to return from *Nueva* York in a grand style and their repeated disappointment. Yunior notes that "The year Papi came I was nine, we expected nothing. There was no sign to speak of" (77). Rafa cautions him that even though they receive a letter, Papi might not come at all: "It ain't the first time he's made that promise" (82).

As an adult narrator, Yunior is as bitter as the teenage Rafa. He resents his father's deferred literal arrival due to his failed metaphorical *arrival*: "On the days I had to imagine him—not often since Mami didn't speak of him anymore—he was the soldier in the photo. He was a cloud of cigar smoke, the traces of which could still be found in the uniforms he'd left behind. He was pieces of my friends' fathers, of the domino players on the corner, pieces of Mami and Abuelo. I didn't know him at all. I didn't know that he'd abandoned us. That this waiting for him was all a sham" (70). The boy's father looms large in these stories, but readers do not learn his name or what actually happened to him until the final story, "*Negocios.*" By this time, the boy's mother has resigned herself to a life of hard work with an adulterous husband. The boys have become aware of their father's extramarital affair with a Puerto Rican woman as well as his bigamous marriage to a Cuban woman. When Yunior enters high school, his father has left both of his families, only to enter a cycle of migration between the families, showing up every few months asking for money.

The only story in which Yunior's father is conspicuously absent—neither present nor mentioned—is in the title story, "Drown." The story depicts Yunior's life once he immigrates. In patches of neighborhoods and people, he narrates this cyclical immigration within the United States. He and his family experienced migration related to economics within the Dominican Republic; in New Jersey, their migration also reflects a number of emotional resignations. One of these resignations introduces an element that appears only one other time in the collection: homosexuality. Yunior describes his friendship with Beto, another young man who is doubly marked: he is gay and he leaves *el barrio* for college. Yunior introduces Beto with familiarity, suggesting he had completely identified with him: "He's a *pato* now, but two years ago we were friends and he would walk into the apartment without knocking, his heavy voice rousing my mother from the Spanish of her room and drawing me up from the basement, a voice that cracked and made you think of uncles or grandfathers" (91).

Since Yunior's father has been so absent, Yunior associates Beto with the only male figures he has known. The absence of Yunior's father is sanctioned; the father is the one who can leave, because it is understood that the absence is necessary to create more opportunities for his family. This absence, however, suggests the vulnerability of Yunior. His father's über-heterosexual masculinity would have been a cultural and physical barrier to Yunior's socialization with Beto. Indeed, in the cultural discourse on Dominican sexuality, Beto would not belong in his neighborhood and he would not be welcome in Yunior's house.

Yunior describes his nights out with other boys, without Beto, because "Beto would usually be at home or down by the swings, or wouldn't be around at all. Out visiting other neighborhoods" (102). Yunior recalls Beto telling him, "You need to learn how to walk the world...There's a lot out there" (102). It is also likely that these excursions had to do with his homosexuality; he would not be safe in his own neighborhood if he was "out." When Beto was around, he and Yunior would go to their favorite spot, the community pool. The pool is the metaphor for his relationship with Beto, simultaneously empowering and threatening.

His memories of the pool trigger his confession about his sexual relationship with Beto: "Twice. That's it" (92). The community pool is the one space youth of different ethnicities share without overt racism or violence. It is also the space that differentiates people like Beto, the ones who get out, from people like Yunior, those who do not seem to try. While Beto comes and goes, Yunior visits the pool for so long that kids of his own age do not go there anymore: "Many of the kids here are the younger brothers of the people I used to go to school with. Two of them swim past, black and Latino, and they pause then they see me, recognizes the guy who sells them their shitty dope" (92). The water, like their friendship, is an imperfect oasis: "While everything above is loud and bright, everything below is whispers. And always the risk of coming up to find the cops stabbing their search lights out across the water" (93).

Any Edenic imagery that the scene opens with, though, is quickly undermined by the diction—stabbing—implying police brutality and foreshadowing a rift between the friends. As Yunior expects, Beto shows up. They swim together, but their conversation reveals the fracture between these two "friends." When Yunior knows what the word "expectorating" means, Beto gets angry and asserts his physical strength: "He put his hands on my shoulders and pushed me under. He was wearing a cross and cutoff jeans. He was stronger than me and held me down until water flooded my nose and throat. Even then I didn't tell him; he thought I didn't read. Not even dictionaries" (94). This scene recalls Yunior's anxieties about his literacy and his masculinity. Despite the fact that Beto is literally drowning him, Yunior does not meet Beto's demand to tell what he knows.

This aspect of Beto's character is very important because Díaz employs it to contrast widely accepted stereotypes about homosexuals, particularly within Anglo American culture, that gay men are passive and incapable of violence. After they return to Beto's house to watch a pornographic film, Beto starts to masturbate Yunior. Yunior doesn't resist, but he leaves right after he ejaculates. He fears that he'll "end up abnormal, a fucking *pato*" (95). Yunior's fear may be rooted not just in the notion that having sex with a man makes you gay, but in the more specific discourse on homosexuality within Latin American culture, which suggests that the receiver of homosexual action is gay, not the giver.[18] Yet, Yunior returns to the pool the next day, cognizant Beto could do this again. Beto offers Yunior a coded escape: "Let's go, he said. Unless of course you're not feeling good" (105). Yunior provides Beto sexual permission when he says, "I'm feeling fine" (105). Once they enter the apartment, Beto assumes the active sexual role and Yunior assesses his sense of self: "After I was done, he laid his head in my lap. I wasn't asleep or awake, but caught somewhere in between, rocked slowly back and forth the way the surf holds junk against the shore, rolling it over and over" (105).

The drowning metaphor performs two ethnical interventions. First, Beto represents another part of Yunior's life that he cannot control, one that leaves him feeling caught, like the "junk," between his desires for men and women. He is caught between his love for his friend and his culture's demands that he disassociate himself from Beto entirely, again revealing the ruptures in belonging within Caribbean Latina/o America. Perhaps more importantly, Beto is a catalyst to Yunior's realization of his socio-economic drowning. Though his mother can usually make the rent and he can pay for utilities by selling pot, Yunior becomes painfully aware that he "wasn't like [Beto]. I had another year to go in high school, no promises elsewhere" (92). The story ends with Yunior throwing away a book, not even having read the inscription, which Beto gives him before leaving for college.

The gift being a book is an important intervention on the author's part: Díaz suggests that Yunior throws away a potential guide out of the *barrio*. The modernist notion that education will allow each generation to succeed more than the previous one is undermined considerably here. Presumably, both boys have equal access to education because they are from the same school district, but Yunior does not seem able to access the resources that Beto has accessed. Beto might have been trying to make up for belittling Yunior's literacy and ultimately could have been an important role model. Díaz criticizes individuals who are offered potential sources of empowerment but reject them without considering the consequences. By depicting characters that fail to choose or fail to act, Díaz forcefully challenges the modernist notion that immigrants are victims of a hostile environment. He also distinguishes Yunior's experiences from those common in exile narratives, where adolescents are victims of institutional discrimination.[19] Díaz addressed his concern about self-defeating actions in an interview: "There's no state in the world that can facilitate all the ambitions of its underclass. So it throws up obstacles—plenty of intoxications, bad schools, aggressive cops, no jobs—and depends on us to do the rest. You don't know how many times I saw a person escape institutional discrimination only to knock themselves down with self-hate and self-doubt" (Céspedes and Torres-Saillant 893).

"Drown" begins a *denouement* of sorts and the collection moves toward Yunior's ruminations about his father's and his own inability to *make it home*. Ultimately, he meets his father's other wife, Nilda, to learn exactly how his father could have started a new family. Realizing, however, that he is never going to know exactly what happened in those years his father was gone, he accepts that his father simply was not a great man whom *Nueva* York defeated. The plot concerning his father goes beyond established tropes of familial separation in modernist immigrant fiction. Díaz revises the reunion of long-lost parents and children into a narrative about paternalism, nationalism, and citizenship.

Yunior's obsession with his father is a well-crafted political narrative about patriarchy in the Dominican Republic. Trujillo's self-aggrandizement was so extensive that he required his picture appear in every citizen's home.[20] Toward the end of Trujillo's reign, citizens who initially supported him realized he had become a brutal tyrant whose economic policies were ineffectual. In several places, Yunior refers to the United States 1965 invasion of the Dominican Republic, especially the smell of the tear gas used to subdue resistors. The "Yanquis" enacted their own brutality in the forms of these gas attacks and water-hosing people, but their presence underscored Trujillo's failings prior to his murder. While Díaz was born in the Dominican Republic after Trujillo was assassinated, the memories and legacies of his rule remain with the nation's people. Moreover, we know that the only image Yunior has of his father is when he is dressed as one of Trujillo's *guardia*. As an author from a nation that does not like to discuss Trujillo with outsiders, Díaz fractures a profound silence on the failure of patriarchy as governance and parallels the personal father-son rupture with the national one.

The final story from *Drown* I discuss here is "How to Date a Brown Girl, Black Girl, White Girl or Halfie." This story appears, at first, to be a technical manual on succeeding in interracial dating. The narrator has worked out a bitter and humorous, if not misogynist, system for addressing the racism that persists within the Spanish Caribbean diaspora and between African Americans, Anglo Americans, and Spanish Caribbeans. Díaz's attention to the racism amongst peoples of color, despite their shared experiences of discrimination and second-class American citizenship, is critical. Of course, racism has been prevalent between Anglo American groups and ethnic minorities; however, it has also been prevalent among Iberian-descended people. In actuality, racism against darker-skinned Hispanics originated in medieval Spain, was legislated in the New World, and became commonplace in the Caribbean and the United States following the Cuban-Spanish-American War (1896–1898).[21] Rather than reading the overt racism and class distinctions within the story as matter-of-fact descriptions of interracial relationships, one can consider how effectively Díaz illustrates the process by which skin-color supersedes nationality and facilitates internalized racism. This story is the collection's exemplar of the problem of belonging in Caribbean Latina/o America.

In contrast to the collection's other narrative voices, Yunior addresses the reader directly, using a very familiar second-person voice and assuming a shared class background: urban Spanish Caribbean poor. Make no mistake; this group has its own subdivisions. Yunior gives particular advice on how to deal with a girl from various sub-*barrios*: "Clear the government cheese from the refrigerator. If the girl's from the Terrace stack the boxes behind the milk. If she's from the Park or Society Hill hide the cheese in the cabinet above the oven...Take down any embarrassing photos of your family in the *campo*, especially the one with the half-naked kids dragging a goat on a rope leash" (145). We can discern the socio-economic stratification amongst Spanish Caribbean people; though many in Yunior's area might be on welfare, the importance of hiding that fact varies by where the girl lives. Yunior fractures the idea of a monolithic economic background of Dominicans by emphasizing the origins as urban or from "*el campo*," so that leaving a picture of yourself in the *campo* would immediately signify your class as rural poor in the Dominican Republic. Here, Díaz emphasizes the wide disparities among Dominicans on the island that migrate with its inhabitants.[22] There is no puritanical shedding and self-reconstruction for such immigrants, nor is there the privilege of acceptance as a temporary, exotic exile.

Yunior also reveals his linguistic impotence. As a Dominican who immigrated as an adolescent, Yunior could either retain his Spanish or be English-dominant. In another story, we learned that when he left Santo Domingo at age nine, he couldn't write his own name. Thus, speaking in Spanish is just as much a class marker as the government cheese. For example, he notes, "You have choices. If the girl's from around the way, take her to *El Cibao* for dinner. Order everything in your busted-up Spanish. Let her correct you if she's Latina and amaze her if she's black. If she's not from around the way, Wendy's will do" (145). Redefining the linguistic practices often assumed about first-generation immigrants is especially important. Under a modern European immigration model, first-generation immigrants would have difficulty acquiring English. Within Spanish Caribbean exile narratives, language acquisition is viewed as an aid in temporary acculturation, not the catalyst for a loss of identity. Yunior's educational background in the Dominican Republic switches this model, leaving him not only illiterate in English, but also unable to speak his native language. This linguistic distance from other Dominicans has significant consequences: Yunior cannot "rap" to women from his own nation or from other parts of Caribbean Latina/o America.

The instructions provide the reader with an increasingly unflattering portrait of Yunior's racial and sexual hierarchy, which asserts, "If she's a whitegirl you know you'll at least get a hand job," and "a local girl may have hips and a thick ass but she won't be quick about letting you touch" (147). Clearly the object is to get as close to having sex as possible on the date, and this—ironically—becomes more complicated the closer the girl is to Yunior racially. In very deft lines, the narrator sets up rules for conversation that are based on a strategy of non-confrontation and emotional distance: "A halfie will tell you that her parents met in the Movement, will say back then people thought it a radical thing to do...She will appreciate your interest...Black people, she will say, treat me real bad. That's why I don't like them. You'll wonder how she feels about Dominicans. Don't ask" (147).

Here, Yunior marks the distances between racially mixed people and those who identify as black. The effect of black on black racism is profound: Yunior assumes the girl won't like him if she thinks he is more "black" than Dominican. Racially, Dominicans have a higher percentage of dark-skinned people with African physiognomy than do Puerto Ricans or Cubans, but all groups use a system of racial preference based on desirable qualities like fair skin, "good hair," or small lips. Each of these qualities is synonymous with more whiteness. His physical characteristics prevent him from passing as white Spanish Caribbean, superceding his nationality, ultimately marking him as black.

Such internalized racism is painfully clear when Yunior notes, "tell her that you love her hair, that you love her skin, her lips, because in truth, you love them more than you love your own" (147). This is perhaps Díaz's most engaging intervention as author; it challenges the reader, especially a Spanish Caribbean reader, to think about why Yunior is aware of, yet persists in, self-hate. By showing a clear linkage between racial preferences and self-hate, Díaz is critiquing his own community for its acceptance of this internalization of racism.[23]

5.3   Redefining Cultural Membership: Making It Home

Díaz's focus on internal racism, intra-ethnic racism, and classicism illustrate the varying stories' effectiveness as *narratives of fracture*. Díaz's strategy of ethical intervention defines the new ethics of the Spanish Caribbean immigration narrative: *making it home*. What distinguishes more recent narratives such as those of Díaz from modernist narratives is the characters' engagement with the concept of *arrival*. In the former, characters recognize the impossibility of *arrival*, but that recognition does not result in a movement out of cultural stasis. In some ways, Díaz's collection does mirror the immigrant narratives of second-generation immigrants or those who came to the United States with no memory of their native country. Unlike modern narratives, though, Díaz's protagonists acknowledge a lack of connection to their nation of origin. Rather than depicting a traumatic rejection of an old world, his writing represents a movement toward a self-conscious search for a present home. Díaz's principle narrator, Yunior, illustrates the psycho-cultural migration intrinsic to people who immigrated at an older age. This is a striking example of contemporary immigrant literature that defines the need to create an intermediary space where characters can negotiate aspects of each culture into a third cultural membership. This need is so clear because neither culture—minority or majority—is an adequate or consistently empowering place to incorporate all the experiences involved in *making it home*.

Notes

1. Within the United States, the term "Latina/o" is more commonly used to refer to individuals of any variation of Iberian descent. I will use the term "Caribbean Latina/o" for regional references and use Dominican, Puerto Rican, or Cuban for specific national references.
2. While Dominicans, particularly women, have begun to migrate to Spain and Puerto Rico in larger numbers, these migrations also serve as a stepping stone to the United States, with the final desired migration being the return to the Dominican Republic.
3. This essay condenses a chapter of my manuscript in progress, *New Memory: The Ethics of Latina/o Literature*. For details on the concept of *arrival*, see Irizarry, Chapter 1.
4. For a discussion on the three-generation model of immigrant acculturation, see Sollors, Chapter 7.
5. For a detailed discussion of the *narratives of fracture* and *new memory*, see Irizarry, "Introduction."
6. For examples, one might consider the work of Mary Antin, Anzia Yezierska, Upton Sinclair, or John Dos Passos.
7. Puerto Ricans were made U.S. citizens in 1917; their citizenship does not allow them to amend their constitution, vote for U.S. presidents, or elect their own governor. In 1966, the 'one-foot-rule' established instant political asylum for Cubans who reached U.S. soil. Dominicans enjoy no facilitated visa or asylum process; to obtain visas they often work for years to save enough money to buy false visas or to bribe officials into giving them extended tourist visas.
8. This is a principal theme in Santiago's memoir, *When I Was Puerto Rican*. Díaz discusses this in interviews. For Díaz's comments, see Céspedes and Torres-Saillant. Also, this is Oscar Wao's principle trauma—the loss of his *Dominicanidad*, which is only recuperated with a physical return to the island.
9. See Chapters 1 and 9 of Bhabha.
10. I find this to be true of other writers; in my manuscript, I use Puerto Rican authors Judith Ortiz Cofer and Ernesto Quiñonez and Cuban author Elias Miguel Muñoz, among others, as examples.
11. For examples of work concerned with acculturation to the Anglo American mainstream, one might consider work by Piri Thomas, Richard Rodriguez, and early novels by Oscar Hijuelos, Esmeralda Santiago, and Julia Alvarez.
12. See Harpham's entry for "Ethics," in Lentricchia and McLaughlin.
13. For a comprehensive study of Spanish Caribbean immigration and community establishment, see Arreola.
14. For a detailed discussion of U.S. neo-colonialism in the Hispanic Caribbean, see Irizarry, Chapter 1.
15. A similar narrative pattern develops in Cofer's novel, *The Line of the Sun*, which depicts one family's cyclical movement between the city and the country. The novel ends in the United States, where another cycle of migrations begins.

16. For analysis of Dominican/Haitian relations, see Wucker or Howard. In fiction, see Danticat, Llosa, or Rosario.
17. Significant differences in the immigration patterns and degrees of acculturation exist among Puerto Ricans, Cubans, and Dominicans. These differences can be attributed to Puerto Rico's status as a 'free associated state' (1952) and the immediate political asylum afforded to Cubans since the Cuban Adjustment Act (1966). Dominicans, unlike both groups, have no special entrance to the United States; their visa process is long and complicated by their civil laws, making it very difficult to emigrate. In 2002, President Bush affirmed the asylum granted to Cubans. See Canedy.
18. For a discussion of male homosexuality specific to Latin American culture, see Almaguer.
19. This trope is particularly recurrent in contemporary Puerto Rican and Cuban American fiction.
20. Julia Alvarez's novel, In the Time of the Butterflies, does an excellent job of representing how Trujillo encouraged this political and spiritual nexus based on Catholicism's patriarchy and his encompassing rule.
21. Categories were developed in response to the expulsion of the Moors and Jews. See Gutierrez for a description of colonial record keeping and racial identification.
22. See Céspedes and Torres-Saillant for Díaz's comments that he remains outside of the Dominican elite due to his class origins.
23. Díaz has discussed the "erasure" of Dominicans in interviews. See Céspedes and Torres-Saillant, and Collazo. Please note that the URL for the Collazo article is a dead link; I have been unable to locate a live link for it.

Works Cited

Almaguer, Tomás. "Chicano Men: A Cartography of Homosexual Identity and Behavior." Differences 3.2 (1991): 75–100.
Alvarez, Julia. In the Time of the Butterflies. New York: Plume, 1996.
Arreola. Daniel D., Ed. Hispanic Spaces, Latino Places. Community and Cultural Diversity in Contemporary America. Austin: University Press of Texas, 2004.
Bhabha, Homi K. The Location of Culture. Durham: Duke University Press, 1994.
Canedy, Dana. "Bush Remark Gives Advocates Hope for Release of Haitians." New York Times. November 8, 2002, late ed.: A14.
Céspedes Diógenes and Silvio Torres-Saillant. "Fiction is the Poor Man's Cinema: An Interview with Junot Díaz." Callaloo 23.2 (2000): 893.
Collazo, Michael O. "Interview with Junot Díaz, Part II." Latino News Network. <http://www.latnn.com/grafico/interview/articles/junot2.htm> January 1999.
Danticat, Edwidge. The Farming of Bones. New York: Soho Press, 1998.
Gutiérrez, Ramón A. When Jesús Came, the Corn Mothers Went Away: Marriage, Sexuality and Power in New Mexico, 1500–1846. Stanford: Stanford University Press, 1991.
Howard, David. Coloring the Nation: Race and Ethnicity in the Dominican Republic. Oxford: Signal Books, 2001.

Irizarry, Ylce. "Making It Home: The Neo-colonial Ethics of Chicana/o and Latina/o Literature after Arrival." diss. Pennsylvania State University, 2002.

Lentricchia, Frank and Thomas McLaughlin, Eds. *Critical Terms for Literary Study*. 2nd ed. Chicago: University of Chicago Press, 1995.

Llosa, Mario Vargas. *Fiesta del Chivo*. New York: Farrar, Straus, & Giroux, 2001.

Ortiz Cofer, Judith. *The Line of the Sun*. Athens: Georgia University Press, 1989.

Rodriguez, Richard. *Hunger of Memory: The Education of Richard Rodriguez*. New York: Godine, 1982.

Rosario, Nelly. *Song of the Water Saints*. New York: Vintage, 2002.

Santiago, Esmeralda. *When I Was Puerto Rican*. New York: Vintage, 1997.

Sollors, Werner. *Beyond Ethnicity: Consent and Descent in American Literature*. New York: Oxford University Press, 1986.

Wucker, Michele. *Why the Cocks Fight: Dominicans, Haitians, and the Struggle for Hispaniola*. New York: Hill and Wang, 1999.

6

Days of Awe and the Jewish Experience of a Cuban Exile: The Case of Achy Obejas

Carolyn Wolfenzon

From its title, Cuban American writer Achy Obejas' novel *Days of Awe* alludes to the period of introspection, repentance, and atonement for sin that the Jewish tradition calls *Yamim Noraim*. During these days the individual is meant to evaluate the actions made in the last year as preparation for being judged by God. They are the ten days between the New Year's holiday (*Rosh Hashana*) and the Day of Atonement (*Yom Kippur*). The days of repentance, Days of Awe, are not part of the Hebrew calendar: they are in fact out of time, or are part of a time outside linear, normal time, an intermezzo for reflection and personal evaluation between one year and the next. The Days of Awe are a borderline separating past from present, old from new. They are an ambiguous and complex territory for personal, interior exile. Obejas chooses this space as a metaphor of diasporic Cubans and explores it as a conflictive but enriching place where the multiple elements that constitute identity can become integrated.

In *Days of Awe*, a novel published in 2001, author Achy Obejas chronicles the saga of the San José family of Sephardic crypto-Jews; Jews who carry on their religious faith in private in spite of their public conversion to Catholicism. (In Hebrew they are called "*Anussim*" and in Spanish, from medieval times, they were known as "marranos," literally meaning "pigs.") The story told is that of the last four generations of the San José family—the grandfather Ytzak, his son Luis and his grandson Enrique, who is the father of Alejandra, the narrator. The family is continuously moving. From the Oriente region in Cuba, a rural zone in the countryside, they move to Havana, and then the younger members migrate to the United States. All of them are doubly exiled: the first members of the San

José family arrived in Cuba after being expelled from Spain; the last ones go to America fleeing Fidel Castro's regime. Because of political circumstances, both share the fact of being part of a certain diaspora.[1]

Alejandra, the protagonist, is part of the Cuban American San José family. From the United States she travels three times to Havana, first for a job, and then because she starts to feel involved with her family history. The third trip coincides with the celebration of the Days of Awe, which is crucially important among Spanish and Portuguese Jews (Sephardic Jews in general) since medieval times, as an affirmation of the Jewish faith among those forced to convert to Catholicism. The protagonist herself explains the importance of the Days of Awe: it is a time "to ask God to forgive and annul promises not kept. It was designed specifically to reconcile those Jews who converted to other faiths under threat of violence or death and, having survived wished to return. It is a necessary preamble to atonement" (354). Initially, Alejandra thinks of herself only as an American. The novel traces back, or rebuilds, the long-obliterated links to her Jewish faith and her Cuban origin. The Days of Awe will become not only the traditional and religious time out of time, but also a more secular version: a time to reflect on identity in terms of culture, history, nation, and even sexuality.

Each historical moment marks the San José family in a different manner, many times through traditional heritage. In the fragmental diary that is the text of the novel, intertwined with historical research, Alejandra recounts the five hundred years of persecution by the Inquisition in order to explain the formation of the first community of crypto-Jews in the Oriente province of Cuba, one of whose members was her great-grandfather Ytzak. Everyone there had a double life: publicly Catholic and privately Jewish. "Historically," the novel explains, "Jewish presence in Cuba was illegal because Jews were never allowed in Spanish Colonies. Thus essentially illegal, formally nonexistent, survival required compromising the most basic aspect of their souls: to survive as Jews they had to pretend to be otherwise" (121). The Cuban Revolution in 1959, the year in which Alejandra is born, forces the family (Enrique, the father; Nena, the mother; and the newborn Alejandra) to migrate to Chicago. The first years of the Revolution are in general hard on religious manifestations, and that explains why the crypto-Jews who remain in Cuba keep on hiding their faith, something they had been doing anyway during the six decades after the Cuban independence from Spain, never believing that historical prejudice could cease due to a political change. What happens to Enrique and his daughter, Alejandra, the narrator of the novel, is quite interesting. They settle down in Chicago, apparently free of either religious or political persecution and prohibition, but Enrique decides never to tell Alejandra that they are Jewish. He becomes another sort of crypto-Jew: one whose Jewishness is primarily hidden from his child, and then from the world around. Alejandra discovers this only as an adult, and her father becomes in her eyes, as she calls him in several passages, "the secret Jew." The interesting phenomenon is that, from the moment of that discovery, she too will be, in a way, retrospectively, a "secret Jew." How is this possible?

It was, curiously enough, another Jew of Sephardic origin, the philosopher Baruch Spinoza, who wrote that the religious and legal rituals of everyday life transform the individual into a subject and a believer. He who practices the rituals of a religion is part of it; faith is a consequence of action. Identity, to put it this way, goes from the material world to the spiritual world. Think of the false *converso* and the crypto-Jew; Enrique, Alejandra's father, surrounds himself, like his parents did, with crucifixes and Catholic altars, Virgin Mary icons, images of saints, and even symbols of Santería, the Creole transculturated version of Christian and Afro-Cuban religions. In private, though, he has a profound Jewish faith and fulfills the rituals of his Jewish life: he wears a *tefillim* to pray on the *Sabbath*, and when he reveals his secret to Alejandra, and knows that his death is near, he asks her to recite the *Kaddish* in his name. That last gesture is, but, a confusing and very unorthodox one, since the *Kaddish* is a prayer only men are supposed to say during the eleven months following the death of their fathers. It is possible to say that, after the long years of hiding, Enrique has styled a Judaism all of his own. Just as he questions his national Cuban identity, his Spanish origin, and rejects the sole possibility of considering himself American, Enrique sees himself as a Jew but needs his own rules. Private and public rituals conflict in him: his identity is a perpetual bifurcation. His private Jewishness is condemned to ask forgiveness for his public Catholicism. His life is thus permanently inserted in a long, always unfinished time out of time; his life is *only* made of Days of Awe. It could be argued that the character of Enrique establishes a polemical dialogue with Gustavo Pérez Firmat's classic book *Life on the Hyphen*, a canonical interpretation of the process of insertion of diasporic subjects, where indetermination could not be a permanent state.

In Pérez Firmat's analysis of the different stages a Cuban exile passes through during his adaptation process upon arriving in the United States, he focuses on the Cubans who were born on the island and moved to the United States during their infancy or adolescence. They are the "1.5 generation" because they have a bit of both worlds and are, like the symbolic figure of the hyphen proposed by the title of the book, uniting two identities in one being. Alejandra, in Obejas' novel, would be part of this group. There are certain stages that all of the "one-and-a-halfers" go through in their process of inserting themselves into the United States. The first is the "substitutive" phase and consists of the exile's need to create spaces similar to those he left behind in his country of origin; substitutes, or copies of his original culture. This explains the proliferation of substitutive enclaves that have arisen in large North American cities such as "Little Havana," "Little Haiti," "Little Italy," or the replicas of rural Puerto Rican houses such as those studied by Juan Flores in his essay "Salvación casita." The latter, exemplified by "el Rincón Criollo" in Spanish Harlem in New York, have become important centers for transmitting Puerto Rican culture. This first stage is loaded with deep nostalgia manifested by a strong and intense desire to return to the motherland. The second stage through which an exile travels is dominated by destitution, a feeling of not belonging, where the person realizes that these fabricated spaces are not his place of origin, but rather something else, always incomplete and different, when "the enclave is no longer *en clave*. The substitutive fantasy collapses. No amount of duplicate landmarks can cover up the fact that you are no longer there, and what's more, that you may never return" (Pérez Firmat 9).

Finally in Pérez Firmat's analysis comes the institution stage because one cannot live in a non-space forever. The feeling of being on the outside ends at some point, becoming the here and now. This is exactly what, for Pérez Firmat, makes Cuban American culture a bicultural mix (hence his interest in phenomena such as mambo, whose fragments accompany every chapter of his book because it is a musical genre born in Cuba but produced in the United States). According to this analysis, the need for a place and a time is essential in order to have an identity. Pérez Firmat himself denies the possibility of living always in an indeterminate state, which is precisely what the Days of Awe are, and which is also the essence of the character of Enrique and a space where Alejandra's identity will be forged. This, as I have pointed out, is the suitable space from which Enrique, and later Alejandra, find their multiple identities. It is not surprising then that Achy Obejas draws a parallel between the diaspora of Jews and that of Cubans because, unlike what Pérez Firmat maintains, Jews, like the Cubans after Castro's Revolution, are the quintessential displaced people who live with the eternal hope of someday returning to their homeland, whether it be a physical or utopian return. Steven Vertovec analyzes in detail the definition of the concept "diaspora":

> The "Diaspora" was of course, at one time, a concept referring almost exclusively to the experience of Jews, invoking their traumatic exile from an historical homeland and dispersal throughout many lands. With this experience as reference, connotations of a "diaspora" situation were usually rather negative as they were associated with forced displacement, victimization, alienation, loss. Along with this archetype went a dream of return. (Vertovec 2)

Vertovec maintains that this term refers to any population that considers itself "deterritorialized" or "transnational," including such diverse groups as immigrants, ethnic minorities, and those displaced by wars, both internal and external.[2] Nowadays the term refers to peoples as diverse and heterogeneous as Armenians, Palestinians, Cubans, Turks, Africans from the Maghreb, and Chinese, but earlier the concept referred directly to Jews.

Diaspora, exile, and double identity are signals all the San José members bear, sooner or later. For Achy Obejas, the author, those are also the connections between the Cuban people and the Jewish people. "Other Latin Americans," Obejas writes, "and some Americans who've had contact with Cubans, call us the Jews of the Caribbean. It's not a phrase much known in Cuba itself, but it has a familiar currency in exile. Like Jews, we are people in diaspora and like Jews, we are people concerned with questions and answers and the temperament of a God that could make us suffer, like Job, so inexplicably and capriciously" (104).[3]

There are other ancient parallels between Jews and Cubans shown in the narration. One is the Jewish rebellion of Masada, when the Jews, at the sight of their fortress about to be taken by the Roman invaders, decided to commit mass suicide instead of surrendering. Alejandra compares this to the episode of the Taino natives in Cuba who killed themselves *en masse* to avoid being captured by the Spanish. Both stories are oral traditions. The first is not in the Talmud, just as the second is not in Cuban history books, but both are powerfully present in their cultures: the notion of renouncing to everything, even life, in order not to become different. And of course there is the main similarity: the desire to return home. In Obejas' novel, Cuba and Israel are both Zion, both are promised lands: "As a child," tells the narrator, "I held Havana out to myself like a secret hiding place, a trump card, the Zion where I'd be welcomed after all my endless, unplanned travels in the diaspora"(55).[4] It should be underlined that this is a feeling Alejandra had before knowing she was in fact a Jew. The desire to return is revealed in the novel through constant allusion by both Jews and Cubans. The narrator says, "Cubans and Jews both were obsessed with a country in the Third World, both lived in the subjunctive, and both, quite frankly, thought they were the chosen people" (104). The desire to return is also explicitly present in the popular Jewish phrase "L'Shana Haba'ah b'Yerushalayim" ("Next year in Jerusalem") which in the novel is rephrased as "L'Shana Haba'ah b'Havana" or "Next year in Havana" and "El próximo año en La Habana." In *Days of Awe* both cities are promised lands, and both "next years" are an unknown, uncertain, mythical future, at once a desired and an almost unimaginable future. In fact, mythical time in Hebrew is referred to by the word "owlam"—that which another American Jew, Bob Dylan, translated in the title of a recording in 1997, as "time out of mind." Zion, be it Havana or Jerusalem, is for the people of the diaspora both a time out of time and a time out of mind. Pure desire, pure faith.

Being for most of its history a nation without a state and a territory, the Jewish people have maintained a strong sense of identity. Spinoza himself attributed this to the fact that the Jewish religion is more an earthly civil code, a set of habits, than a transcendent metaphysical scripture. Achy Obejas' novel deals with the ways in which these features of Judaism go across geographical boundaries; but in doing so, it applies a similar notion to explaining the ways that *cubanidad*, Cuban belonging and identity, are kept by people in the exile community. The building of enclosed collectivities allows for the fragile delusion of a world unchanged, transforming exile into an inner enclosure. Diaspora is both an external travel and an internal seclusion, and thus it needs rituals, practices, and the staging of a representation of the past in the present. One of the reasons why the San José family relocates in front of a lake in Rogers Park, Chicago, is because they feel the need to live surrounded by water, and with an urban center nearby, Rogers Park is not only a Cuban neighborhood, but also a Jewish one. Jews seem to be there reproducing the environment of European ghettos, minus the threat of external force and anti-Semitism. Exile, then, shows the core of its fugitive nature. One flees a place because it is or seems dangerous, goes to another place and builds a safer imitation of the previous one, but that second place is just the stage in which one is able to dream about a third one, an archetypical promised land, the impossibly simultaneous replica of the other two and its sublimation.

In the novel Cuba is somehow reproduced, reinterpreted, and reenacted. The Spanish language is the foremost vehicle, since it is the only language allowed in the San José home. But there are also many icons of Cuban Christianity and *Santería*, as I mentioned, and during the repeated walks along the lake shore in Rogers Park, the family members act as if they were promenading along the *Malecón* in Havana's waterfront. Textually, the novel itself is also a fabric of references to Cuban literature. In the Oriente province chapters, there is a kid named Celestino, who is originally the protagonist of *Celestino antes del alba* (*Celestino before Sunrise*), a novel by Cuban author Reinaldo Arenas. The boy named René, main character of *La carne de René* (*René's Flesh*), a novel by Havana author Virgilio Piñera, also makes an appearance here. So does José Farraluque, the writer who is a character in Lezama Lima's *Paradiso*, one of the pillars of the Cuban literary canon. Other well-known fictional Cubans to appear here include Pilar Fuentes, protagonist of Cristina García's *Dreaming in Cuban*, and Teresa Rodríguez, out of the novel *Tres tristes tigres*, by Guillermo Cabrera Infante. The intertextual presence of these characters in Obejas' novel is not a simple accumulation of quotes and interpolations. Arena's Celestino is a boy who rewrites other people's poems on the surfaces of trees; Enrique, Alejandra's father, is translating Lezama Lima's character's work into English; García's character, Pilar Fuentes, protests, from Miami, against Castro's regime in English but permanently daydreams of Cuba in Spanish; and Teresa Rodríguez, the character extracted from Cabrera Infante's novel, is, tellingly, a translator. The Cuba Alejandra obsessively thinks of is thus made out of other people's memories and fictional renditions of the country, and is to a large extent a translation. Since the novel is divided into sections narrating Alejandra's three trips to Cuba and fragments referring to her dreams of Cuba when she is in Chicago, the narration seems to describe a character that is always somehow in Cuba, be it in fact or as a figment of her imagination. Alejandra is also a character who can never establish a durable contact with the immediate world, never integrating herself into the community in which she lives and, as the novel progresses she becomes more and more introspective, building an inner space where the acceptance of a plural identity will become possible to her.

Benedict Anderson's concept of the "imagined community" seems to resonate here since the communities to which Alejandra wants to belong are almost entirely imagined—realms of the mind, one might say—transmitted by literature, myth, and oral tradition, but physically alien and most of the time far, far away from the one who imagines them. However, the novel seems to tell us that they *are,* after all, Alejandra's real origin. Her identity is a product of the mind, the multiple discourses she chooses to believe, and the discourses of tradition she can hardly refuse once she discovers them.

If *Days of Awe* is a reflection on Cuba from exile, exile itself does not seem to be a limitation for being connected to the language, culture, and life of a country from which the character is absent. The novel focuses on the act of memory and the fact of reconstructing the history of a people, which is also the history of a family with the peculiarity of being always displaced and wandering, but attached in different ways to practices originated in their previous lives. Opposite to Alejandra and her father, Enrique, other characters like the great-grandfather, Ytzak, and his Cuban neighbor, Moisés Menach, always assume doubleness as an inalienable feature of their identities. "We are Cubans and Jews," they say (143). This doubleness will be accepted also, toward the end of the novel, by Alejandra and by Enrique, who will ask his daughter to cremate him and throw his ashes in the Havana Sea. That the novel's characters finally arrive at the acknowledgment of an identity doubleness as the closest way to think of their own way of belonging is perfectly harmonious within the ideological scope of a novel that conceives its subject matter always as hybrid. There is temporal hybridity in the flashbacks and prolepsis that form the mechanics of the narration; there is stylistic hybridity in its pastiche of historical tales, myths, orally transmitted stories, travelogue, etc. Hybridity is at the core of the novel because the novel is the dramatization of an active memory, both a chaotic reality and a cosmic, ordering impulse. The act of writing itself stands for this process. Remembering and writing down fragments in a notebook is the dramatic counterpart of the narrated subject; the work of remembering and writing is identity in the making, active and dynamic. Memorizing and writing, Obejas seems to say, as she did in her previous novel *Memory Mambo*, are indispensable activities for surviving in exile because they imply opening new spaces and building new places.

In *Memory Mambo* the protagonist, Juani Casas, whose path to the United States is similar to that of Alejandra in *Days of Awe*, is trying to reconstruct her past and discover the personalities and secrets of all the members of her family. The only information she receives are lies, versions, stories, and contradictory answers from each one: "Everybody in our family is a liar. Mami and Papi make up stuff about the duct tape fortune, Caridad lies about Jimmy, Jimmy lies about everything, Patricia lies about Titi, god knows Tio Raúl and Pauli both have tons of secrets" (*Memory Mambo* 194).[5] Because of this collage of lies, she is not able to distinguish fact from fiction and she decides that her only possibility of surviving in the diaspora is to abandon the family business of the laundromat, a building where all of her relatives live as well, to become independent and write her own story. The critic Julio Ramos, in his essay "Migratories," argues that "the home constructed by writing would seem to find a compensatory place built against the grain of external pressures, including that of the 'danger' of more or less contact with other languages" (Ramos 54). One of the characteristics of life in the diaspora is dual memory, because a man in exile "is someone who inhabits one place and remembers or projects the reality of another" (Seidel ix). This is just what happens to Juani Casas, who has snippets of her history and that of her relatives and whose function in the novel is to discover, investigate, and later give proper cohesion to the versions that they tell her of Cuba and their mysterious lives in Chicago, where they actually live. All these stories are like rhythms of a fragmented mambo, counterpoint sounds with no common thread until she proposes to find one.

For Linda Craft, who analyzes in detail how memory and fiction function in exile in this first novel of Obejas, the reconstruction of the saga and the absolutely dysfunctional family history of the Casas family are part of the building of the identity of the protagonist. "One has to ask whether her father and family are really so dysfunctional or whether their mythmaking is a necessary part of the creation of identity, the family story, and psychological survival" (Craft 378). One of the characteristics of memory in exile, according to Marcus Embry in his study of *Memory Mambo*, is temporal duality and this is precisely what Juani experiences as well as Alejandra and Enrique in *Days of Awe*.

The actual state or experience of exile is like a dream, condensed and tightly wound. When the exilic subject, occupying a space that is not

home, produces writing or performance after exile, that production—
which in this analogy has been identified as exilic memory—unravels
a life world of singular cohabitation and dual temporality. Exilic
memory is the unraveling and actualization of the phenomenon of
exile. (103)

The characters in Obejas' stories cling to their writing because they need
the fragments of their stories to be able to reconstruct their own lives.
For all of them memory is converted into an alternative space, a type of
home. Michel Seidel, in his book *Exile and the Narrative Imagination*,
affirms that "for the exile native territory is the product of heightened
and sharpened memory and imagination is, indeed, a special homecoming" (Seidel xi). This takes us back to one important issue in *Days of
Awe*: translation. Even if the two traditions explicitly compared in the
text are the Jewish and the Cuban, the book, and so the character's memories and reconstructions, are written in English.

Language is a leading theme of the novel. In Chicago, Enrique is a college professor and a literary translator from Spanish into English. He is
constantly amazed by the difficulties of finding precise and literal translations from one language into another, and understands the discrepancies between them as irrecoverable gaps and holes. For him English is
a temporarily useful tool whereas Spanish is a territory linked not to
Cuba, but to the far past, the almost mythical past of Sephardic Spain.
Translation is for him the meeting of a present in which he does not want
to be and a past in which he never was. The blurred space in between,
the gap, the hole, the lost meaning, is his life in Cuba, the object of his
denial. Symbolically, Enrique's impossible translations are the cipher
of all the meanings lost with his own migration to the new language.
"For my father," writes Alejandra, "translation was a spiritual return to
Spain—although he never went there in real life, never booked a tour,
demurred every time he received an invitation. It was a way of creating and preserving Spain. That travel ban was not extended anywhere
else but to Cuba" (91). Alejandra is an interpreter at an NGO, working
with Latino people. For her, initially at least, translation is an easy business. There is an English word for every Spanish one and vice versa: her
world is biunivocal. This is the way she describes her work: "'I'm an
empathy,' she says. 'I slip my client's words through my mouth as if they
were formed by the electrical impulses of my own brain. When I am in
my reverie, I have no clue about what I'm actually saying. It's all aaaaa-
uuuhhh-eeeee'" (92).

These two visions of translation carry with them two different ideas
about identity. In both cases there seems to be a void between both languages. Enrique is conscious of the gap. The intermediate values, the
frontier, the blank spaces, that which cannot be named are what he looks

for in every text. In recognizing the difficulty of building the bridge, he sees at least the fleeing space in which the bridge should be placed.[6] It is not until the end of the novel that Alejandra will be able to notice this. Symptomatically, she will not understand it directly from her father's case, but by reading one of the ancient Sephardic Spanish poets Enrique and Ytzak admire. Even more curiously, this meeting point for father and daughter will be the work of a poet who wrote in Hebrew, Arabic, and Ladino—a mixture of Hebrew and Spanish—the medieval Cordobés writer, Judah Halevi.

The name of Halevi is frequently repeated throughout the novel. He is Enrique's and Ytzak's favorite author and lines from his poems constantly intertwine with the narration. Halevi was born in Spain and lived there during the First Crusade, suffering various persecutions due to the intolerance of the Almoravid, a Muslim fanatic group greatly influential in Cordoba and Toledo. After witnessing the death of many Jews, Halevi decided to migrate to Zion, developing from his life experience and his readings of the *Torah* the idea that it was impossible to be a true Jew outside of the Holy Land. Halevi started the journey to Israel, traveled across Egypt, but died before arriving in Jerusalem. Legend has it that it was as soon as he saw the city in the distance that he died, and his last words are the elegy "Zionide," one of the traditional foundations of Zionist discourses, whose crucial idea is that Jewish identity cannot be fulfilled without physical appropriation of the Israeli land. The novel, though, will progressively deny Halevi's notion, opposing to Halevi's Zionist principle of territoriality as a *sine qua non* requisite for identity, a principle of cultural reformulation as a mechanism for survival, and in doing so it will also postulate an identical mechanism for the transmission and appropriation of Cuban identity.

In *Days of Awe*, the male members of the San José family are the ones who pass down the Jewish tradition to their descendants and keep it alive over a period of a hundred years. Even Enrique, who first hides his Jewishness from his daughter, finally resorts to the same pattern. Until the very last moment, the female members of the family, conversely, are far removed from Jewish traditions: they are real converts, not crypto-Jews. Significantly, according to Jewish tradition, that should be the end of it. The women's conversion to Catholicism should mean the end of the Jewish heritage, since Judaism is of matrilineal inheritance. The novel modifies this automatic principle of belonging and possession of the Jewish identity in order to depict a kind of perseverance of belonging that goes beyond private rules and privative principles of inheritance. Passing down Judaism as a religion and Jewishness as an identity implies, in the novel, modifying both in order to keep them alive.[7] It is not the preservation of an unchanged tradition, but adaptation to reality that becomes crucial. In the absence of what is needed for matrilineal inheritance, men are willing to fulfill the female roles and so women should be ready to do the opposite. And that is just what happens. Ytzak kidnaps his son Enrique and takes him to Havana to be circumcised without his mother's approval, and keeps him there until he is thirteen and goes through his Bar Mitzvah.

Many years later, Enrique, approaching his death, will ask Alejandra to say the *Kaddish* for him, wearing a *tefillim*, knowing perfectly that both things are strictly forbidden for women in the Jewish tradition. It is also forbidden to cremate a body, but that is the third request Enrique has for Alejandra. In fact, after confessing to his daughter that he is a Jew, *everything* Enrique does at the end of his life in order to die and leave the world as a good Jew is forbidden by Judaism. So is everything Alejandra does at the beginning of her own life as a Jew. It is not the nature of those prohibitions that turns out to be significant, but the reasons for the modification, and its consequences. Once Enrique publicly acknowledges his Judaism, he becomes able to deal with his Cuban past also, since the main reason for his conflictive relation to Cuba was the fact that the island had been a major obstacle for his openly embracing the religion. After a life conflicting with this, he discovers a way to integrate Cuba and his Judaism into one whole signifier. When he asks Alejandra to cremate him after his death and to sing the *Kaddish* for him, he also asks her to throw his ashes in the Havana Sea. Alejandra, willing to comply with her father's wishes, travels to Cuba. She enters the Havana synagogue and is confronted by the rabbis. How does she dare wear the *tefillim*? After she is expulsed from the temple, she goes to the ocean and throws the ashes in the water, and instead of repeating the traditional *Kaddish*, she chooses to pronounce a verse by Judah Halevi and adds, "Judah Halevi may or may not have made it to his Zion, but here, through me, my father is at rest in his" (320). The final act of Enrique's existence is the ritual transformation of Cuba into his symbolic Zion, and his return to it. That is also the founding act of Alejandra's new life as a Jew. Halevi's nationalist Zionism is resignified, reconstructed as a spiritual ideal, turned into a metaphor. One can be a Jew without returning to Israel, as long as one has some personal place to return to. Jewishness turns out to be a kind of intimate nostalgia, never to be wholly cured. Enrique's body will not be buried in Cuba, but immersed in the intermediate space between exile and return, in the Cuban sea, which is a way out and a way in, or just a frozen space in between: time out of time, time out of mind. The French philosopher Jean-Luc Nancy wrote about burial as the ultimate gesture of integration into the community. Enrique is never buried. A Jew is not the one who returns, seems to say Obejas, but the one who wants to return. Jewish heritage is not land, but a form of desire, and Jewish community is a commonality of desire. And that is the core of identity for exiles, as the Jewish Cuban exile Alejandra learns from her father.

Notes

1. Upon publishing her first book of stories—*We Came All the Way from Cuba So You Could Dress Like This?* (1994)—Achy Obejas declared to Tatiana De La Tierra her desire some day to write a great novel about the relationship between Jews and Cubans. That project is, without a doubt, *Days of Awe*. "Obejas hopes to one day write the great Cuban-Jewish novel. She has had fascination and identification with Jewish culture since she was a child. In Michigan City, IN, the Jews were the only other people who had accents, ate strange food, spoke a foreign language, where obsessed with a foreign country, and who thought they were white" (De la Tierra 39).

2. William Safran expands upon Vertovec's definition and defines diaspora as "expatriate minority communities" that have the following characteristics: "1. that are dispersed from an original 'center' to at least two 'peripheral' places; 2. that maintain a 'memory vision, or myth about their original homeland' 3. that 'believe they are not—and perhaps cannot be—fully accepted by their host country'; 4. that see the ancestral home as a place of eventual return, when the time is right; 5. that are committed to the maintenance or restoration of this homeland; 6. that its consciousness and solidarity as a group are 'importantly defined' by this continuing relationship with the homeland" (Safran 83–84). For Safran the Jewish diaspora is the "ideal type" of diaspora because all six of the mentioned characteristics occur. James Clifford sees the last two points of Safran's list as problematic given that "the notion of 'return' for Jews is often an eschatological or utopian projection in response to a present dystopia" (Clifford 248). This is precisely what Enrique, Alejandra's father, feels.

3. For Vertovec, there are three characteristics of all peoples in a diaspora: a social grouping that implies a displacement from the original land, having a common past or a group consciousness, and having a similar type of cultural expression.

4. In an interview with Jorjet Harper, Achy Obejas confesses that she lives in the United States but she is almost simultaneously in Havana. "In fact, I'd obsessed about Havana to the point that some years ago I'd even memorized the map of the city and all the bus routes. So when I got there I knew where I was going all the time. And in some ways I belonged right away, but I realized I didn't belong there attitudinally" (Harper 2).

5. Obejas' work has been studied principally from a homosexual perspective, connecting the openly declared lesbianism of the author with that of her characters. That explains why her least studied work is *Days of Awe* where Alejandra's bisexuality is not the central theme. In her two previous works the protagonist's lesbianism is relevant. In the case of *Memory Mambo*, Juani Casas is not understood because of her homosexuality and that is clearly one of the factors that marginalize her within her community and within her family. In *Memory Mambo* Maite Zubiaurre proposes that the function of memory and the reinvention of the past as a core theme of the novel not only serve as an identity mechanism, but also as a motive for proposing the reconstruction of a new female-centered country. The idea of relating and reconstructing Cuba from the United States is connected to the intention of narrating or establishing a feminine nation.

6. Maya Socolovsky analyzes in detail the aspect of the different visions that father and daughter face in order to translate texts. "Enrique is not just a translator; he is a crypto-Jew engaged in the act of translation for whom meaning emerges only through absence and *différance*. If translation is a way of determining or creating presence in language, it is also in practice dependent to continual replacement and *différance* for the production of meaning" (Socolovsky 230). The author concludes that the entire novel is written through Enrique's silences, his secret (the fact that he is Jewish) is never directly revealed. Quite the contrary. The story is narrated through a series of displacements and new meanings

7. A central theme of the novel is the necessity of adapting one's traditions to be in accord with the context in which one lives the diaspora, and this is just what the 1,500 Jews who still live in Cuba do today. The documentary *Havana Naguila* and the article by Caren Osten Gerzberg published in *The New York Times*, "In Cuba, Finding a Tiny Corner of Jewish Life," show how the few Jews who stayed on the island, in spite of the religious prohibitions imposed by Fidel Castro until 1992, practiced Judaism in secret and had to reformulate some of their traditions due to the shortages, the risks, and their poverty. Some of the necessary changes were: "The Jewish community of Cienfuegos gathers each Friday night for *Sabbath*, services in the front room of Rebecca Langus's second-floor apartment." Moreover, the lack of men to form the *minyán*—the minimum number of ten adult men to be able to begin a prayer—meant that the Torah acted as a man. "There where so few Jewish people coming to pray that the Cuban *minyan* was born, counting each *Torah* as a qualifying member to make prayer possible." Finally, among the changes that the journalist mentions, the community had no rabbi, but Joseph Levi acted as one.

Works Cited

Anderson, Benedict. *Imagined Communities: Reflections on the Origin and Spread of Nationalism*. London: Verso, 1993.

Clifford, James. "Diaspora." *Routes: Travel and Translation in the Late Twentieth Century*. Cambridge: Harvard University Press, 1997. 244–277

Craft, Linda. "Truth or Consequences: Mambos, Memories and Multiculturalism from Achy Obejas's Chicago." *Revista de Estudios Hispánicos* 35.2 (May 2001): 369–387.

De la Tierra, Tatiana. "Achy Obejas: All the way from Cuba." *Deneuve* 5.2 (1995): 38–39.

Embry, Marcus. "Cuban Double-Cross: Father's Lies in Obejas and Garcia." *Double Crossings = Entrecruzamientos: antología de artículos presentados en el Noveno Congreso Internacional de Culturas Latinas del Norte*. New Jersey: Ediciones Nuevo Espacio, 2001. 97–107.

Flores, Juan. "'Salvación casita': Space, Performance and Community." *Negotiating Performance: Gender, Sexuality and Theatricality in Latino America*. Durham: Duke University Press, 1994. 121–136.

Harper, Jorjet. "Dancing to a Different Beat: An interview with Achy Obejas." *Lambada Book Report* 5.2 (September 1996): 1–3.

Obejas, Achy. *Days of Awe*. New York: Ballantine Book, 2001.

———. *Memory Mambo*. Pittsburgh: Cleis Press, 1996.

Osten Gerszberg, Caren. "In Cuba, Finding a Tiny Corner of Jewish Life." *The New York Times*. Sunday, February 4, 2007. 3.

Pérez Firmat, Gustavo. *Life on the Hyphen*. Austin: University Press of Texas, 1994.

Socolovsky, Maya. "Deconstructing a Secret History: Trace, Translation, and Crypto-Judaism in Achy Obejas's *Days of Awe*." *Contemporary Literature* 44.2 (2003): 225–249.

Seidel, Michael. *Exile and the Narrative Imagination*. New Haven: Yale University Press, 1986.

Ramos, Julio. "Migratories." *Re-Reading Jose Marti (1853–1895): One Hundred Years Later*. Ed. Julio Rodríguez-Luis. Albany: State University of New York Press, 1999. 53–67.

Safran, William. "Diasporas in Modern Societies: Myths of Homeland and Return." *Diaspora* 1.1 (1991): 83–99.

Vertovec, Steven. "Three Meanings of 'Diaspora', Exemplified among South Asian Religion." *Diaspora* 7.2 (1999): 1–37.

Zubiaurre, Maite. "Hacia una nueva geografía feminista: nación, identidad y construcción imaginaria en *Dreaming in Cuban* (Cristina García) y en *Memory Mambo* (Achy Obejas)." *Chasqui: Revista de Literatura Latinoamericana* 28.1 (May 1999): 3–15.

Filmography

Havana Naguila: The Jews of Cuba. Dir: Paull, Laura. Schnitzki & Stone Production, 1995.

III

Gender Crossings

A Community in Transit: The Performative Gestures of Manuel Ramos Otero's Narrative Triptych

Mónica Lladó-Ortega

7.1   Toward a Poetics of Transit: The Multiplying of the "I" and of the Island

The three short story collections of Puerto Rican author Manuel Ramos Otero, *Concierto de metal para un recuerdo y otras orgías de soledad* (1971), *El cuento de la mujer del mar* (1979), and *Página en blanco y staccato* (1987) in conjunction form a triptych of performative gestures that proposes a poetics of transit. This narrative triptych explores the effects of colonialism and migration on subjectivity and conjures an alternate community created through transit, migration, and difference in opposition to the insular discourses of nationalism and colonialism that subsume difference by imposing totalizing metaphors and symbols based on fixed geographical boundaries and essentialist notions of identity. I propose that all three collections of stories through the performative gesture each represents, mutual eviction/the duel/ and reconciliation, inscribe the author's poetics of transit that through the narrative strategy of autobiography as a pretext for the multiplication of the "I" and of the Island conjure through the transit of difference an alternate Trans Puerto Rican community.[1]

My concept of performative gestures arises not only from the notions of performativity as proposed by Judith Butler but also from Ramos Otero's own notion of autobiography as a pretext for exploring subjectivity and life through writing.[2] In an essay titled "Ficción e historia: texto y pretexto de la autobiografía" Ramos Otero explains his idea of autobiography as a narrative strategy of self-liberation paradoxically linked to fiction:

> Yo estoy entre mi ficción y la historia, no estoy fuera de ninguna de las dos sino entre ambas, y todo lo que he escrito, todo lo que escribo es un intento de atrapar, irónicamente, la voz de mi liberación, esa voz que al aprehender las otras voces de los otros cuenteros de la historia definirá mejor los bordes temporales de la lengua…(22)

Ramos Otero's proposal is that the writer or *cuentero* ("yo") is always already in between fiction and reality("historia") and it is from within that ambiguous and paradoxical space that freedom is sought, affirmed and apprehended. Moreover, this proposal affirms that the *cuentero*'s voice contains the voices of the others. The "I" is multiplied in two ways: first because it acknowledges within itself the voices of the other writers or "cuenteros" he/she has read or encountered;[3] and second, the voice of the "I"(first person) also contains the voices of the others who participate in the (his)story. From the first person, traditionally conceived as conveying the singular voice of the individual, Ramos Otero proposes a plural voice that is collective in the sense that it includes the others. In his case the others are those excluded from the canonical third person that homogenizes and erases difference. For Ramos Otero, the "I" is a political stance that affirms difference and multiplicity against the discourses of the homogenizing "we" of sameness. The "I" is multiplied through the inevitable interconnectedness of otherness-difference: "*Sí*, el acento se pone sobre la vida individual, pero el acento siempre ha estado puesto sobre el *Yo*, que también es *Tú*, que además es *Él* y que siempre es *Ella* cuando nos genera con el acento fundamental de la diferencia" (emphasis in original, 23). In that way, the author conceives his writing to be in transit between fiction and history and, as he explains further in the essay, it also moves between the individual and the collective (138). In her book *Giving an Account of Oneself* (2005) Judith Butler articulates a similar proposal to Ramos Otero's autobiography as pretext. Her theory of the subject affirms its connection to the "community of others," since it is in the relation to the other that the subject forms. At the moment of narrating the "I" or "giving an account of oneself": "we become speculative philosophers or fiction writers" (78). Narration, be it written or oral, becomes a simultaneous fiction and reality that is at once individual and collective.

In his essay Ramos Otero explains his narrative strategy while he implicitly addresses the critiques of some of the Island's literary critics who consider his insertion of the autobiographic as a symptom of either a lack of distance of the author from his work or as narcissistic solipsism (González, Ríos Ávila). The tendency to read his writing as too autobiographical is partially due to the fact that Ramos Otero inserts himself in his texts, literally, through the pictures of himself and of his mother on the covers of the books and through the insertion in the stories of his last names and the names of people in his life, friends and lovers, as well as his preference for first-person narrators that in most of his stories and poems thematically explore homosexual love. These readings of his work also respond to the fact that the canonical texts of Puerto Rican literature have traditionally sought to construct the nation through paternalistic totalizing metaphors privileging the house and the family and using third-person narrators that conjure a unifying we, prohibiting the enunciation of the "I" (Gelpí).

In response, Ramos Otero proposes autobiography as a pretext for the exploration of being, but not in the ontological sense of encountering the essence of self nor as a means to dehumanize and convert subjectivity into an abstraction. Through his narrative strategy of autobiography he multiplies the "I" so as to conjure a space of in-betweeness that simultaneously pluralizes the place of the subject and of the nation-island. Hence, traditional notions of "I" as an ontological enunciation of the individual are challenged precisely through the movement inscribed through its multiplication. Furthermore, Ramos Otero's poetics of transit distances his work from all ontological notions of self, of nation, and of gender and sexuality. In fact, the author uses this strategy precisely to articulate the oppression of the colonial-marginalized subject and in that way access the power of writing as the power of being, or more precisely, of becoming. The purpose of this strategic writing is really twofold; to use writing as a means to affirm the denied humanity of the colonized subject (Gates, Fanon) that in most cases is also a migrant subject; and to challenge the imposed limits between fiction and reality, self and other in order to reveal the discourses of identity (national/sexual) as fictions. In this way, writing in Ramos Otero represents a search for freedom: the freedom to live and write.[4]

It can be said that Ramos Otero critiques the canonical notions of authority manifested in the paternalistic discourses of the nation and evicts himself into an abject and abstract outside of the literary canon, and of the metaphoric house-nation (Arroyo, Barradas, Cruz-Malavé, Montero, Ríos Avila). Nonetheless, I propose that the apparent eviction is in fact inscription, an overwriting, so to speak, that inscribes, transforms, and multiplies the island. In other words, this narrative strategy of the autobiographical as pretext of the multiplication of the "I," simultaneously multiplies the island or nation as well. Instead of an excluding paternalist totalitarian space of fictional sameness it becomes a multiple place of diversity. Writing and storytelling are the means through which to negotiate exclusion-marginalization and conjure within the text a new notion of self and nation that is inclusive and non-normative, where movement and difference translates into the liberty to become the self/ nation of Trans Puerto Ricanness.

As I will explain in the following sections, Ramos Otero's three collections of short stories form a triptych of performative gestures that through the praxis of autobiography pluralize the self and the Island while inscribing a poetics of transit that expands the archipelago.

7.2   Mutual Eviction: Concierto de metal para un recuerdo y otras orgías de soledad

The first collection of stories, *Concierto de metal para un recuerdo y otras orgías de soledad*, represents the performative gesture of mutual eviction. This apparent eviction is reflected in the book's cover graced with a photo of Ramos Otero in a desolate place, suggesting the short stories therein are about the author's life. In 1968 the author literally migrates and leaves the Island of Puerto Rico to live and write in New York City. As the author expressed in an interview, he left because of the rejection he experienced on the Island because he was openly gay (Costa 59).[5] In turn, the author in this collection appears to reject the Island and exclude it from his stories by not making any explicit references to it. In this way, the stories in this collection reflect the author's migration from the Island to the diaspora. Nonetheless, this book can be said to have the least autobiographical elements of the three, confirming the narrative strategy of the autobiographical as pretext.

Although this performative gesture of mutual eviction, of being outside and without a home, is apparent in all thirteen stories in the collection through the urban and anonymous effect that is created by establishing the place of action in external and public spaces and by the emphasis on solitude and death as recurrent central themes, ironically what is explored is the inevitable interdependence of self and other. An example of solitude and death as an exploration of this interdependcy of self and other can be seen in the story with the same title as the book: "Concierto de metal para un recuerdo." In this story subjectivity and individuality are explored through two anonymous characters, who do not have names and only identify themselves through numbers as if they were objects, in fact they appear to be cyborgs: half human and half machine. Everything in the story is anonymous, dehumanized, and cold. The place of action referred to in the text as the agency is totalitarian and repressive.

In the story subjectivity and solitude become one and they are achieved through being outside of the collective represented here by the agency. Solitude also represents difference and in the story it symbolizes the recuperation of humanity through feeling, and in that way, through breaking the rules of the agency. Though solitude is the means toward individuality and humanity, it is through the interaction of both characters that this is brought about. One of the characters expresses feelings of envy, happiness, tears, and the other recognizes these as illegal acts that must be penalized by death ("fundición"), but witnessing the feelings of the other awakens the character's desire to express her own individuality: "vio aquel cuerpo diferente del suyo, vio aquellos ojos sumidos en llanto. Vio aquellos labios comerse todas las sonrisas para sonreír. Vio que era diferente. Vio que no era igual que los demás camaradas de la sociedad... vio que era distinta y le gustó su unicidad" (84).[6] Even though solitude is proposed as the means to accessing individuality, subjectivity, and ultimately liberty from the totalitarian-collective and its dehumanizing rules (the agency), it is through the interaction with the other character that the desire to be different from the rest arises. This confirms in a Lacanian sense the interdependence of self and other because it is revealed precisely through the image and difference of the other.[7] At the same time, this creates an ambiguous and paradoxical effect because the characters become subjects through solitude and death:

> A su lado pasaban aquellos con el uno y dos...uno y dos...y no corrían. Todos eran iguales, asquerosamente iguales. Sólo ella diversificaba la muchedumbre. Entonces sintió un gozo muy interno al saberse que no era igual. [...] Y entonces le pareció extraño lo demás. Al mirar su cuerpo sintió asco de su metálica existencia, y mientras aspiraba la naturaleza se quedó estática...(85)

In the agency everyone is "disgustingly the same," they are not subjects, but rather machine-like objects. Here individuality is achieved through solitude and difference that arises by breaking the agency's rules and rejecting the homogenous collective. At the end of the story she manifests her maximum gesture of freedom, embracing her humanity by "breathing in nature" and becoming a subject in a paradoxical act of self-liberation through death contained in the double meaning of the word *"estática"*: to be still or inert and to be in ecstasy or overflowing with joy. If ecstasy is the liberty produced when one becomes conscious of one's own existence or being, that is to say, that ecstasy arises from knowing who one is, as Martin Heidegger proposes, then this story resignifies subjectivity, being, and community since it is through death that symbolically and simultaneously a subject and an alternate community is created.[8] In fact, the deaths of the two protagonists of the story can be read as migrations or exiles that also conjure the community of the diaspora.

This story is not only an implicit critique of colonialism, but also a critique of the foundational discourses of the nation-Island, that in Puerto Rico manifest themselves through the totalizing metaphor of the family that seeks to homogenize and erase difference while establishing a patriarchal hierarchy of authority. This seemingly solipsistic story hides a differential notion of community because, ultimately, it is through the interaction with the other that the protagonist arrives at the solitude that makes subjectivity possible. The word community is resignified and instead of meaning the agency, that totalitarian place where everyone is subsumed in sameness ("asquerosamente iguales"), it refers to an alternate community of difference created through the multiplication of the "I" in its interdependency with the other, suggesting the simultaneous multiplication of the Island by inscribing within it the other island of difference, migration and diaspora. Thus, Ramos Otero's poetics of transit is traced through the movement between the self and the other, and paralleling the transit in between the Island and its other community of migrants.

In the stories of this collection the pluralizing of the self and the Island symbolically reveal a paradoxical simultaneous rejection of and desire for the Island-home, which render the eviction a performance that becomes inscription. Though there is a rejection of the Island and its excluding and marginalizing totalitarian discourses, there is at once a desire for inclusion. However, this inclusion is not a submission to those discourses, but rather an inclusion into a new collective that conjures a new Island-home. Hence, the multiplying of the Island in this collection of short stories occurs through the implicit critiques of Puerto Rico's discourses of the nation and its inscription of the other Island of difference and transit: the diaspora.

The last story of the collection "La casa clausurada" confirms the paradoxical performative gesture of mutual eviction and the author's poetics of transit. Here the image of transit is inscribed not only through the *cuentero*'s name, *Roberto Bracero D'Paso* ("Bracero" as migrant workers are also called and "D'Paso" as in passing by), but also because his mother's death-migration can be read to symbolize the displacement of the Island as place of origin (Arroyo). The narrator's affirmation that "la familia es mamá" (70) can be read as a challenge to the patriarchal discourse of the nation by displacing the father and the Island, inscribing in its place the other Island of the diaspora and the others who have migrated. The transit of migration questions the notion of a fixed place of origin, and of an identity tied to this physical geographical space. The conflictive paradoxical relationship of the *cuentero* and the Island is revealed through his indecision to enter the house or in other words, return to the Island. In this way, the mutual eviction of this short story collection that at first glance appears to be solipsism, given the emphasis on solitude in the texts, is really an exploration of self or subjectivity in order to arrive at the other, affirming the implicit collectivity of every subject and connecting these narratives symbolically and simultaneously to the Island and the other island of exile and diaspora. The narrator's affirmation of "la familia es mamá" and the abundant presence of feminine characters in the stories of this first collection connect it to the second book, *El cuento de la mujer del mar*, that reflects in its title an alliance with women and adds yet another dimension to Ramos Otero's poetics of transit.

7.3   The Duel: El cuento de la mujer del mar

The fact that the cover of the second book of short stories, *El cuento de la mujer del mar*, is not a picture of the author but of his mother inscribes Ramos Otero's strategy of the autobiographical as pretext and in this case pluralizes the self through the inclusion of his mother: announcing an alliance with women as the marginalized and excluded other of the Island. The hierarchies of the Island-patriarchy that impose the paternalistic metaphor of the family are challenged through this cover. Though the cover could suggest a matriarchy as a substitution for patriarchy, this would only fortify the binary father/mother and the notions of the masculine and feminine they represent. In this way, the performative gesture of this book can be articulated as a duel against the paternalist discourses of the Island and the notions of gender they seek to impose. The duel inscribes the author's poetics of transit in this collection through the transit of transvestism.[9] Hence, the poetics of transit in this collection, is manifested through the criss-crossing, dressing, and undressing of the *cuenteros* between the poles of the feminine and the masculine, that become masks they use to move through what these spaces represent so as to challenge the idea of a fixed and definable sexual, cultural, and national identity. Through this transit the traditionally marginalized voices of the other are inscribed in non-dualistic terms.

In all the stories included in this collection, the voices of the storytellers are multiplied by the transit to and from first person to third person, feminine to masculine, and in some cases, the narrators and characters are drag queens: *Alana-Alan*, in "Peregrinación por un eclipse"; *Miseria*, in "La última plena que bailó Luberza"; and *la emperatriz china* in "Inventario mitológico del cuento." In conjunction, these transits between the two sides of the binary multiply the "I" and the Island, identity and gender are pluralized and produce a queer subject and nation in transit. It is queer precisely because through its transit it ungrounds itself in opposition to the norms inscribed in each side of the binary, and simultaneously proposes an identity and nation without essence, signaling the impossibility of an ontology of the self and, for that matter, of the nation.[10]

In the story "Inventario mitológico del cuento" two characters in particular can be said to queer the subject and the Island while tracing the alliance of this book to the excluded-marginalized others of Puerto Rico: the transvestite character of *la emperatriz china* who represents the queering of the subject; and *la Corteja de la Vida* who represents the queering of the Island. *La emperatriz china* is queered through both her/his literal transvestism and also her/his simultaneous connection to two mythological goddesses: *Atabex* (155) and Athena (163). *Atabex*, Taíno goddess of mother earth, the sea, and the moon is the mother of *Yocahú* who has no masculine ancestor; and Athena, warrior goddess of wisdom, as the Greek myth describes, is born through Zeus' assimilation and incorporation of the goddess Métis' body, making him her father and mother simultaneously. The double identification of *la emperatriz china* with *Atabex* and Athena connect her/him to the spaces of the feminine and masculine through transit-transvestism while simultaneously questioning what each represents. This symbolic union of these seemingly opposite spaces in this story becomes an erotic transit between both, producing a queer subject in transit.

The queering of the island occurs through the character *la Corteja de la Vida* who represents the Island of Puerto Rico. She is Betty, the first lady, who dies of breast cancer and has requested to be buried between *las Tetas de Cayey*. The queering occurs throughout the story through the alternative practices of the multiple narrators that represent those excluded from and marginalized by the national project because of their gender or sexual orientation: the cook *Carmen Cachete*; the poet *Ola Sola*; the writer *cuentero Ramos*; and *la emperatriz china*. Together they inscribe on *la Corteja*'s body, which appears as a double for the Island, the writing of the story and the voices of otherness each represents. Through these inscriptions of otherness, liberation from, and the transformation of the Island is sought. The hierarchies of the Island's patriarchy that privilege the father-man as authority-author represented in the story by the characters *Conde Carlos* and *Cortázar* are challenged through the multiplied self of the subaltern voices that "disarm the machista canon" and seek to assassinate the author-father from the space of otherness and difference represented by the women, the gay, the mulatto, and the writing itself (Cruz Malavé 258). Moreover, I propose that it is in the transit of crossing and cross dressing that a queering of the Island is manifested through the inscription of the other Island of otherness. In this way, an alternative community is conjured that includes not only those marginalized by the totalitarian discourses on the Island, but also those who have been excluded because they have migrated to the other Island of the diaspora. This queering of the Island occurs in the story when *Cortázar*'s phallic airplane transits across the Island-*Tetas de Cayey* and in this crossing or transit, transforms the funeral of *la Corteja de la Vida* into the murder and queering of *Conde Carlos-Cortázar* and of patriarchy:

> Se sacudió la tierra como cambiándose de lado [...] el avión (helicóptero tal vez) con el asesinado no asesinado todavía cruzaba sobre

la tumba de la Corteja de la Vida y el asesino pensaba de inmediato: ¡maldita Corteja de la Vida, tomas el viento de pretexto para largarte volando! [. . .] el avión—helicóptero tal vez—se posaba como una mariposa, como un bicho de sombras, sobre el ataúd y pensó que ya era hora, que ya podía vestirse con la ropa de luto y ser cuentero, para poder contarlo todo sin omitir detalles. (166)

A double queering of the father and the Island occurs through the transit of the Plane-helicopter that crosses-penetrates *la Corteja*-Island-*ataúd*. The father represented by *Cortázar*'s plane is queered through its transit across the body of *la Corteja* and inscribes both the feminine, helicopter-round/ "mariposa," and the masculine, airplane/ "bicho de sombras." The body of *la Corteja de la Vida* is in turn liberated ("se largó volando") through the queering of the totalizing discourses of the patriarchal national project in what can be read as a symbolic and simultaneous migration and inscription of the other Island of the excluded others. In that way, the Island is multiplied and queered and *la Corteja* becomes the *asesino-cuentero Ramos* who can from that space of otherness access storytelling and writing as the tool for conjuring the alternate community constituted through otherness and difference: the Trans Puerto Rican community.

Throughout the stories of this performative gesture of the duel, Ramos Otero's poetics of transit are inscribed as a queering of the subject and the nation, confirming the interdependency of self and other, and of the individual and the collective: "uno sale de uno mismo para reencontrarse en el amado" ("El cuento de la mujer del mar" 216). Additionally, the photo of his mother on the cover and the insertion of biographical allusions to Puerto Rican poets, Julia de Burgos and Clara Lair, as well as to the historical figure of *Isabel la Negra* in the stories "El cuento de la mujer del mar," "El romance de Clara Gardenia Otero," and "La última plena que bailó Luberza," respectively, not only confirm Ramos Otero's strategy of auto/biography as pretext, but also his inclusion of those marginalized from both inside and outside the space of the nation-Island and its history and literature.

The duel as performative gesture is not a dehumanizing abstraction of the dichotomies of Island/diaspora, self/other, man/woman, but rather, as the character *la Corteja de la Vida* suggests in her name, an exploration of subjectivity and identity as paradoxical spaces of articulation. In this way, writing as the search for being is also the search for the freedom to be or become, and in Ramos Otero both are conceived as transits, as never-ending processes. What is conjured and inscribed implicitly in this transit of the second book of short stories is the Trans Puerto Rican community that in the third performative gesture will be emphatically and explicitly manifested as the inhabitable place of difference and otherness.

7.4   Reconciliation: Página en blanco y stacatto

The third book of short stories, *Página en blanco y staccato*, represents the third performative gesture of the narrative triptych: reconciliation. On the cover, a portrait of the author painted by Puerto Rican artist Angel Rodríguez Díaz, connects this book to New York, "La otra isla de Puerto Rico," as the first story of the collection is titled. This gesture represents reconciliation with the Island and the diaspora, the initial eviction of the first book with the apparent absence of the Island and the constant transit-transvestism of the second that inscribed an implicit Island of the other are now transformed into an explicit and paradoxical desire to embrace the multiple Islands.

This book represents the author's symbolic return to the place of origin, the Island of Puerto Rico, and the acceptance of the inevitable future and return to his origins in a different sense: death. This third performative gesture closes the cycle of life with death and reconciles itself with the first gesture of apparent eviction by multiplying the island of Puerto Rico through the image of a floating, migrating island that also represents home. The expansion of the Puerto Rican archipelago, that from the outset of the triptych has been implicit, becomes explicit here in the first story of the collection directly through its title and the image of a migrating island:

> Puerto Rico es [...] un barco de remeros bilingües [...]; cada remero solitario de las olas caribes, pensando en el otro y el otro remero solitario que por siempre navegará las dulces venas de los ríos isleños y la preciosa sal de las bahías, en indisoluble hermandad de yugos achicharrados en un claro de bosque, libertad de soledades mutuas en la nave que siempre revoluciona a sus guerreros, y ahora, [está] detenida en su curso... (16–17)

Puerto Rico is a boat of solitary bilingual rowers united in "indissoluble brotherhood/ sisterhood" and though it is "detained" by colonialism the rowers keep rowing "forever." This could be seen as a poetic summary of the performative gesture: the reconciliation of these solitary soldiers who fight for survival as colonial subjects. Through these stories, Ramos Otero seeks to transform the separation and distance into closeness through the sea that unites the floating, migrating islands and its rowers. The sea as isolation as emphasized in Antonio S. Pedreira's canonical text *Insularismo* (1934) is transformed into a space of movement, connection, and aperture. The action of rowing represents the act of writing and storytelling that transforms what appears fixed on maps into something mobile; just as the narrators of the first story comments: "por la posición en que se encontraba ese día la isla de Puerto Rico," as if the island had floated ("La otra isla de Puerto Rico" 12).

From the first story to the last, the gesture of reconciliation manifests itself through this image of the moving island of Trans Puerto Ricanness that multiplies the Island into the Islands of the Trans Puerto Rican community. This Trans Puerto Rican community inscribed by Ramos Otero in his work is constructed from the mobile, diverse, and multiple instead of the imagined fiction of a homogenous us where differences are subsumed and erased.[11] I propose the term Trans Puerto Rican because it articulates Ramos Otero's poetics of transit: it inscribes the constant transit of Puerto Rican people and artifacts in between geographic, linguistic, and ideological spaces and reveals its transnational character.[12] In this way, Ramos Otero explores the paradox of a community in transit that constantly displaces the Island, as place of origin, and builds itself on the difference of those traditionally marginalized by the identity politics of the insular national project.

Hence, this third collection of stories, through the performative gesture of reconciliation, seeks to insert the stories of the excluded by transiting between the spaces of reality and history, and autobiography and fiction. All the stories of this third book explore the colonial status of Puerto Rico in varying degrees through the stories of exile and migration. Ramos Otero's storytellers insert the voices silenced by colonialism, exile, and migration into the "official stories" of the paternalistic metaphors of the family and the house (Montero).

For example, the forgotten rebellions and migrations of the others of the Island are remembered in the *Memorias* of José Usbaldo Olmo Olmo and the storytelling of his twin sister Liboria, in the story "La otra isla de Puerto Rico." The voices of the brother, sister, and the narrator tell the story exploring the history of Puerto Ricans in New York: "estamos en medio de los otros de la otra isla de Puerto Rico, más de un millón de fotografías ignoradas en los archivos de emigrantes" (20) and "ocho nacionalistas acaban de ser encarcelados por conspirar para derrocar el gobierno de Estados Unidos en la otra isla de Puerto Rico" (22). The voices of the characters represent different elements of historiography and storytelling: the written is represented by José Usbaldo's *Memorias*, the oral is represented by Liboria's stories and the narrator represents the translation implicit in the acts of reading, hearing, and writing stories. Together the three voices simultaneously multiply the "I" and the Island and inscribe a new form of historiography and literature.

In "Vivir del cuento," there are also multiple voices that narrate three different stories in one and move between the limits of history and reality, and fiction and illusion. The character Monserrate Álvarez represents the biographical and he tells his-story of a Puerto Rican in Hawaii through his letters that Norma, another Puerto Rican in Hawaii, integrates into a literary conference. The *cuentero* and Magali (allusion to Ramos Otero's friend Puerto Rican author Magali García Ramis) represent the translation of history and reality into fiction. And the third story within the story is a third-person narrative of the colonial history of Hawaii that simulates a historical text. The presence of the other stories of Monserrate and Norma and the fictions that arise from them, evoke implicitly the image of the migrating island and propose both storytelling and writing as means to affirm the denied humanity of the colonized-marginalized subject and simultaneously challenge the imposed limits between fiction and reality. The title of the story "to live by/from story telling" merges writing and storytelling so as to acknowledge both the written and oral stories of migration and inscribe them through Ramos Otero's notion of the *cuentero* who is both writer and storyteller. In the last two stories of this third book, titled "Página en blanco y staccato" and "Descuento," the floating island becomes central to the notion of the performative gesture of reconciliation with both spaces, Puerto Rico and the diaspora, transforming them both into inhabitable places. This image of the floating-migrating island challenges identities tied to geographical places of origin and multiplies the Island revealing in its transit the paradoxical relationship of simultaneous rejection and desire of the home or place of origin.

For example, in "Página en blanco y staccato," the two protagonists are both in transit between communities: Sam Fat is a black Chinese Puerto Rican born in New York ("desde el momento que vió al recién nacido, supo que el niño sufriría la agonía del rechazo" 76) and the narrator, a gay Puerto Rican, is in between the gay community in New York and the community of the Puerto Rican diaspora, not fully belonging to either. Both characters challenge identity categories that intend to define and fix individuals through totalizing, essentialist notions of national, cultural, and sexual identities. Both characters displace any notions of a stable or fixed place of origin based on geographical boundaries and spaces (Martínez-San Miguel). The characters represent Ramos Otero's poetics of transit that through the multiplying of the "I" and the Island produce a subject and a community in transit.

The last story of the collection, "Descuento," closes both the book and the triptych of performative gestures. It serves as an epilogue by narrating the origins of the stories of the book and connecting each with the biography of the *cuentero*. The narrator pluralizes the self and the Island while transiting to and from the multiplied identities explored in the other stories of the collection. It is precisely through the mask of the autobiographical and the historic that the stories of this collection transit from the individual to the collective and reveal the relation of writing and storytelling to life and death and the urgent need to create an inhabitable place, a home. The narrator of this story affirms that the reality of HIV "reclama volverse literatura" (92). In this way, writing and storytelling are proposed as a simultaneous search and desire for the home and for the freedom to live and write. Through the poetics of transit the gesture of reconciliation proposed by Ramos Otero and his storytellers transform both the Island and the diaspora into the homeland, so as to be able to die in peace and simultaneously remain alive in writing.

Hence, this third book in its performative gesture inscribes the collective biography, history, and narrative of the Trans Puerto Rican community, inserting the stories of the other Puerto Ricans that inhabit other islands: it is a Puerto Rico in transit in between geographies and words. And it is through this poetics of transit that Ramos Otero seeks reconciliation with the Island and the diaspora. Tracing an image of a floating and migrating island inhabited by bilingual rowers, who in spite of colonialism, migration, and exile continue rowing and thinking of the other rowers and in that way form an alternate community where everyone with their differences can inhabit the multiple shores of the islands.

The Trans Puerto Rican community conjured in the narrative triptych of performative gestures of Manuel Ramos Otero reflects the circular migration of Puerto Ricans and of the other islands of Puerto Rico, expanding its archipelago, through a literary poetics of transit that combines history, auto/biography, and fiction in order to produce a literature of reconciliation that multiplies the self and the nation, transgressing the imposed limits of national, cultural and sexual identities. Through this poetics of transit and the multiplying of the "I" and Island, the interdependency of self and other, of individual and collective is revealed and affirmed. For Ramos Otero writing-storytelling as transit, far from being a dehumanizing abstract space of articulation, becomes a means to ponder life as a paradoxical embrace of otherness.

Notes

1. Jossianna Arroyo explores transit in Ramos Otero's poetry as a means to inscribe the displacement and absence created by exile, proposing a poetics of homosexual desire that erases the other: "*La corporiedad del poema es el único signo posible, mientras que el amante/cuerpo como referente y nombre se desvanece*" ("Exilio y tránsito entre la Norzagaray y Christopher Street: acercamientos a una poética del deseo homosexual en Manuel Ramos Otero" 51). Also see Arroyo's "Itinerarios de viaje: Las otras islas de Manuel Ramos Otero" where she proposes a reading of Ramos Otero's work through the image of the "*viajero.*" Juan Gelpí has defined Ramos Otero's writing as "*una escritura a la intemperie*" and "*transeúnte*" that represents the space of exile as being outside of the house of the nation and the literary canon ("La escritura transeúnte de Manuel Ramos Otero" in *Literatura y paternalismo en Puerto Rico* 145).

2. See Judith Butler's *Bodies That Matter* (New York: Routledge, 1993). Subjectivity as performance in Ramos Otero is found both inside and outside his literary work as Oscar Montero affirms: "en vida del escritor, para bien

o para mal, la ficción se nutre de los gestos del cuerpo; en el caso de Manuel Ramos Otero, esos gestos fueron frecuente y deliberadamente teatrales" (39).

3. This idea of writing as rewriting of the texts the author has read was culti-vated by Jorge Luis Borges and Julio Cortázar; both were very influential in Ramos Otero's work.

4. Ramos Otero's notion of subjectivity is similar to Michel Foucault who pro-poses that it is a paradox: "the individual is an effect of power, and at the same time, or precisely to the extent to which it is that effect, it is the element of its articulation. The individual which power has constituted is at the same time its vehicle" (*Power/Knowledge* 98).

5. For an analysis of Ramos Otero's work as a reflection of the experience of first-generation Puerto Rican gay migrants see Larry La Fountain-Stokes "Autobiographical Writing and Shifting Migrant Experience" in *Queer Ricans*. (Minneapolis: University of Minesota Press, 2009).

6. All citations of the stories from the books *Concierto de metal para un recu-erdo* and *El cuento de la mujer del mar* will be from *Cuentos de buena tinta* (San Juan: Instituto de Cultura Puertorriqueña, 1992).

7. See article "El estadio del espejo como formador de la función yo [je]..." in Jacques Lacan, *Escritos I* (México DF: Siglo Veintiuno Editores, 2001).

8. See Martin Heidegger. *Being and Time.* (Albany: State University of New York Press, 1996).

9. Transvestism has been identified by other critics of Ramos Otero's work as one of his narrative strategies (See Arroyo, Barradas, Cruz Malavé, Montero).

10. I use the notion of queer as it is defined by David Halperin in *Saint Foucault* (New York: Oxford University Press, 1995): queer identity need not be grounded in any positive truth or in any stable reality. As the very word implies, "queer" does not name some natural kind or refer to some deter-minate object; it acquires its meaning from its oppositional relation to the norm. Queer is by definition whatever is at odds with the normal, the legiti-mate, the dominant. There is nothing in particular to what it refers. It is an identity without essence (Emphasis in original, 62).

11. The fiction of national discourses and communities has been explored by Benedict Anderson in *Imagined Communities* (London: Verso, 1983) and Etienne Balibar in *Race, Nation, Class: Ambiguous Identities* (London: Verso, 1991).

12. For more on Puerto Rico as a transnation see Jorge Duany's *Puerto Rico: Nation on the move* (Chapel Hill; London: The University of North Carolina Press, 2002); Yolanda Martínez-San Miguel, *Caribe Two Ways* (San Juan: Ediciones Callejón, 2003); and Agustín Laó, "Islands at the Crossroads: Puerto Ricanness Traveling Between the Translocal Nation and the Global City," in *Puerto Rican Jam*, Eds. F. Negrón-Mutaner and R. Grosfoguel (Minneapolis: University of Minnesota Press, 1997).

Works Cited

Anderson, Benedict R. O'G. *Imagined Communities: Reflections on the Origin and Spread of Nationalism.* London: Verso, 1983.

Arroyo, Jossianna. "Exilio y tránsito entre la Norzagaray y Christopher Street: acercamientos a una poética del deseo homosexual en Manuel Ramos Otero." *Revista Iberoamericana* 67.194–195(January–June 2001): 31–54.

———. "Historias de familia: migraciones y escritura homosexual en la literatura puertorriqueña." *Revista Canadiense de Estudios Hispánicos* 26.3 (2002):361–378.

———. "Manuel Ramos Otero: las narrativas del cuerpo más allá de *Insularismo*." *Revista de Estudios Hispánicos* 21 (1994): 303–324.

———. "Itinerarios de viaje: Las otras islas de Manuel Ramos Otero." *Revista Iberoamericana* 71.212 (July-September 2005):865–885.

Balibar, Etienne. *Race, Nation, Class: Ambiguous Identities*. London: Verso, 1990.

Barradas, Efraín. "Manuel Ramos Otero o del homenaje sacrílego." *Homenaje a Manuel Ramos Otero*. New York: City University of New York, 1992. 26–38.

Butler, Judith. *Bodies that Matter*. New York: Routeledge, 1994.

———. *Giving an Account of Oneself*. New York: Fordham University Press, 2005.

Cañas, Dionisio. *El poeta y la ciudad: Nueva York y los poetas hispanos*. Madrid: Cátedra, 1994.

Costa, Marithelma. "Entrevista: Manuel Ramos Otero." *Hispamérica* 20.59 (August 1991): 59–67.

Cruz Malavé, Arnaldo. "Parar virar al macho: la autobiografía como subversión cuentística." *Revista Iberoamericana* 59.162–163 (January-June 1993): 239–263.

———. "Toward an Art of Transvestism: Colonialism and Homosexuality in Puerto Rico." *Entiendes? : Queer Readings, Hispanic Writings*. Eds. Emilie L. Bergmann and Paul Julian Smith. Durham: Duke University Press, 1995. 137–167.

Duany, Jorge. *The Puerto Rican Nation on the Move: Identities on the Island and in the United States*. Chapell Hill; London: The University of North Carolina Press, 2002.

Fanon, Frantz. *The Wretched of the Earth*. New York,: Grove Press, 1968.

Foucault, Michel. *Power/Knowledge: Selected Interviews and Other Writings, 1972-1977*. Brighton, Sussex: Harvester Press, 1980.

Gates, Henry Louis, Jr. *Race, Writing and Difference*. Chicago: University of Chicago Press, 1986.

Gelpí, Juan. "Historia y literatura en *Página en blanco y staccato*." *Enfoques generacionales/Rumbos postmodernos*. Ed. Carmen Cazurro García de la Quintana and Mario R Cancel Sepúlveda. Aguadilla: Quality Printers, 1997. 61–71.

———. *Literatura y paternalismo en Puerto Rico*. San Juan: Editorial de la Universidad de Puerto Rico, 1994.

———. "Página en blanco y staccato" *La Torre* 4.14 (April–June 1990): 245–250.

Halperin, David M. *Saint Foucault: Towards a Gay Hagiography*. New York: Oxford University Press, 1995.

Heidegger, Martin. *Being and Time*. Trans. Joan Stambaugh. Albany: State University of New York Press, 1996.

Lacan, Jacques. "El estadio del espejo como formador de la función del yo [*je*] tal como se nos revela en la experiencia psicoanalítica." *Escritos I*. México, DF: Siglo Veintiuno Editores, 2001. 86–93.

La Fountain-Stokes, Larry. "Autobiographical Writing and Shifting Migrant Experience" in *Queer Ricans*. Minneapolis:University of Minesota Press, 2009. 19–63.

Laó, Agustín. "Islands at the Crossroads: Puerto Ricanness Traveling Between the Translocal Nation and the Global City," in *Puerto Rican Jam* Eds. F.Negrón-Mutaner and R. Grosfoguel. Minneapolis: University of Minnesota Press, 1997. 169–188.

Martínez-San Miguel, Yolanda. *Caribe Two Ways: Cultura de la migración en el Caribe insular hispánico*. San Juan: Ediciones Callejón, 2003.

Montero, Oscar. "Manuel Ramos Otero." *Homenaje a Manuel Ramos Otero*. New York: City University of New York, 1992. 39–45.

Pedreira, Antonio S. *Insularismo: Ensayos de interpretación puertorriqueña*. San Juan: Biblioteca Autores Puertorriqueños, 1936.

Ramos Otero, Manuel. *Concierto de metal para un recuerdo y otras orgías de soledad*. 1a. ed. San Juan, P.R.: Editorial Cultural, 1971.

———. *El cuento de la mujer del mar*. San Juan P.R.: Huracán, 1979

———. *Cuentos de buena tinta*. San Juan: Instituto de Cultura Puertorriqueña, 1992.

———. "Ficción e historia: Texto y pretexto de la autobiografía." *El Mundo* October 14, 1990, sec. Puerto Rico Ilustrado: 20–23.

———. *Página en blanco y staccato*. Madrid: Editorial Playor, 1988.

Ríos Avila, Rubén. "Dislocaciones caribeñas." *La Raza Cómica: Del sujeto en Puerto Rico*. San Juan: Ediciones Callejón, 2002. 223–244.

8

A Revolution in Pink: Cuban Queer Literature Inside and Outside the Island

Ana Belén Martín Sevillano

The sight of a Gay Parade in the streets of Havana in May 2009 was perceived by many Cubans as an optical illusion. For those who have internalized the institutional homophobia launched by the Revolution it was an odd mobile stage, a delusion. Yet for those who suffered persecution over the years due to their sexual preference, for those condemned to self-repression and silence, it was more like a brief mirage in a tropical desert. The march was the first of its kind in Cuba, made possible only because it was organized by the invigorated CENESEX (National Center for Sexual Education). Created in 1989, this institution was originally in charge of educating the youngsters on sexual prophylaxis; however, recently it developed a high-profile campaign by legally claiming rights for the Lesbian, Gay, Transsexual, and Bisexual (LGTB) minority and actively working for a respectful popular attitude toward homosexuality. The CENESEX initiatives and achievements are indeed remarkable (e.g., legalization of transsexual surgery within the health system), and indispensable for the potential regeneration of an otherwise exhausted system that has for too long convicted homosexuals as criminals. The fact that the director of this center is the daughter of Raúl Castro makes this socially complex and controversial project viable. Certainly, such a politically contentious endeavor could not have been undertaken by someone whose loyalty to the system could be questioned along the way.

Despite these official accomplishments, advocacy for homosexual rights in the public sphere, that is, outside of State control, is still persecuted; and civil associations, such as "Fundación LGTB Reinaldo Arenas," remain illegal. Furthermore, the initiatives taken by the CENESEX are far from spontaneous, but they respond to the debate about homosexuality that has taken place within a sector of the Cuban society in the last two decades. As many other thorny issues, homosexuality started to be discussed in the cultural and literary fields during the late eighties and early nineties, decades in which artists positioned themselves politically by voicing the concerns of Cuban minorities and representing the outcasts of the Revolution. Since any gay-related depiction or behavior had been absolutely forbidden during the previous decades, the construction of a homosexual subject became a necessary step toward the opening of a much-needed plural Cuban society (Martín-Sevillano).

Thus, in the last decade of the twentieth century, the literary text in Cuba became an active space where homosexual subjectivity was discussed and constructed. New authors drew on the considerable array of homoerotic works written in Cuba since the 1920s. Although from quite early on the Revolution opposed the publication of any text in which homosexuality was positively portrayed or even considered in depth, there is no gap in the representation of the homosexual subject in contemporary Cuban literature, mainly due to two distinct reasons. On the one hand, there were a few authors who, despite never deserting the country, dared to face unassumingly the official dogma by either writing about homosexuality or by openly acknowledging their own (homo)sexual preference. This would be the case of José Lezama Lima and Virgilio Piñera, respectively. Not surprisingly both suffered internal ostracism for their refusal to accept the dogmatic cultural policies of the Cuban government. On the other hand, authors such as Reinaldo Arenas or Severo Sarduy moved to exile to be able to explicitly define themselves as gay, and to write about their own subjectivity and identity. Hence, for decades exile became the main territory where the self could be understood and constructed as queer and as Cuban; a territory in which crucial Cuban literary works were published. In the case of Arenas and Sarduy, the floating province of exile, in the United States or in France, enabled them to develop a homoerotic poetic that would produce a major textual *corpus*. Later on this would be a vital reference for authors who, within the geographical boundaries of the island, decided to openly protest the discriminatory policies set up by the Revolution against homosexuals. As a liberated region of the geographically restricted nation, exile escapes the contingencies that specific political regimes or historical situations might impose within its limits. As part of the nation, exile presents a similar interaction of forces in the different fields of production; however, its strength might be very different or even have the opposite sign. In this light, cultural production of exiled artists should not be considered apart, under rubrics such as "literature of exile," but as an integrated part of the national *corpus*.[1]

In the case of Cuba, the homoerotic literary works of contemporary authors writing and publishing in the island, such as Pedro de Jesús López (b.1970), would be very different without the legacy of exiles such as Arenas and Sarduy. Furthermore, the 2009 Gay Parade in Havana might very well have not happened if Severo Sarduy had not left for Paris in 1960 or if Reinaldo Arenas could not have made his way out through the El Mariel boatlift in 1980.

In order to offer a clear picture of a historic process, this paper will first recount how the homosexual debate evolved in the Cuban cultural field during the nineties. Next, it will focus on how contemporary Cuban literary production in the island has fully absorbed the works of Reinaldo Arenas and Severo Sarduy, both written and published in exile, and both with sound formulations of queerness and homoeroticism. Specifically we will analyze the work of Pedro de Jesús López that has focused particularly on the construction of a homosexual subjectivity, largely drawing on the work of Arenas, Piñera, and Sarduy. With this analysis the paper will show how López's texts are indeed a space where different voices, discourses, and places meet, confirming the continuity between the works of several authors who, despite writing from different geographical locations, belong to the same literary tradition.

8.1   Recovering Voices: The Discussion about Homosexuality in the Cuban Literary Field

In the literary field, the debate about homosexuality was open in Cuba in 1988 with a number of works from the new generation of writers, the so-called *Novísimos*. In that year, Roberto Urías (b.1959) published his short story[2] "¿Por quién llora Leslie Caron?" and Norge Espinosa (b.1970) won the Caimán Barbudo poetry prize with a collection of poems that included the renowned "Vestido de novia." In the first, a transsexual exposes the feeling of suffering and inadequacy that he experiences for lacking rights and social respect just for being who he is. The use of stream of consciousness provides the reader with an otherwise impossible closeness to a marginalized social subject. Significantly, this specific story was repeatedly reproduced in the numerous anthologies of short stories that appeared during the early nineties in Cuba and abroad. Yet, the author never published the volume to which this story belonged, and he went into exile in 1995, after being fired as editor of Casa de las Américas in Havana. Just like the title of Urías' story, the poem "Vestido de novia" is a long open question about the impossibility for a queer teenager to truly know himself and find a suitable social position.

These works were followed by many, such as the poem "Desnudo frente a la ventana" by Abilio Estévez (b.1954) or the short-story "El cazador" by Leonardo Padura (b.1955), both published in 1990. However, the short-story "El lobo, el bosque y el hombre nuevo," published in the same year by Senel Paz (b.1950), was the most celebrated instance of the discussion about homosexuality in Cuba. Its popularity was due to the fact that it was chosen by Tomás Gutiérrez Alea to be the basis for the *Fresa y chocolate* script. Senel Paz's work tells the story of a friendship between a middle-aged homosexual artist and a young heterosexual revolutionary, who is the narrator. Thus, the story is presented from the view of a politically orthodox subject, who nonetheless states the need to reconsider the strict behavioral paradigms that define the Revolutionary subject.

The movie screenplay was a substantial improvement on the initial short story, and Gutiérrez Alea's indisputable talent made of *Fresa y chocolate* a compelling reflection on Cuban homophobic political and social culture. The movie offered a national allegory by presenting a symbolic historic subtext with all the different discourses that crossed the Cuban society in the early nineties (Bejel 1994). Clearly the young character, David, embodied the "new man" proposed by Ernesto Guevara and others to establish a behavioral mold that enclosed the political orthodoxy of the Revolution, which implied heterosexuality as the productive and healthy sexual option. This theory came to reinforce the Cuban traditional popular homophobia, and provided authorities with grounds for prosecution, often covering ideological reasons. When writers such as Lezama Lima, Virgilio Piñera, or Reinaldo Arenas were silenced, censored or imprisoned, it was not only because their sexual choice, but also because their literary work did not comply with the norm of socialist realism vertically imposed on the cultural field. In contrast, the Revolution integrated homosexual individuals who fit the political parameters, and this was the case of well-known figures within the cultural field.

During the nineties many writers, such as Roberto Urías, Senel Paz, Abilio Estévez, Leonardo Padura, or Jorge Ángel Pérez, approached the conflict of homosexuality in short stories and novels, but it is Pedro de Jesús López and Ena Lucía Portela (b.1972) who have presented a cohesive work in which the construction of a homosexual subjectivity is the key aspect. Queer or not, contemporary Cuban authors have made an important effort to restore the figures and work of Lezama Lima, Virgilio Piñera, Reinaldo Arenas, and Severo Sarduy. These four queer writers furthered in different ways the construction of a Cuban gay subject, receiving therefore the veto of all the official instances. The process of recuperation of these authors is not only traceable through their influence on contemporary literary texts, but also through the critical work published in Cuba. *Unión. Revista de Literatura y Arte* and *La Gaceta de Cuba*, the most important literary journals in the island, have contributed with frequent articles and occasional complete issues to assess the importance of the work of Lezama and Piñera. Furthermore, there has been an important number of studies about the impact that *Orígenes* and *Ciclón*[3] had on the Cuban cultural field.

Paradiso, the major novel by Lezama published in 1966 in Havana, contained two celebrated chapters that analyzed homosexuality, underlining its foundational character for the existence of the nation (Cruz-Malavé). After its publication, and despite being internationally acclaimed as a masterpiece, its author disappeared from the public stage, and it was twenty- five years later when it was reprinted. Obviously, the Cuban government did not think much of an extremely complex work that refuted in every way the literary patterns of social realism. However, Lezama's own homosexuality remained always a private affair, and the writer led a discreet life with his devoted wife, never verbalizing any political statement. It is probably due to the complexity of his work and the ambiguity of his sexual preference that Lezama, while still claimed by the new generation of authors, has not received the same deference as Virgilio Piñera, an author who openly acknowledged his sexuality and suffered persecution. In addition, Piñera established friendships and literary relationships with other gay authors, such as Reinaldo Arenas, Antón Arrufat (b.1935), and Abilio Estévez (b.1954), who after his death kept his memory alive and organized public celebrations in his honor. Paradoxically, Piñera's work approaches the topic of homoeroticism only occasionally and never directly; *La carne de René* (1952), his most notable work, mostly focuses on the feeling of guilt that desire inflicts, avoiding homoerotic passages and never reflecting on the specific conflict of the homosexual subject. However, in 1955 the author published a controversial article in *Ciclón*, "Ballagas en persona," in which he argued that any appropriate approach to the production of the nationally distinguished poet Emilio Ballagas (1908–1954) must unavoidably consider his homosexuality and the conflict between his desire and his conventional heterosexual social behavior. Piñera claimed the need of considering the body as the main source of subjectivity, which is necessarily involved in the literary process. Yet the Cuban critical discourse was not ready to accept the challenge of broadening or transcending its views (Jambrina). "Ballagas en persona" was only fairly discussed in the nineties, when critics and writers understood the importance of searching for historic representations of the homosexual subject in order to properly demand his social acceptance.

In this process of claiming proscribed queer authors, the figures in exile were more cautiously integrated into the national literary canon than those who had never left the island; and this rehabilitation was only possible if they had not made any public statement against the Revolution. The most notable in this group are Gastón Baquero, Calvert Casey, and in particular Severo Sarduy, who has received considerable critical attention in the periodical literary publications of the island, especially after his death in 1993. Even though he had left Cuba in 1960, not to return, he never explicitly confronted the political regime. This silence made possible an official posthumous recognition that Reinaldo Arenas has not yet received. In contrast with Sarduy, Arenas openly and furiously confronted Fidel Castro, for which his name remains banned from any official Cuban publication.[4] Even if often under a hyperbolic style, Arenas' autobiography, *Antes que anochezca* (1992), gives testimony of the homophobic practices that, during the decade of the seventies, violently censored both his writing and his private life in Cuba. Certainly, it is this writer's determination to behave as a queer in an adverse political and social climate that has inspired younger authors in the island. This would be the case of gay writers such as Pedro de Jesús López, Norge Espinosa, or Jorge Ángel Pérez. In Cuba, thanks to the efficient unofficial exchange of books that counteracts the internal and external embargoes, many readers are familiar with the works of Arenas, especially with *Antes que anochezca*.

The Cuban debate about homosexuality during the nineties found an actual site when Norge Espinosa organized between 1998 and 2000 the "Jornadas de Arte Homoerótico" in the Asociación Hermanos Saíz, a cultural institution for young authors. In these organized sessions, writers such as Antón Arrufat, Pedro de Jesús López, or Víctor Fowler openly discussed the social and literary representation of the homosexual subject in Cuba. Simultaneously, the interest in homosexuality in the literary field materialized in a number of critical works (Fowler, Suquet, Jambrina, Alonso Estenoz, Bejel 2000) that reviewed the literary construction of the queer subject in Cuban literature. Two of them, *La Maldición. Una historia del placer como conquista* by Víctor Fowler, and *Gay Cuban Nation* by Emilio Bejel, offer a comprehensive view of the topic in light of the concept of the nation. Both books underline the appearance of homoeroticism as a recurrent topic in Cuban literature, highlighting the novels *El angel de Sodoma* (1928) by Alfonso Hernández Catá, and *Hombres sin mujer* (1938) by Carlos Montenegro, as the first to reflect on the condition of homosexuality in a hostile social environment. Fowler's book was published in Cuba where the author lives, and for this reason it does not include any analysis of Reinaldo Arenas' work. In contrast, Bejel, a Cuban exile professor who works and publishes in the United States, examines extensively Arenas' final autobiographical work. At the end of their analyses, both critics point to Pedro de Jesús López as one of the most prominent contemporary queer writers, and Bejel actually dissects this author's first published collection of stories, *Cuentos frígidos (Maneras de obrar en 1830).*[5]

8.2   Voices from Inside, Voices from Abroad: The Literary Work of Pedro de Jesús López

Pedro de Jesús López's *opera prima* was indeed one of the first published-in-Cuba literary works that exclusively focuses on the complexities of the gay imaginary in the context of the Cuban tradition and society. The title reveals two main literary influences to be found in the volume: that of Virgilio Piñera, author of *Cuentos fríos*, and that of Stendhal and his *The Red and the Black: A Chronicle of 1830*. Piñera's influence is wide and recurrent, but it is mostly his figure that inspires the author to represent a subject erased long ago from the Cuban social scene. In contrast, Stendhal's work seems to be a reference in terms of the intricacy of the narrative instances.

All the pieces in the volume converge in what is at once the central subject and the plot: homoerotic desire, used to construct a homosexual subject driven by the force of the body, both his own and that of the object of desire. The body is in Pedro de Jesús' work the main sign of identity; throughout his work the reader can easily observe how the body generates subjectivity, which varies depending on the situated conditions it experiences. In "Ay, esa música (La importancia de ir hasta el final)" one of the characters discusses the necessary sexual condition of the human being, and the impossible separation between the being and the desiring body:

> ACTOR 1 (Indignado, casi gritando.) ¿Qué quieres que te diga? (Se para y vuelve a sentarse) ¿Qué necesito una pinga? (Pausa. Tensión. Dramatismo) ¡Pues no, necesito una persona, un ser humano...(Pausa. Tensión. Dramatismo) Que tenga pinga, sí, porque me gustan las pingas, si no, no fuera maricón! (30–31)

As experience, subjectivity moves, adjusting to the different emotional and physical situations the body goes through (Braidotti). Significantly, in this author's work sexual desire seems to be connected to the game of imagination, and specifically, of writing, conveying that the only possible reality is the textual one.

In the story that opens the volume, "Instrucciones para un hombre solo," the reader finds most of the views and themes that will be presented in the rest of the volume: the uncertainty of gender in identity, loneliness as final truth, homoerotic desire and sex to escape the ultimate emptiness of being alive, and simulation as a strategy for survival. In a parody of the *Divina Commedia*, a character that carries the same name as the author travels accompanied by Virgilio (this time Piñera) in a quest for the ideal man. However, both master and disciple are aware that ideals do not exist outside imagination, so they will soon realize the impossibility of their initial mission:

> 26. Que Virgilio agregue: "Pero es obvio: lo que buscamos en realidad no son hombres ideales."
> 27. Asentir de nuevo—nosotros, no sé si ustedes.
> 28. Fingir—ellos—que empiezan a conocerse, que es un éxito la cita. Emborracharse allí mismo. Arruinarse. Pagar los servicios de la agencia. Irse.

29. Regresar. Como quien regresa de un vacío a otro vacío. Como quien apenas se ha movido nunca. (11–12)

As writers, these characters will also find out that fiction is not the space for sentimental utopias either as the textual encounter with René (main character in *La carne de René* by Piñera) becomes also a disappointment. In this collection of stories, Pedro de Jesús, like Sarduy in "Pido la canonización de Virgilio Piñera" or Arenas in *Antes que anochezca*, pays homage to a man who suffered the consequences of being personally and intellectually honest. But the symbolism of Piñera as guiding father is finally dismissed by both characters, Piñera and Pedro de Jesús, which share similar views and values, and understand the ultimate solitude of beings. Thus, the end of the story appeals to the power of silence either to fight the rigor of social standards, or to satisfy the inner self, which also represses its own desire. Formally, the structure of the story points toward the fragmented condition of reality that affects not only the disposition of the chronological line of events, but also the quality of an ambiguous narrator, delivering a cubist textual image.

"La Carta," the second story of *Cuentos frígidos*, presents again many of the previously mentioned strategies. However, it is a more complex piece in which the narrator swings from third to first person, disappearing when the characters break out with their dialogue. From a bifocal point of view, the storyteller articulates a plural discourse. On the one hand a line of narrative presents the impossible affair between a woman and a gay man, a relationship that sometimes seems to be a desire, and sometimes seems to be a past event, which enters the sphere of imagination. In the space of the text, the heterosexual relationship is not only impossible, but also described as a simulation where subjugation is the only bond. The second narrative line presents a dispute between the woman and the man's lover, who is protesting about his description in a letter that the woman addressed to the first man. The characters argue over the importance of possessing a full textual identity, implying once again that the only reality is that of the text.

The rest of the stories in the volume share many compositional similarities with the previous ones in terms of conflict, characters, and textual strategies (fragmented structure, multiple narrative instances, meta/intertextuality) while presenting original plots that sustain an enjoyable reading process. The last piece of the collection, "El Retrato," has been widely reproduced and cited, very likely due to its detailed sexual descriptions. As in some of the previous stories, this short story recounts two parallel erotic narrative lines that converge only to generate violence, chaos, and solitude. In the first one, Ana is a painter who usually finds inspiration through sexual encounters, her last one being with a taxi driver. The second narrative line focuses on the relationship between

Hector and Gabriel, friends of Ana. In order to help her creative process, Hector offers Ana a place where she can put together art and sex.
However, Hector's hidden agenda is to seduce Jorge, the taxi driver.
Hector's betrayal causes Gabriel's despair and, in a hysteric seizure, he
destroys Ana's works and induces Jorge to flee. The story transcends the
homosexuality/heterosexuality debate in order to reflect on gender and
sex, pointing toward the cultural construction of gender. These characters do not possess a fixed identity, their contradictory and multiple experiences challenge socially assigned roles and question the notion of an
essential and stable subjectivity. Thus, while constructing a homosexual
subject, the author still resists any characterization of gender or sexual
behavior, leaving an open door to difference and change.

Some of the above-mentioned characteristics (i.e., the uncertainty of
gender, simulation as a strategy for survival, the fragmented/void condition of the being and of reality) inevitably reveal Severo Sarduy's back-
stage presence. While Virgilio Piñera remains an inspiring figure, Pedro
de Jesús López seems to inquisitively draw on the literary work of Severo
Sarduy, re-exploring textual avenues opened up in some of his novels,
such as *Cobra* or *De donde son los cantantes*. Particularly, he emphasizes
Sarduy's ideas on the tragicomic and theatrical condition of existence, sex
remaining the decisive performance to defy an otherwise boring stage.
Certainly, in the exhilarating company of the Parisian post-structuralist
group, Sarduy developed a sound theoretical view that guided his writing. Pedro de Jesús López has studied this view meticulously, and has
clearly pointed out both the merits and the flaws in Sarduy's texts. A
lucid and concise article published in 1995 by the author, "Los estereotipos en Sarduy," began with the following sharp paragraphs:

> Aún hoy, después de permitida la conversación pública y oficial sobre
> ella, la obra de Sarduy debe soportar el peso de dos enormes incon-
> venientes para su recepción y asimilación en Cuba: uno, haber sido
> escrita en el exilio, el otro, hallarse ostentosa y cínicamente plagada
> de lugares comunes.
>
> Mientras lo primero la hace curiosa, mito apetecible tras el cual los
> lectores corren en una búsqueda casi enfermiza, casi snob; lo segundo
> la torna frívola y aburrida. La obra de Sarduy transita, por una y otra
> razones, de la reverencia al escupitajo, o peor, al olvido. (37)

In this article, López compares Piñera to Sarduy, reflecting on the fact
that both writers considered emptiness and void to be the ultimate truth.
However, Pedro de Jesús argues that while Piñera believed the being
had a deep consistency, Sarduy considered it to be only the surface, pure
simulation. It is specifically in the space in between both perceptions of
existence where Pedro de Jesús López places his work, shifting from one

to the other, reflecting on emptiness as the material that gives beings both weight and lightness. The author renders a poetics of contraries, where lightness does not exclude depth, and where the body is not the last but the first contingency. This tension between opposite signs turns out to be a trait in this author's work, where life is portrayed as a festive but anxious simulation, with characters that inescapably suffer as they celebrate the very fact of being alive. This is easily noticeable in *Sibilas en Mercaderes* (1999), a novel that pays homage to Severo Sarduy, who even materializes in it as a character. As it has been noted by Margarita Mateo (2002), *Sibilas en Mercaderes* shares with many other contemporary Cuban pieces its liking for intertextuality, with references to well-known national and international authors. However, it is Sarduy who emerges through most of its lines as the novel displays characters, images, and references that directly refer to his works. *Sibilas en Mercaderes* suggests that, given the essential emptiness of the being, simulation becomes the only possible strategy to defeat the force of the void, an idea that Sarduy thoroughly developed through his novels and poems, and explicitly articulated in *La simulación*.

The three main characters in *Sibilas en Mercaderes*, Cálida and Gélida—both echo of the dioscural Auxilio and Socorro from *De donde son los cantantes*—and the photographer Jan van Luxe voice the considerations about the nature of fiction and artistic representation that the author had already presented in his previous work. As nomadic subjects (Braidotti), Pedro de Jesús' characters mutate their identity restlessly, emerging in many evoking, but simulated images. Similarly, place seems to be transforming continuously, denying its very existence; Havana becomes Paris or Kuala Lumpur, and the ambiguous land of Bambula is simultaneously everywhere and nowhere: "[…] pero los caminos, cualesquiera que sean, conducen siempre a Bambula. Estar aquí es igual a estar en otro sitio. Bambula es una aspirina. El mundo es una aspirina" (101). With this statement the narrator is not only considering the vital itinerary of Jan Van Luxe, but also suggesting that the nation is always within oneself. Exile is, therefore, another possible geography of the nation.

In one of his eloquent analyses of Sarduy's work, Roberto González Echevarría offers an interpretation of *De donde son los cantantes* that nuances the thesis we are supporting here about the condition of exile:

> En su borde último esta novela es sobre la imposibilidad de ser, y de ser de o en algún lugar. *De donde son los cantantes* expresa, pues, la nostalgia del exilio como condición generalizada en la era actual. Es un exilio permanente que se niega aun a sí mismo porque abolir el origen y posibilidad de regreso anula su más poderosa razón de ser. Si todo es exilio, ¿cómo puede haber exilio? ¿Exilio de qué? ¿Exilio de dónde? (1591)

Aesthetically and conceptually *Sibilas en Mercaderes* becomes a literary game where the author reflects about the validity of Sarduy's views on the essential simulation of the being and his struggle for presenting a convincing image. Location, therefore, depends on the character's determination to be in a particular place, reason why Cálida and Gélida in Havana converge with Severo Sarduy in Paris without any transatlantic displacement, which suggests the fallacy of an exclusive geographically limited nation. Certainly, Severo Sarduy, as Reinaldo Arenas, was only able to produce his singular work because he moved to exile. Once there, writing became an effective tactic to wipe away the limits of the nation and the restricted conditions of possibility it allowed. His work was therefore inextricably linked to national cultural production. Thus, exile becomes a need of the geographically trapped nation, allowing the possibility of existence to subjects and thoughts that would otherwise never fully develop under specific adverse political or cultural conditions.

In his last published work, the collection of stories *La sobrevida*[6] (2006), Pedro de Jesús López abandons the rhetoric of images, as well as his previous predilection for ambiguity and narrative intricacy. He gives himself to the pleasure of telling, composing intriguing plots, and developing attractive characters with a concise, sharp, and evocative language. As the title suggests, the stories in *La sobrevida* speak of characters that more than living are surviving. Lack of housing, lack of money, lack of medical assistance, or lack of safety or trust...scarcity is the main setting in these tales. However, this social twist in the work of Pedro de Jesús López does not dominate the plots. Previously favored topics, such as homoerotic desire and homosexual subjectivity are still central here. Clearly the author has mastered his talent for erotic descriptions, smoothly delivering gentle ("El cuento menos apropiado") or intense ones ("Fiesta en casa del maître"). As in *Cuentos frígidos*, homosexuality is a focal subject in this collection, but the author offers here a different perspective on it. On the one hand, men's homoerotic desire is presented as an instinctive masculine longing that can be shamefully denied ("El cuento menos apropiado") or joyfully verbalized and exorcised ("Tormenta en el paraíso"). On the other hand, lesbianism becomes the central subject matter in the volume's two longest pieces ("Ángeles y La Muda" and "La última farsa"). The characters' complex and incisive depictions open up in the text a reflection about women's subjectivity, revealing the socio-cultural taboos and stereotypes that surround lesbianism. With *La sobrevida*, the author contributes significantly to textually developing a still marginal subject in Cuban society.

While *La sobrevida* implements a more personal approach to literature, one of the presences that gracefully resonates through some stories is that of Reinaldo Arenas, especially when the author skillfully uses sarcasm and irony to irreverently resolve conflictive situations, or in the depiction of sexually eager subjects. That is the case of "Mientras llega el chico a lo punk," where the narrator observes from a hidden position a couple's interaction in which a man seems to be courting a waitress. The narrator cannot actually hear the dialogue between them so he dubs the scene in a process that corresponds with writing. But the reason why the narrator is hiding from view is not to observe the couple and find a plot for a story, but to have a sexual encounter. Here the creative process of telling and writing imposes itself as much as the body's desire, and both processes take place simultaneously. The two scenes evolve in parallel: while the man in the bar seduces the waitress, the narrator waits for his much anticipated meeting. Willingly, the narrator foresees two sexual scenes: one in the bar between the couple he is observing, and one in his hiding spot, between himself and his awaited new lover. Unfortunately, necessity is stronger than desire, and both scenes end up being a robbery instead of a sexual encounter. The tone throughout the story is always jovial and fresh, with a final reference to a popular song in Cuba, "Todos nacimos ángeles" by the duo Buena Fe, that serves as an ironic counterpoint.

The aforementioned characteristics certainly make of *La sobrevida* a telling example of the author's literary maturity. Not surprisingly this book won the 2006 Alejo Carpentier short-story prize in Cuba. Every one of its pieces reveals a personal, distinct style that has finely incorporated previously overshadowing influences. However, the figures of Reinaldo Arenas, Virgilio Piñera, and Severo Sarduy still illuminate the author when he elegantly addresses certain subjects or when he resolves tricky situations.

8.3   Queer Women in Cuba: The Quest for Voices

If the Cuban literary imaginary of masculine homosexuality was gradually developed during the twentieth century thanks to the work of authors inside and outside the island, lesbian subjectivity has only recently been approached in fictional works. The Revolution had a substantial impact in advancing women's liberation in a traditionally patriarchal society, but its political project remained almost exclusively masculine. This is easily perceptible in the literary field, where for decades there was a minimal presence of women writers, and the published works did not present women's conflicts (Campuzano). Thus, the new generation of authors faced the task of building women's subjectivity in their artistic and literary work. The construction of this subjectivity fought the fixed image that the Revolution provided: a politically engaged woman who never forgot her maternal duties. Many contemporary writers have devoted part or most of their work to opening up in the text different possibilities for women's subjectivity and social roles. Standing out among them are Anna Lidia Vega (b.1968), Karla Suárez (b.1969), and especially Ena Lucía Portela, who focuses particularly on the construction of lesbian subjects.

In a critical, selective, and complex literary technique, Portela carefully portrays unconventional feminine characters. As in the case of Pedro de Jesús López, her production favors experimentation, making use of fragmented compositions, complex narrative voices, or intertextuality. A significant characteristic of her work is the recurrence of two distinctive themes: violence and lesbianism. In this last regard, Portela refuses the idea of a fixed subjectivity excessively articulated around terms such as "feminist" or "lesbian," leaving her characters an ambiguous margin where gender and sexual identity could easily shift.

Initially, Portela looked for inspiring women's voices within the Cuban literary tradition, discovering the lesbian poet Lourdes Casal (1938–1981), who had moved to the United States in 1962 and returned to Cuba in 1973. During her time abroad, Casal was actively involved in cultural and political activities that supported the dialogue between exiles and the government in Havana. Her most famous poem, "Para Ana Veldford," included in the collection *Palabras juntan revolución* (Casa de las Américas Prize for poetry in 1981), expresses the feeling of inadequacy the poet experienced in exile. Despite the fact that she did not hide her lesbianism, she never addressed the subject in her poetic work nor made any political claim against the Revolution's homophobic policies (Negrón Muntaner & Martínez San Miguel). Significantly, the title of Ena Lucía Portela's first collection of stories, *Una extraña entre las piedras*, is a line from the poem "Para Ana Veldford." Besides, the figure of Lourdes Casal inspires the main character in the most important piece in the collection, a story that shares the title "Una extraña entre las piedras." Here an exiled Cuban writer recalls the emotional events that took place upon her arrival to New York, where she lives. As in many of this author's stories, the piece analyzes a couple's relationship, in this case two women. The structure of the story plays around with the dichotomy essential/dispensable by putting in parallel two love stories: a toxic short-term one and a secure long-lasting one that, however, does not interest the narrator. The story displays different points of view that either anticipate or recall the ephemeral relationship the narrator had with a radical feminist. The author uses this last character to caustically criticize the rigidity of some elements of the feminist dogma that prevent flow in everyday women's lives. Furthermore, she attacks the political attitude of Western intellectuals on the left who have been unable to abandon the idea of a socialist utopia, unconditionally supporting Fidel Castro. Portela shares some of her experiences with the narrator/character of "Una extraña entre las piedras," such as that of the Caribbean women writers' conference that took place in Hunter College in 1998. There, writers and academics considered the importance of developing a feminist credo in the frame of the text. However, the narrator refuses any identification with a feminist subject that traps all women in a false preset identity. Thus, Portela refuses any dogmatic approach to women's or lesbian subjectivity, defending a more embodied notion of it, where the physical experience shapes the mental state. The lesbian subject is an experimenting subject, who changes as it comes across different settings.

Ena Lucía Portela has published extensively: a second collection of short stories in 2006, *Alguna enfermedad muy grave,* and four novels: *El pájaro: pincel y tinta china* (1997), *La sombra del Caminante* (2002), *Cien botellas en una pared* (2002), and *Djuna y Daniel* (2007). With the exception of her last novel, Portela has consistently addressed Cuban subjects, using the local vernacular. Still, she has always declared her interest in different literary traditions that provide her with a more suitable set of references than the Cuban one (Camacho). This would be the case of the Anglo feminist literature, where writers such as Virginia Woolf, Sylvia Plath, or Djuna Barnes have intensely approached women's and lesbian's conflicts. Precisely, in Portela's last work, the author fictionalizes the life of the American writer Djuna Barnes. Anticipating academic interpretations, she has explicitly declared that she does not intend to build any lesbian subjectivity in her work, but just to consider the implications of any given experience (Portela, 2007). Still, this novel moves in a zone of experience that gives voice to subjects traditionally labeled as queer, and specifically to queer women. Even if relying on a different literary canon and tradition, Ena Lucía Portela along with Pedro de Jesús López in his most recent work, are opening spaces for the representation of lesbian subjects in Cuba: spaces that before were not only nonexistent, but also culturally and socially prevented.

As a fundamental part of the Cuban nation, exile has determined the quality of its cultural and artistic production. The Cuban regime's regrettable policies during the sixties and seventies (which have been repeatedly called "the black decades") led many writers and intellectuals to live abroad, with no return possible. These writers contested those policies in their work, not necessarily by denouncing them, but by bringing to life in the text those ideas and subjects that the policies were trying to eradicate. Today they are inspiring figures for those who never left the island, and especially for the generation of authors that since the early nineties has challenged the Revolution's orthodox discourse with irreverent textual pieces. Narrative has been the site for a political activism oriented to give voice to marginalized subjects, such as homosexuals, but also the mentally or physically sick, the dissidents and the exiles. Among these authors Pedro de Jesús López stands out in reestablishing the outstanding Cuban literary tradition, recovering the work of literary figures who, from inside or outside the island, work toward the recognition of individual rights, and develop a sound literary work. In that sense, the voices from abroad resound clearly in Cuba.

Notes

1. Exile is intimately linked to the formation of the Cuban nation and its culture. Rodrigo Lazo and Rafael Rojas, among others, have considered the importance of exile in the political and cultural manifestation of the Cuban nation. During the nineteenth century, not only did canonic literary authors such as José María Heredia, Cirilo Villaverde, and Juan Clemente Zenea live, write and publish in exile, but also did four major intellectual figures: Félix Varela, José Antonio Saco, José María Heredia, and Domingo del Monte. Moreover, the most prominent national political figure, José Martí, lived most of his adult life in exile. During the twentieth century, exile is again home for some of the most renowned Cuban writers, such as Guillermo Cabrera Infante, Severo Sarduy, or Reinaldo Arenas, and an important experience in the life of others, such as Alejo Carpentier or Virgilio Piñera.
2. Short story was the literary genre of choice during this period for its ability to present a conflict succinctly, but effectively, in parallel with the visual arts. The genre enjoys a vigorous tradition in Latin America and in Cuba, where it becomes especially significant after 1959 (Antonio Benítez Rojo, Alejo Carpentier, Calvert Casey, Jesús Diaz, Norberto Fuentes, Virgilio Piñera, and Julio Travieso among others contemporary writers, dedicated an important part of their work to short story).
3. These were two of the most important literary journals in Cuba and in Latin America during the decades of the 1940s and 1950s. *Orígenes* was edited by Lezama and *Ciclón* by Piñera.
4. Together with that of Arenas, the names of Guillermo Cabrera Infante and Heberto Padilla remain absent in any official literary account.
5. The book was initially published in 1998 in Spain, and two years later in Cuba.
6. The title evokes a renowned poem by one of the most emblematic poets of the Revolution, Roberto Fernández Retamar.

Works Cited

Alonso Estenoz, Alfredo. "Tema homosexual en la literatura cubana de los 80 y los 90: ¿renovación o retroceso?" *La Habana Elegante* 11 (2000). <http://www.habanaelegante.com/Fall2000/Pasion.htm>.

Bejel, Emilio. "*Fresa y chocolate* o la salida de la guarida." *Casa de las Américas* 196 (1994): 10–22.

———. *Gay Cuban Nation.* Chicago: University of Chicago Press, 2001.

Braidotti, Rosi. *Nomadic Subjects. Embodiment and Sexual Difference in Contemporary Feminist Theory.* New York: Columbia University Press, 1994.

Camacho, Jorge. "¿Quién le teme a Ena Lucía Portela?" (interview). *La Habana Elegante* 33–34 (2006). <http://www.habanaelegante.com/SpringSummer2006/Angel.html>.

Campuzano, Luisa. "La voz de Casandra." *La Gaceta de Cuba* 4 (1996): 52–53.

Cruz-Malavé, Arnaldo. *El primitivo implorante. El "sistema poético del mundo" de José Lezama Lima*. Atlanta: Rodopi, 1994.

Espinosa, Norge. "Vestido de novia." *Mapa imaginario*. Ed. Rolando Sánchez Mejías. La Habana: ICL, 1995.

Fowler, Víctor. *La maldición. Una Historia del Placer como Conquista*. La Habana: Letras Cubanas, 1998.

González Echevarría, Roberto. "Plumas, sí: *De donde son los cantantes* y Cuba." *Severo Sarduy. Obra Completa*. Eds. Gustavo Guerrero and François Wahl. Madrid: Galaxia Gutenberg & Círculo de Lectores, 1999.

Jambrina, Jesús. "Sujetos *queers* en la literatura cubana: hacia una (posible) genealogía homoerótica." *La Habana Elegante* 11 (2000). <http://www.habanaelegante.com/Fall2000/Pasion.htm>

Lazo, Rodrigo. *Writing to Cuba. Filibustering and Cuban Exiles in the United States*. Chapel Hill: The University of North Carolina Press, 2005.

López, Pedro de Jesús. "Los estereotipos en Sarduy." *Unión. Revista de Literatura y Arte* 25 (1996): 37–39.

———. *Cuentos frígidos. Maneras de obrar en 1830*. Madrid: Olalla, 1998.

———. *Sibilas en Mercaderes*. La Habana: Letras Cubanas, 1999.

———. *La sobrevida*. La Habana: Letras Cubanas, 2006.

Martín Sevillano, Ana Belén. *Sociedad Civil y Arte en Cuba. Cuento y Artes Plásticas en el Cambio de Siglo*. Madrid: Verbum, 2008.

Mateo Palmer, Margarita. "La narrativa cubana contemporánea: las puertas del siglo XXI." *Anales de Literatura Hispanoamericana* 31 (2002): 54–64.

Negrón Muntaner, Frances and Yolanda Martínez-San Miguel. "In Search of Lourdes Casal's 'Ana Veldford'." *Social Text* 92, 25.3 (2007): 57–84.

Paz, Senel. "El lobo, el bosque y el hombre nuevo." *Unión* 12 (1991): 27–37.

Piñera, Virgilio. "Ballagas en persona." *Ciclón* 1.5 (1955): 41–50.

Portela, Ena Lucía. "Algunos rumores sobre *Djuna y Daniel*." *Pie de Página* 12 (2007). <http://www.piedepagina.com/numero12/html/ena_lucia_portela.html>

———. *Una extraña entre las piedras*. La Habana: Letras Cubanas, 2007.

Rojas, Rafael. "Insularidad y exilio de los intelectuales cubanos." *Estudios. Filosofía-Historia-Letras* 43 (1996). http://biblioteca.itam.mx/estudios/estudio/letras43/notas1/sec_1.html/.

———. *Isla sin fin: contribución a la crítica del nacionalismo cubano*. Miami: Universal, 1998.

———. *Motivos de Anteo: patria y nación en la historia intelectual de Cuba*. Madrid: Colibrí, 2008.

Sarduy, Severo. *La simulación*. Caracas: Monte Ávila Editores, 1982.

Suquet, Mirta. "Apuntes sobre el homoerotismo masculino y femenino en la literatura cubana de los 90." *Lectora* 5–6 (2000): 37–48.

Urías, Roberto. "¿Por quién llora Leslie Caron?" *Anuario de Narrativa*. La Habana: Unión, 1994.

9

Gender Pirates of the Caribbean: Queering Caribbeanness in the Novels of Zoé Valdés and Christopher John Farley

Omise'eke Natasha Tinsley

Though familiar to Americans primarily as a laid-back beach destination, Jamaica is hardly idyllic. The country has the world's highest murder rate. And its rampant violence against gays and lesbians has prompted human-rights groups to confer another ugly distinction: the most homophobic place on earth.

—Tim Padgett ("The Most Homophobic Place on Earth?" Time, April 12, 2006)

At the turn of the millennium, the Caribbean entered North American LGBT publications as a beautifully sea-splashed, tropically blooming tourist destination—but one shadowed by strong warnings. Even as affluent gays sought "friendly" vacation spots to pleasurably spend dollars and Euros, magazines on airport stands informed them of a wave of same-sex loving migrants traveling in the opposite direction, fleeing the Global South for the North. In these years Caribbean queer migration to Europe and North America made stark headlines on LGBT news services worldwide. Gay, lesbian, and transgendered Caribbeans filed high-profile asylum cases in London, New York, and Miami, claiming that their northward migration was a matter of life and death—that if they returned to countries like Jamaica, Trinidad, and Cuba, their sexuality or gender put them at risk of being attacked and murdered. "I would be dead now in Jamaica," one asylum seeker put it simply to a human rights organization (Bentham). Reports like these fed into a spiral of media condemnations of Caribbean sexual "underdevelopment" that reached a crescendo in *Time*'s 2006 declaration of Jamaica in particular, and the Caribbean in general, as the "Most Homophobic Place on Earth."

Such provocative headlines bold print what Jasbir Puar, in her ground-breaking *Terrorist Assemblages,* calls the discourse of Global Northern *sexual exceptionalism.* This imperialist discourse, which builds on long, troubled traditions of North American exceptionalism, positions the United States (and other Northern countries) as world leaders in the tele-ological march toward sexual freedom, while the Caribbean, the Middle East, and Africa lag culturally and temporally behind in a state of sex-ual savagery that drives women and queers to desperation and "illegal" migration. This imagined division, which subtends both LGBT rights platforms that proclaim the need to save Global Southern queers and nationalist rhetorics that justify military and economic policies marginal-izing "sexually backward" (Islamic, communist, debtor) nations, works by "glossing over its own policing of the boundaries of acceptable gender, racial, and class formations" (9). For this reason, she calls emphatically to her readership: "Unraveling discourses of U.S. sexual exceptionalism is vital to critiques of U.S. practices of empire…and to the expansion of queerness beyond narrowly conceptualized frames" that foreground gay visibility and consumerism as indexes of "progress" (9–10).

This essay offers close readings of two texts that take on this work of unraveling. In years of accelerating "gay" migration, Cuban-born Zoé Valdés, now resident in Paris, and Jamaican-born Christopher John Farley, now resident in New York—and a senior editor at *Time* when "The Most Homophobic Place on Earth?" went to press—chose to imagine the Caribbean as a harbor from Global Northern homophobia: a place where North Americans and Europeans migrated to live out riotous, complex gen-ders and sexualities suppressed in their homelands. These authors did so by writing historical novels about an infamous eighteenth-century female pirate who raided and loved on the Caribbean Sea as a swashbuckling man: Ann Bonny, aka Bonn. Valdés' *Lobas de Mar* (2003) and Farley's *Kingston by Starlight* (2005) excavate piratical histories that strategically re-imagine the region as a crosscurrents of endless trajectories for fluid gender, sex-ual, racial, and class identities. Countering hegemonic mappings, Valdés' and Farley's novels scan the seas to find space to *think* what Michel-Rolf Trouillot calls *unthinkable* histories, and express the *possibility* of what Gayatri Gopinath calls *impossible* desires—that is, histories and desires that cannot be contained in dominant discourses of imperialism and sexu-ality without exploding them. As Philippine studies scholar Kale Fajardo notes, piracy disrupts so-called "smooth flows" of globalization; and these fictionalized pirate stories attempt a parallel narrative disruption, over-turning smooth narratives of global sexual inequalities.

In what follows, I contrast reflections on two high-profile gay asylum cases with extended analyses of Valdés' and Farley's novels in order to think through the complex twenty-first-century politics of representing queer Caribbean transnationalism and migration. These readings suggest how diasporic writers use their positions abroad to reverse dominant imaginations of (im)mobility, configuring the Global North—where they live—as a site to leave behind, and the Caribbean—where they're from—as an ideal destination, one where multiple fluid identities push and dissolve national, racial, and sexual boundaries. As history and fiction, literature and commentary, these provocative queerings challenge popular, literary, and scholarly discourses to map unexpected confluences of race, nationality, sexuality, and gender in the Other Americas. But as they do, they leave another set of problems and questions. In replacing journalistic "ugly truths" with the ribald positivity of pirate utopias, where do these authors find openings into submerged ways of knowing imperialism and sexuality? And where do their inverted visions of the Caribbean as the *most queer-friendly place on earth* stumble into one more too-simplistic rendering of the sexual, racial, and gendered complexities of the region?

9.1   A Cuban Asylee in Miami: Fidel Armando Toboso-Alfonso

"Attorney General Janet Reno today issued an order that would allow homosexuals from other countries to seek political asylum in the United States," announced the *New York Times* on June 17, 2004. On that day—marking "another turn in the Clinton Administration's seemingly uneven approach to gay rights issues"—Reno directed asylum review officials considering the claims of same-sex loving applicants to use one landmark case as a guide: that of Cuban Fidel Armando Toboso-Alfonso, who arrived in Miami during the Mariel boatlift and sought asylum on the grounds that he was persecuted in Cuba due to his sexuality (Johnston). Toboso-Alfonso testified to relentless surveillance by the Cuban government, which he said kept files on homosexuals and regularly detained him for days to review his sexual activities; and relentless threats from civilians, ranging from shouts that all queers should leave the country to a hail of eggs and tomatoes rained on him by neighbors. His case was appealed by the INS but upheld by the Board of Immigration Appeals (BIA) in 1990, then elevated to immigration law precedent by Reno four years later—a precedent that still stands.

The BIA's decision was based on two considerations. First, it agreed with the original immigration judge's finding "that homosexuality is an 'immutable' characteristic"—one the applicant couldn't simply change to avoid further persecution—and that there was no "evidence or argument that, once registered by the Cuban government as a homosexual, that

that characterization is subject to change" (*Matter of Toboso-Alfonso*). Building on this, the Board opined that, (supposedly) unlike U.S. laws against gays' military service, marriage, and parental rights, the Cuban government's legalized homophobia was also immutable. Cuban officials' threats against Toboso-Alfonso were cited as proof of "the government's desire that all homosexuals be forced to leave their homeland," and the BIA found no evidence that this *ever would* change (*Matter of Toboso-Alfonso*). Persecution of same-sex loving people joined the list of human rights violations that U.S. courts leveled against Fidel Castro's Cuba, and stood in opposition to the apparent beneficence of their capitalist neighbors offering refuge to its victims.

The politically motivated beneficence of the BIA's ruling would, over the next decade, benefit a few same-sex loving and Caribbean migrants. By 2003, 686 men and 87 women were offered sexual orientation-based asylum, less than 1 percent of pleas granted in that period (Randazzo 43). But the premises on which the precedent-setting decision were based proved as problematic for queer Caribbeans as the *yolas* on which migrants crossed the sea proved dangerous. The writing into law of homosexuality's immutability codifies what Michel Foucault documents as the invention of the homosexual *as species,* a group essentially, inherently Other—an invention hegemonic institutions systematically deploy to stigmatize and disempower that "species" even as they offer nominal protection. And the writing into law of Cuban homophobia's intransigence codifies ethnocentric fantasies of the Caribbean's explosively macho, passionately public sexual primitiveness. As it does, it naturalizes global inequalities that position the capital-rich U.S. as a destination for same-sex loving exiles and other migrants, and the capital-poor Caribbean as a site emigrants fight to flee—insidiously suggesting that the Global South's economic "behindness" is a reflection of its sexual "backwardness." Transnational migration, such logic suggests, is the result—not of exploitative economic globalization, but—of the South's cultural lag behind the North. Who would want to live *down there* in the sexual savagery of Cuba when they could live *up here* in the tolerant latitudes of the United States?

9.2   A North Carolina Pirate in Cuba: Ann Bonny

Who, indeed. In Valdés' *Lobas del Mar,* the answer to this question is Ann Bonny, the Irish-born seafarer who fled her North Carolina home to become a female pirate passing as a man on rocky Caribbean seas. Imagining Ann's eighteenth-century "illegal" migration to waters where governors ceaselessly hunt her down, Valdés' portrait of *la pirata* closely follows contemporary documents, notably Charles Johnson's *General History of the Pyrates* (148–165). (Johnson even appears as a character in *Lobas*, traveling on the pirate ship to document its mates—and Valdés clearly agrees with those who believe this author was a pseudonym-disguised Daniel Defoe). The details Valdés reproduces from Johnson's account include Bonny's attack on a North Carolina maidservant, her marriage to (then desertion of) a sailor, her affair with pirate Captain "Calico" Jack Rackham, and her erotic interest in fellow female-to-male pirate Mary Read. Valdés' refusal to imagine too far from the "official version" also takes more metaphoric, more problematic forms. Much of the novel sticks closely to dominant gender scripts, creating for Bonny a conventional, gown-loving femininity that she eases into when not on deck; and to dominant racial scripts, backgrounding the region's black population to focus on a lily-white pirate crew. But there's one scantily documented episode in Bonny's life—absent from Johnson's *History,* granted only a sentence in other accounts (Klausman 206)—which Valdés develops in ways that veer widely outside any historical record and puncture the normativity threatening to settle into her text. She dedicates a 40-page chapter to elaborating improbable, wonderful details about Bonny's possible sojourn in Cuba, where she's rumored to have given birth to her first child. In Valdés' novel, this interlude becomes a "queer time and place" (Halberstam) that opens new possibilities not only for her protagonist's sexual and racial affiliations, but also for understanding queerness in the endlessly inclusive contours she traces for Caribbean cultural geographies.

In Cuba, Ann develops two new and (given the story so far) surprising interests. The first is in the welfare of enslaved Africans, a concern to which this violent pirate has previously seemed unmovably indifferent. When, before temporarily leaving Ann, Rackam meets with a Cuban landowner to negotiate the sale of recently captured human "cargo," Ann angrily interrupts their proceedings—shocking both by demanding justice for the captives and insisting Rackham mistreat them only "por encima de mi cadaver": "Ambos hombres se interrogaron con la mirada, asombrados del súbito y raro acto de humanismo" (Valdés 133). Her second unexpected Cuban interest is in other women, who to this point have only appeared as antagonists (including the servant she stabs to death). But during her island sojourn Ann develops an unprecedentedly tender erotic friendship with Rackham's ex-lover Lourdes Inés, who agrees to raise her child. When they meet, Lourdes greets the pirate by offering, "Ann, eres muy hermosa" (Valdés 140). Ann returns the compliment, going on to murmur the syllables *Lourdes Inés* until she reforms them in her a mouth to create a new name for their "intimidad" (Valdés 140). *Lunes,* she calls her: signifying on another Defoe text, *Robinson Crusoe,* whose protagonist renames his island companion *Friday*—but reversing that renaming's connotations by imagining this woman as the beginning of her week, of her Cuban time.

Ann's two interests converge when she overhears nocturnal drums and tracks down a Santería *bembé* (ceremony), where the rhythmic, kinetic, embodied liberty of dancing blacks fascinates her. After threatening her host Diego with violence, she convinces him to introduce her and her now inseparable friend Lunes to the ceremonies, where they become nightly dancers. Ann's participation is immediately marked as "queer"— disruptive to normative cultural logics of sexuality and (racialized) gender—in more than one way. First, she experiences *bembés* as scenes of sensual opening and same-(as well as other-) sex eroticism. Opening mouths to sing and drink together, arms and legs to dance together, Ann and Lunes deepen their connection amidst smoke and sweat as Ann twirls barefoot and Lunes "aprendío a contonear la cintura, hip-notizada" and "pareció liberarse" (Valdés 143). Less literally and more powerfully, Ann's *bembé* nights read as racially queer—eccentric, unsettling, non-normative—activities for a reproductive European female like herself, scenes that move her decidedly outside the time (day) and space (plantation house) she's supposed to occupy comfortably. Exploding racialized gender norms, Ann spends third trimester nights dancing with enslaved blacks, *mulatos*, and maroons, and becomes excited "hasta perder los sentidos" watching black women's drumming and *cimarrones'* scarred, dancing bodies (Valdés 142). Ever pirate-spirited, Cuba-inspired Ann desires to *be with* all the wrong people…women, blacks, black women; and desires to *be like* all the wrong people…*negras, mulatas,* and maroons who have—like her—escaped a normative colonial order based on genocidal racial and sexual violence.

But the queerness of this pirate's Santería interval appears most provocatively at the end of her island time, after her daughter is born and Rackham comes to return her to their ship. As she leaves, a maroon smuggles her the written transcription of a *dilogún* (cowry shell) reading. Committed to paper by a man of African descent—who, according to slave law, should never be able to read or write, but can both read what Henry Louis Gates theorizes as the Yoruba writing system of *dilogún* (13), and compose the colonizer's language, Spanish—this reading, like (and quite unlike) a court judgment, becomes a document by which readers can interpret the protagonist's travels through waters, genders, and sexualities. The reading falls in Oshé Ojuani, a sign where Cuba's patron saint Oshún, *orishá* (divinity) of sweet water, femininity, and eroticism, offers her blessings. This letter, the transcript explains, communicates a strong relationship with Yemayá, *orishá* of seawater, maternity (like Lunes, she raises children that Oshún bears) and—depending on story and storyteller—Oshún's sister or lover (Connor and Sparks 74); but also indicates a bond with Shangó, *orishá* of lightning, masculinity, and strategy, another of Oshún's lovers. Finally, the letter offers a key to understanding the endless mutability not only of Ann's desires, but of her appearance: "*En Oshé Ojuani...es donde nace la apariencia...no puedes dar tu verdadero rostro*" (Valdés 147).

This Oshún-saturated paper that Ann takes back to sea attests to what Antonio Benítez-Rojo might call "a certain kind of way" (19) of knowing sexuality, gender, and (non)identity that she could only learn in Cuba, and that will serve her throughout her pan-American travels. This way maps an Afro-Caribbean cosmology/epistemology underpinned—or better, left productively unmoored—by the divine mutability of sexuality and gender. The divinity of sexuality's sexuality "naturally" moves both seaward and skyward, in same-sex and other-sex currents; and her gender emerges as equally mobile, this paragon of Cuban femininity showing herself to be something very different from the fixed definition of womanness that stifled Ann on the continent. Rather, part of Oshún's blessing is to encourage this gender-complex *pirata* in her ability to change self-presentations—to navigate between masculine and feminine, hiding her "verdadero" body as she passes for male on the high seas. Santería chroniclers note that pansexual Oshún often serves as a patron of sexual as well as gender fluidity, protecting same-sex loving and transgender devotees. And practitioners recognize certain *diloggún* letters, notably those related to Yemayá and Oshún—and especially to the two in relationship to each other—as speaking *orishás'* sanction of sexual and gender variance (Conner and Sparks 130). So while the letter of U.S. law codifies queers as a marginalized species, *dillogún letras* write sexual and gender complexity into the cosmic plan of the universe's unstable flow. Sealed with this multiply signifying reading, while the rest of the novel is about sailing on high seas, Ann's Cuban interlude becomes about diving into what Glissant imagines as the submarine realm of submerged Afro-Caribbean epistemologies (67): a space where reading is done with shells rather than books or legal writs, and where what the North considers "identity" emerges as endlessly, powerfully in flux as the ocean those shells come from.

This submerged epistemology surfaces in Valdés' novel not as only anti-heteronormative but as powerfully anti-racist. Her experience with *orishás* and their empowered devotees undermines racial hierarchies as it erodes distinctions between desires and genders; Oshún's lesson to Ann is to not be fooled by *any* appearance or construction of Otherness. When she finishes reading the maroon's note, "Ann sonrió y se dijo que serían los esclavos los que un día se levantarían y salvarían a ese país de la avaricia y de la invidia.—¡Vaya usted a saber! A lo majer...un día se unirá todos" (Valdes 148). As her queer Cuban time draws to its conclusion, Ann comes to understand fluency in Afro-Cuban epistemology—not any discourse of the Rights of Man—as that which will enable slaves to free themselves and Cuba by unifying inhabitants across race, class, gender, and sexuality. Valdes' language here, her evocation of (capitalist) greed and exhortation for all to unite, echoes rhetoric of her homeland's twentieth-century communist revolution. But she imagines that what's uniquely revolutionary about Cuba is housed not in the institutions of Castro's government—institutions that Toboso-Alfonso fingers as homophobic—but in resistant systems of thought that can never be contained within them. In *her* revolutionary Cuba, not only is homophobia far from immutable and closer to non-existent; racism and colonialism, those violences the United States still institutionalizes in immigration law, are danced out by the force of multiracial, multisexual bodies.

Finally, Ann's Cuban interlude imagines an idyllic Caribbean space where the power of *los negros* meets the power of the feminine and the queer to choreograph a different, egalitarian social order where Cuba emerges as centuries "ahead" of the Global North. Pushing beyond verisimilitude as does much of *Lobas,* Valdés' Santería fantasy spins a rosily romantic view of Cuba's racial and sexual politics. On the one hand, her hyperbole, like Ann's overstated threats to Rackam and Diego, reads as a literary tactic—a way to imagine aggressively against the North's fantasies of Caribbean sexual savagery. On the other, though, this idyll dances away from any opportunity to critique Caribbean slavery and the racism which, despite Castro's rhetoric, continues in "revolutionary" Cuba—or to complexly render the racial and sexual patriarchies that intertwine historically as well as in the present. Despite the location of this episode in a place that Valdés knows well, rather than a return to a recognizable Caribbean, her Cuban interlude leaves readers gazing at what Foucault sees in utopias: "society itself in a perfected form, or else society turned upside down, but in any case...fundamentally unreal spaces" (1986, 4).

9.3   No Evidence: Marcia Forrester's Exile to Jamaica

"Jamaican Lesbian Convict Denied Asylum: Immigration Officials Say Torture Treaty Doesn't Cover Community-Fueled Anti-Gay Violence," the *Gay City News* lamented in April 2005. The convict in question was Marcia Forrester, a New York denizen who obtained legal resident status in 1992 but was convicted of drug dealing in 2003—grounds for deportation in post-9/11 immigration law. Indeed, George W. Bush's administration witnessed spiraling anti-immigrant and anti-gay laws that made the climate when Forrester arrived in court a perilous one. But since deportation can be forestalled if the accused shows serious risk of injury upon return, Forrester filed a claim asserting that, as a masculine lesbian, she feared "being raped, victimized, and humiliated by the locals and the police" and should be protected under the Convention Against Torture (Leonard 2007b). While immigration judge Walter Durling initially granted her claim, finding it " 'almost a virtual certainty' that Forrester would suffer torture" if returned to Jamaica and that the Jamaican government wouldn't intervene, the BIA overturned his ruling on appeal. "The BIA noted that notwithstanding Forrester's obvious masculinity and lesbian status, she failed to offer any evidence that she was tortured or arrested on any of her four visits to Jamaica," wrote Judge Michael Chagares. He noted that while the BIA took no issue with Durling's finding on "the intolerance of Jamaican society toward homosexuals," the "society's" violent homophobia was a problem the government shouldn't be implicated in: "even assuming arguendo that Forrester would suffer some sort of harassment or violence based on her sexual orientation [...] there was no evidence that the Jamaican government would acquiesce to such mistreatment" (Leonard 2007b).

Exemplifying a growing tide of anti-migrant legal decisions in the years since Toboso-Alfonso's watershed case, this ruling also highlights why males have received asylum nearly eight times as frequently as females. As Randazzo documents, the kinds of violence that immigration law counts as torture—such as incarceration and beating, Chagares' examples—are most often experienced by males, while forms of intimidation leveled against females—forced marriage, rape, shunning—are considered "private" affairs in which the state won't intervene (43–44). Even more to the point here: though several male-to-female transsexuals have filed successful asylum claims, courts remain less likely to take the violence leveled against female gender variance seriously. While Forrester's sexual orientation is judged as "immutable," her "obvious masculinity" is treated as a surface characteristic (not a "status") and dismissed as a possible cause of oppression in the same sentence where it's introduced—leaving no opening to consider what social violences, including lack of opportunities for legal employment, may have resulted from her female masculinity (IGLHRC). Instead of being given substance in Chagares' report, gender variance floats in the proceedings' margins—hovering in dependent clauses, never emerging into the foreground.

At the same time, the appeal verdict exemplifies workings that disadvantage claimants from U.S.-supported governments and favor those from nations with which it maintains strained or no relationships. Contemporary U.S. documents including the Human Rights Watch's *Hated to Death: Homophobia, Violence, and Jamaica's HIV/AIDS Epidemic* (2004) scrupulously record the Jamaican government's impunity in ignoring police brutality against gays, refusing to prosecute gay bashings, maintaining sodomy laws, and underfunding HIV/AIDS initiatives. (All abuses of which the U.S. was accused prior to *Lawrence v. Texas*.) Yet Chagares goes to great trouble to exculpate the Jamaican state—which, not coincidentally and quite unlike Cuba, consistently aligns itself with U.S. interests—from any human rights abuses, while inculpating the Jamaican populace as the "real" source of homophobia. The state is just, Chagares suggests, but the population incorrigibly unendingly violent. As surely as the BIA's earlier condemnation of the homophobia of Castro's Cuba, its support of the gay rights stance of Patterson's Jamaica demonstrates the rationalization of capitalism at work as one heteropatriarchal capitalist state records its approbation for another. Just as surely, its suggestion that Jamaica's "common man" is the problem for people like Forrester—that the average Jamaican is less evolved regarding sexual difference than the average North American, and what can either government do about it?—reinvents the racism evident in the Toboso-Alfonso case while adding a layer of classism and sexism. What can be done, the BIA's report suggests, besides returning Forrester to the protection of Jamaican law, and hoping that her country's association with the U.S. will bring her compatriots more enlightenment?

9.4   Evidence Imagined: Bonn's Queer Jamaican Haven

What can and must be done to push transnational imaginations beyond these narrow straits, suggests Farley's *Kingston by Starlight,* is, first, to distrust all official narratives of border-, gender-, and other transgressions. To navigate the multiple crossings of time, space, and gender that he undertakes as "a man passing himself off in his fiction as a woman who is passing herself off as a man" (Farley 327), Farley imagines far wide of all historical documentation on Bonny (whom he calls Bonn). While he uses official histories as a "skeleton" (Farley 327)—and echoes the skeleton's meaning on the Jolly Roger, where it signified vigorous transgression against norms of imperial "life" (Rediker 166)—he not only makes up numerous episodes not recorded anywhere, but imagines that much written down in court reports and pirate histories are fabrications. In *his* story, Rackham's crew valiantly capture a Spanish galleon, but the governor never acknowledges the raid so he can keep the booty when they're captured; the state brings false witnesses to testify at the pirates' trial; and newspapers concoct statements Bonn makes against Rackham's valor (statements that appear in the *General History* as well as Valdés' novel). With strokes like these, Farley plunders official records of Bonn's life to reverse their implicit judgments. And as he does, his tales plunder and reverse those twenty-first century, Global Northern assumptions about Jamaica and its "obviously masculine" females that skew the Forrester decision.

In his unpredictable imagination of gender-crossing, Farley never reverts to painting Bonn's masculinity as inborn or "immutable," a trait always already "obvious." Rather than part of her/his being, Bonn's female masculinity is doing, is *work:* learning to *pass* as a man is like—and part of—learning to *make passage* at sea. When Ann (not yet Bonn) flees her father's house, she escapes to the waterfront to find work. Watching workers from the docks, she muses:

> All who worked the sea—the fishermen and the boatswains, the lighthouse keepers and the captains' boys—were male. Accordingly, large bodies of water, to me, seemed to be churning cauldrons of manhood, stirred at the bottom by long-bearded Poseidon with his scepter; oceans, lakes, and rivers, in my mind, contain'd in their white-flecked crests the very sum of the rages and storms and swells of the other sex. If I could just learn the ways of the water [...] (Farley 47)

Ann's wave-rocked reflections swiftly overturn traditional gendering of the sea as feminine—as well as conventional fictions of gender as a fixed ground on which to build identities. Instead, masculinity is literally fluid here, powerfully changeable like "rages and storms and swells" that rock the sea with the force of the Greek gods whose tales of metamorphosis fascinated Ann in childhood. But unlike those magic transformations, fluid masculinity now surfaces as something whose "ways" she can learn like the work of fishermen and boatswains; and it arouses Ann's desire not to find a man at sea but to become one, to train her body to masculinity like and along with seafaring. And train she does. By the end of the chapter Ann becomes Bonn for the first time—(somewhat clumsily) dressing, flirting, and talking as a man in a sailors' bar—and extends the maritime metaphor to think: "I had dipped my toe in the waters" (Farley 55).

Soon Bonn swims masterfully in these waters, living full-time as a man, and makes his way to sea by joining Jack Rackham's pirate crew with the promise that under the black flag all men are equal, regardless of how (poor, black, female) they were born. The ship sails into Caribbean waters with the final destination of Jamaica; and—again bucking tropes of the region—the closer Bonn comes to Jamaica and the deeper into that island he ventures, the deeper he travels into what seems the *least* homophobic place on earth, a haven for multiple queernesses. Queerness moves beyond signifying same-sex desire in Farley's tale of the pirates' Jamaica to marking wildly colored disruptions to all kinds of pallid colonial norms. Following historical sources in including Bonn's relationship with Jack, Farley nonetheless thoroughly queers their heterosexual but never heteronormative partnership. Their first sexual encounter is sparked by Bonn's thrill at penetrating Jack—at opening a (cunnic) gash on his cheek (Farley 185). The relationship continues with as much pitch and lightning as the seas they travel until, ready to retreat with their hefty booty, the pair retires to Jamaica to farm (another episode Farley draws from imagination). Bonn finds Jamaica an endless erotic paradise, where "all is everlasting emerald" (Farley 246) and the lay of the landscape naturally takes the shape of "homo" desire, as green hills embrace—not their other, not sky or sea—but each other, "naked in the light, like lovers in a bed savoring the last of slumber" (Farley 247). And Bonn and Jack love each other like those hills—as two of a kind, two men. Bonn recalls: "He liked me to dress as a man, and to talk as a man, and so, since that was consonant with my nature, I would wear his breeches and canvas shirts, and together we would talk in the rough cadences of men, even as we shared sweet intimacies" (Farley 250). This interlude, like Valdés' Cuba, paints another colorfully romanticized Caribbean: one where the region's geography itself—masculinely charged sea and homo-desiring land—turns even differently sexed encounters into something queer, non-normative, and piratical. Farley's chapter-long utopia, where the endless sexual summer of Jamaica reads like a brochure for gay tourism, initially poses many of the same problems as Valdés' idealized Cuba. But unlike *Lobas, Kingston* neither begins nor ends the pirates' Caribbean time in this idyll. Instead, the novel continues to traverse a complicated variety of Jamaican social geographies, breaking "gay" paradise open as it intersects with race, gender, and the state to splinter from utopic to heterotopic.

Having queered heterosexuality, Farley's characterization of Bonn—undisputedly Irish in historical records—goes on to queer whiteness. Throughout the novel characters remark on how dark Bonn becomes in the tropics, taking him for mulatto. And finally we learn that he *is* not only gender- but racially hybrid, fathered by Zed, a "Moor" and former corsair who escaped to Ireland. Bonn immediately embraces this news, remembering how Zed taught him boys' sports, told sea stories, and helped him become the pirate that he is: "Is my hair his hair? Is my skin his skin? Do we share the same dreams?" (Farley 310). So Bonn's gender/piracy finally emerges not as something that a European imports to the Caribbean but as a set of masculine "dreams" that Bonn learns from an African traveler—a product of Southern histories of travel and transgression rather than Northern sexual exceptionalism. The unexpected concluding revelations continue in the next chapter, when reproduction is queered, too. Farley follows official sources in narrating that Bonn and companion (Mary) Read are both pregnant when captured by infamous, pirate-chasing Governor Woodes Roberts—and eventually released because of their pregnancies. But he pushes this record by imagining both as pregnant *men,* referring to them with masculine pronouns as they await childbirth. And while Bonn's child is conceived with Jack, Read tells Bonn that his child is conceived in a sexual encounter with Bonn: that one night in prison the wall separating them fell away and, masculinely and maritimely, "I sailed quickly into your harboring arms and you into mine" (Farley 317). While Bonn miscarries and Read dies after childbirth, Bonn goes on to raise his and Read's magically conceived child in Jamaica, naming him William after their pirate ship. The next generation of Jamaica, then, is the child of the novel's multiple queernesses, flowing together the sexual, racial, gender, and maritime transgressions of these boundary-defying pirates.

In the end, not only is Farley's Caribbean a "natural" haven for queerness; the region's populace, far from a bastion of homophobia, is (partly) the offspring of that queerness. Further assailing U.S. narratives of sexually backward Caribbean folk vs. supposedly protective states, the novel's final chapters paint Jamaica's only trans-/homophobic forces as representatives, not of seadogs, settlers, or slaves, but of the imperial law and government who finally capture the pirates. In prison, jailers ascertain Bonn's femaleness and indict his manness as witchcraft ("They're sayin' yer a witch"), feminizing and demonizing his gender piracy (Farley 274). And literally in the hands of the law, restrained by guards en route to court, he suffers the text's only transphobic violence. Onlookers claw, bite, and strip him until he's "standing as naked as African cargo on the deck of a slaver" as a guard sneers, "You look like a woman now." To which Bonn cuts back: "Give me a sword and I'll show you who's a man" (Farley 276–277). Here any public transphobia comes only *when enabled by state agents*, who were first to forcibly restrict Bonn's body and gender. Once he's verbally and physically disciplined into "a woman now," populace and jailers alike can—as in Forrester's case—erase gender complexity as an element of his story that deserves consideration on its own terms. But even while demonstrating the power dynamics of this disciplining, Farley imagines for Bonn something Forrester never gets in Chagares' written judgment: a chance to answer back, taking the last word and aggressively claiming manness even as his female body is exposed and restrained.

As the pirates make their way through the legal system, the state's attack wields even deeper violence against same-sex sexuality. In yet another addition to the historical record, Farley imagines that homophobia—and, indeed, *internalized* homophobia—is the "real" reason that bloodthirsty Governor Rogers hunts pirates down. After Jack's hanging, Bonn learns that he and Rogers, "on some voyage long ago, shared those things that men sometimes share on sea-voyages, when one comes to know one's fellows in a way one never would on land. To John, all flesh was flesh, and this episode was just one of many; but to Rogers, it was a moment of deep ignominy, of weakness, of sin, and it was his drive to purge himself that drove the Governor to destroy John and all who sail'd with him" (Farley 292). So—echoing the controversial history recounted in Barry Burg's *Sodomy and the Pirate Tradition*—Jack's sea experience traces the Caribbean as a region populated not (only) by heterosex, but by sea voyages that breed homosex. And despite/because of this foundational sexual fluidity where "all flesh was flesh," Rogers founds the first stable British colonial government not only on the slavery's racial violence, but on sexual violence that excises queerness in order to stabilize heteropatriarchal imperial domination. While not part of historical records of Jamaican colonization, Rogers' attacks echo the twentieth century state-sponsored homophobia that Jacqui Alexander calls the Caribbean's *heteropatriarchal recolonization*: a system of ideological and material limitations that neocolonial governments impose on citizens' erotic autonomy in order to symbolically solidify their authority over the "body" of the nation (25). The violence meted out to Jack's nation-defying body reads as Farley's narrative counterattack against U.S. rhetoric touting these recolonized states as the legitimate guarantors of "gay rights." Why should they be, when the state's function has *always* been to solidify imperial heteropatriarchy, never to harbor those who sail outside it?

But Bonn escapes the state-sponsored violence that kills Jack, and his long life and lifelong storytelling stand in for a successful strain of resistance to official trans-/homophobia that, the novel suggests, has always—ribaldly, forcefully, piratically—found place in Jamaica's hills, waters, bush, and cities. Since this multiply queer Caribbean history has, like Rackham's crew, been violently excised in service of hegemonic narratives of global sexuality, *Kingston* creates an alternative, imaginative archive where that queerness sails the high seas and populates the landscape, too. The final chapter holds one last surprise. To support pregnant Read, Bonn agrees to write a tome of fictionalized pirate stories for a North American publisher. This is *The General History of the Pyrates,* and Bonn chooses as his pen name a dockside bar term for penis—Johnson—so surreptitiously signing the definitive account of piracy with his transgressive male identification (Farley 313). North America has never known the real story of Caribbean gender piracy "Johnson"'s historical fiction suggests that history is still submarine, and readers must move creatively outside official Northern (non)fictions to navigate it.

9.5   Coda

Valdés' novel ends with an unconcluded search for Bonny's descendants in rural Cuba; Farley's ends with Bonn telling the unfinished tale of his life in rural Jamaica. And like their creative texts, this essay won't attempt to bring closure to the narrative possibilities of piracy. My point, rather, has been to follow openings: to follow how, while undocumented, working-class migrants such as Toboso-Alfonso and Forrester continually risk finding their migration stories forcefully channeled into thickening discourses of U.S. sexual exceptionalism, more privileged diasporic subjects such as Valdés and Farley experiment with using their transnational positions and readerships to speak back creatively, charting countercurrents in global imaginations of how sexual "progress" flows. These countercurrents present their own pitfalls and traps, as authors, caught in flip-the-script responses to the Global North, must move deftly to avoid getting caught in utopian fantasies of *Caribbean* exceptionalism. But they also present possibilities for developing new narrative routes that connect sexuality, gender, race, and colonialism in unexpected ways of knowing—reminding readers of the need to keep postcolonial and queer imaginations perpetually under pressure, perpetually in multiplication and motion. As Bonn sends off his narrative: "Ah, my darling, my loved one, my voyage is far from finished!" (Farley 320).

Works Cited

Alexander, M. Jacqui. *Pedagogies of Crossing*. Durham: Duke University Press, 2005.

Benítez Rojo, Antonio. *The Repeating Island*. Trans. James Maraniss. Durham: Duke University Press, 1992.

Bentham, Martin. "Asylum is granted to gay Jamaicans." *The Telegraph* (October 12, 2002). http://www.telegraph.co.uk/news/uknews/1410018/Asylum-is-granted-to-gay-Jamaicans.html/. Accessed on February 14, 2010.

Burg, Barry. *Sodomy and the Pirate Tradition*. New York: New York University Press, 1995.

Conner, Randy & David Hatfield Sparks. *Queering Creole Spiritual Traditions*. New York: Harrington Park Press, 2004.

Defoe, Daniel. *A General History of the Pyrates*. London: J.M Dent & Sons, 1972.

———. *Robinson Crusoe*. New York: Dover Publications, 1998.

Fajardo, Kale. "Piracy in the Gulf of Aden." (December 9, 2008). http://www.youtube.com/watch?v=sA30hwJpivM/

Farley, Christopher John. *Kingston by Starlight*. New York: Three Rivers Press, 2005.

Foucault, Michel. *The History of Sexuality*. Vol. 1. Trans. Robert Hurley. New York: Vintage Books, 1994.

———. "Of Other Spaces." *Diacritics* 16.1 (Spring 1986). 22–27.

Gates, Henry Louis. *The Signifying Monkey*. New York/Oxford: Oxford University Press, 1988.

Glissant, Edouard. *Caribbean Discourse*. Trans. Michael Dash. Charlottesville: University Press of Virginia, 1989.

Gopinath, Gayatri. *Impossible Desires*. Durham: Duke University Press, 2005.

Halberstam, Judith. *In a Queer Time and Place*. New York: New York University Press, 2005.

Human Rights Watch. *Hated to Death: Homophobia, Violence, and Jamaica's HIV/AIDS Epidemic*. *Human Rights Watch* 16:6 B (2004).

IGLHRC (International Gay and Lesbian Human Rights Commission). *Lesbian Issues Packet*. New York: IGLHRC, 2000. http://www.asylumlaw.org/docs/sexualminorities/Lesbian%20IssuesPacket.pdf.

Johnston, David. "Ruling Backs Homosexuals on Asylum." *The New York Times* (June 17, 1994). http://www.nytimes.com/1994/06/17/us/ruling-backs-homosexuals-on-asylum.html?n=Top/Reference/Times%20Topics/Organizations/J/Justice%20Department/

Klausmann, Ulrike, Marion Meinzerin, & Gabriel Kuhn. *Women Pirates and the Politics of the Jolly Roger*. Trans. Tyler Austin and Nicholas Levis. Montreal: Black Rose Books, 1997.

Leonard, Arthur S. "Jamaican Lesbian Convict Denied Asylum: Immigration officials say torture treaty doesn't cover community-fueled anti-gay violence." *Gay City News* 4.7 (April 17–23, 2005). http://www.asylumlaw.org/docs/sexualminorities/JamaicaSO.pdf/.

———. "Lesbian's Asylum Bid Denied." *Gay City News* (January 4, 2007). http://gaycitynews.com/site/news.cfm?newsid=17671147&BRD=2729&PAG=461&dept_id=568860&rfi=6

Matter of Toboso-Alfonso. United States Board of Immigration Appeals. March 12, 1990. UNHCR Refworld, http://www.unhcr.org/refworld/docid/3ae6b6b84.html

Padgett, Tim. "The Most Homophobic Place on Earth?" *Time* (April 12, 2006). http://www.time.com/time/world/article/0,8599,1182991,00.html/.

Puar, Jasbir. *Terrorist Assemblages*. Durham: Duke University Press, 2007.

Randazzo, Timothy J. "Social and Legal Barriers: Sexual Orientation and Asylum in the U.S." *Queer Migrations*. Eds. Eithne Luibhéid and Lionel Cantú Jr. Minneapolis: University of Minnesota Press, 2005. 30–60.

Rediker, Marcus. *Villains of All Nations*. Boston: Beacon Press, 2004.

Trouillot, Michel-Rolf. *Silencing the Past*. Boston: Beacon Press, 1995.

IV

Racial Migrations

10

Insular Interventions: Jesús Colón Unmasks Racial Harmonizing and Populist Uplift Discourses in Puerto Rico

Maritza Stanchich

Emergent scholarship on Jesús Colón intersects fruitfully with how literature of the Puerto Rican diaspora has become increasingly important on the island in the past two decades, as the intelligentsia continues to deal with the ways in which previous formulations of national culture neglected class, race, gender, sexuality, and, of course, the diaspora itself. Now that the critical mass of Puerto Ricans in the U.S. mainland has superseded the population on the island, and migration from the island today seems heading toward another historic peak, it has become increasingly untenable to exclude the history and literature of the Puerto Rican migration from formal local considerations.[1] Indeed diasporic Puerto Rican literature, broadly construed historically and geographically, often overtly addresses national discourses on the island, even as it was being excluded from consideration there. By drawing distinctions in particular between racial discourses in the United States and a country of the Hispanic Caribbean, literature of the Puerto Rican diaspora profoundly interrogates and exposes the naturalized and reified historical, social, and political discourses in Puerto Rico that have enshrined notions of racial democracy, despite major interventions of the past.[2]

Though diasporic Puerto Rican literature is hardly a monolithic statement, much of the literature questions such crucial and contested affiliations of the nation with race and language (the important linking of language I will bracket for now). Since navigating the racial quagmire often triggered by migration is a central theme in much literature of the diaspora, perhaps one of its most radical contributions is to further expose and illuminate the incommensurability of racial discourses between the United States and Puerto Rico, as Jorge Duany and Isar Godreau have observed in comparing recent insular and stateside racial Census identifications (2002, 2003; 2008). This line of inquiry helps unmask Eurocentric cultural nationalist discourses of a harmonious racial democracy in the making since at least the mid nineteenth century, with the *jibarismo* exemplified by Manuel Alonso's *El Gibaro* (1849), and consolidated into the racial harmonizing discourses of Populist cultural nationalism of the 1940s and 1950s. Hence the previous exclusion of diasporic literature in Puerto Rican canonicity, even while understandably historically grounded against the colonial imposition of English, also serves to mask racial and class affiliations that expose these racial harmonizing discourses of Populist cultural nationalism and *jibarismo* in Puerto Rico.[3]

Indeed as one of the early authors of the Puerto Rican diaspora, also deemed proto-Nuyorican for how his work anticipates 1960s militancy and the thematic concerns of what came to be called Nuyorican prose and poetry,[4] Jesús Colón left a body of work that also functions to critique these powerful insular ruling-class discourses. And unlike Bernardo Vega and later authors of the diaspora, Colón's more mature work refuses tendencies to essentialize, romanticize, and idealize Puerto Rico, in critically unflinching terms not seen until the publication of Miguel Piñero's poem "This is Not the Place Where I Was Born" (1975, 1980). The Recovering the U.S. Hispanic Literary Heritage project's 1993 publication of Jesús Colón's newspaper columns *The Way It Was and Other Writings* expands the Afro-Puerto Rican perspective of the *testimonio, crónica,* and journalism published earlier by Colón and Bernardo Vega, as does a compilation of his Spanish-language didactic poems, epistolary, and polemic journalism in *"Lo que el pueblo me dice...,"* published by the Recovery Project in 2001. His vignettes and columns published as *A Puerto Rican in New York and Other Sketches* in English in 1961, and re-released in 1982, also contain some hard-hitting and nuanced explorations of race. Along with the Recovery Project's translation of Luisa Capetillo's *Mi opinión (A Nation of Women* 2004), and its publication of the memoirs by Colón's brother, Joaquín Colón López (*Pioneros puertorriqueños en Nueva York 1917–1947,* 2002), Colón's writings address blind spots in early diaspora studies traditionally dominated by Vega's *Memoirs* (1972, 1984).

For example, the essays in *The Way It Was* that forge alliances with African American civil rights struggles, such as desegregation battles in Little Rock, Arkansas, as well as those essays that confront racism in Puerto Rico, augment and complicate Vega's critique of U.S. discrimination with a perspective that markedly differentiates Colón's subjectivity from Vega's, whose memoir begins by stating that he was a white *jibaro* from Cayey, also Colón's hometown. While race per se is not the overriding central concern of Colón's work (though its implicit relation to colonialism often is), he takes up the subject of race specifically and forcefully throughout all phases of his decades-long writing career, including early phases in Spanish, which are usefully divided into periods by Edwin Karli Padilla Aponte's introduction to "*Lo que el pueblo me dice*" (2001), and as also evidenced in his archive at the Centro de Estudios Puertorriqueños at Hunter College. Indeed his career and work on racial justice was recognized in a 1999 tribute at a gala event sponsored by the Schomburg Center for Research in Black Culture, in which Colón was named one of the 100 most important blacks in New York history, with a long list of impressive names bestowing honorable mentions.[5] As has been pointed out, this is a different portrait than the conclusion arrived at in Winston James' *Holding Aloft the Banner of Ethiopia* (1998), which ultimately vacates Colón's critiques of racism in comparison to those of Schomburg.

Colón's perspectives on race range widely from biting critiques of internalized racism, as seen in the early satirical didactic poems "Invitación" and "Miss cívica empolvada," both first published in 1935 under the pseudonym Miquis Tiquis for *El Curioso* (2001, 75–81), to denials of internal racism that claim racism in Puerto Rico is a U.S. import and that police Puerto Rican attitudes toward race along essentialist lines, as seen in the 1943 essay "Puerto Rico es también una nación" (141–142) published in *Pueblos Hispanos*. This latter sentiment is also echoed by his brother Joaquín in the section of his memoir titled "Raza de color–El negro en Puerto Rico" (25–29), but adding the compelling argument of how Booker T. Washington's Tuskegee Institute served to indoctrinate students from the island selected to study there. Padilla Aponte points out this shift over time in Colón's work (xxiv), which suggests evolving discursive tensions between tactics of heterogeneity and homogeneity as Colón articulated national anti-colonial concerns. The early didactic poetry is marked by a catchy rhyme scheme and Puerto Rican colloquialisms, as seen in "Invitación": "Fulano de Tal," "un baile social," "…un cine/ llamado crystal," "con olor fatal/ a cañita mala/ y a amonia animal" (2, 4, 9–10, 14–16; 75).

This poem harshly critiques a social event billed as "un baile 'de blancos'" (3, 75) in which the persona in the poem is surprised to instead find "Tipos empolvados/ de manera tal/ que parecían negros/ pintados con cal" (47–50, 76), who are mocked, caricatured, and critiqued as "Pobres ignorantes"… "que en su yo mental/ sienten el complejo/ de inferioridad" (87, 98–100; 77). While the critique of internalized inferiority is valuable, it is accompanied by a derision tainted by classist stereotypes, illustrated in the lines "pobres, tristes diablos,/ tratando escapar/ de sus propios seres…" (77–79, 77), culminating into what would become well-worn stereotypes (along the lines of the 1961 film

West Side Story decades later, for example): "Llovían galletazos/ sonaba 'trompa'/ salía la cuchilla/ presta a acuchillar" (119–122, 78). The poem ridicules the group's phony whitening posture further by contrasting them (as pretentious social climbers from the island) with U.S. elites: "no sabía si echarme/ a reir o a llorar;/…/o llorar de pena/ si un continental/ cree que esa gentuza/ va a representar/ o es la aristocracia/ de mi isla natal…"(135–136, 141–146; 79) and closes with a laudatory reference to George Washington as foundational leader of the U.S. nation. This is a highly unusual move when compared to Colón's later work: "¡Pobre Jorge Washington,/ hombre sin igual/ que ensucien tu calle/ con sociedad tal!/ ¡si estuvieras vivo/ Mandaras a matar/ a toda esa chusma/ pintada con cal!" (159–166, 79). The related poem "Miss cívica empolvada," a portrait that is equally statirical and similarly problematic, with two young ladies espousing "en tono tartamudeado" their club "de la famosa Unión Cívica,/ usted sabe…la de blancos," (22, 25–26; 80) focuses on the same pointed critique, with a young male Latino persona renouncing the club, stating that he would support it only if "no fuera un grupo ecuménico,/ sino de negros y blancos" and deeming the group "enemigo de los hispanos" (37–38, 44; 81). Linda C. Delgado also notes that during an even earlier period, when he published for *Gráfico*, his columns made moral observations, as "he warned his neighbors and cohorts against laziness and the dangers of self-fulfilling prophecies" (72), at a time when stereotypes of and prejudices against the growing Puerto Rican community in New York were becoming virulent, if not calcified. The later essay from this early phase, "Puerto Rico es también una nación," performs an about-face, abandoning problematic depictions of class distinction and internalized racism, and casting Puerto Ricanness in essentialist terms reminiscent of the period:

> Si algo tenemos los puertorriqueños, los VERDADEROS puertor-
> riqueños, superior a los norteamericanos, es la completa ausencia de
> prejuicios raciales en nuestra personalidad como pueblo. El prejuicio
> racial que existe en Puerto Rico hoy, lo importaron los yanquis a Puerto
> Rico, junto con el absentismo que nos pauperiza, y el bilingüismo que
> nos embrutece. El prejuicio racial no es una característica puertor-
> riqueña. (142)

Colón's later work on the subject increases in critical complexity, as well as adopts the use of English, with the powerful vignettes "The Mother, the Young Daughter, Myself and All of Us," (1961, 1982), and "A Bright Child Asks a Question" (1993), and the psychologically compelling "Little Things are Big" (1956, 1961, 1982). In this latter essay, originally published in his column "As I See It from Here" in the *Daily Worker*,[6] gone is the problematic moralizing and stereotyping of working class people from the early didactic poems, and present is a subtler, more nuanced critique of racism's permutations. Yet Colón's by-now entrenched socialist politics do not produce a romanticized working class nobility, as seen in Bernardo Vega's *Memoirs*. Rather, a more complex and intimate portrait of working-class sensibilities emerges. Delgado notes a chronological shift in Colón's positioning on race, suggesting that he was prompted to reconsider his early emphasis on class and nationality over race by the U.S. civil rights movement (81), and also noting that his changes for the second edition of *A Puerto Rican in New York*, republished in 1982, reflect increased nuance in his race analysis (84). James registers a similar arc of development in Colón's race concerns, noting that such self-reflective essays about Colón's own experience with racism as "Little Things are Big," along with "Hiawatha into Spanish" and "Phrase Heard in a Bus," were published in 1956 and 1957, around the time Colón promoted and attended the Pilgrimage of Prayer civil rights march in Washington, DC, in 1957 (1996, 113–114). These pieces and others of this period are usefully analyzed and historically contextualized in the context of U.S. black radicalism in Adalaine Holton's work on Colón, but also with an eye to their Puerto Rican context, which is pronounced. In "The Mother, the Young Daughter, Myself and All of Us," the young daughter told to sit next to the first-person narrator in the only available public seat responds out loud "I won't sit beside no nigger," stunning both adults into silence, and jolting readers to reflect on the stark and sudden interpellation of Puerto Ricans into the U.S. racial schema (118). The vignette "A Bright Child Asks a Question," structured in similar compact brevity (but previously unpublished), approaches the "layered intricacies of race," as Roberto Márquez theorizes comparative diaspora consciousness (19), by invoking the history of *mestizaje* in Puerto Rico (but without using that word) in two simple textbook-style paragraphs, starting with the proverbial arrival of Columbus. Again relaying a scene of a mother and young daughter, though this time Puerto Ricans, and again enacting intersections with African American struggle, the mother teaches the child the lyrics to "We Shall Overcome," when upon hearing the phrase "black and white together," the child asks: "Mother, what am I, black or white?" (46). Both vignettes from distinct vantage points bear witness to Puerto Ricans confronting such "layered intricacies" between the differing histories of hispanophone Puerto Rican and anglophone U.S. racial discourses and the interplay between them through such fraught encounters and epiphanies.

How such racial discourses do and do not travel and translate across these differentiated histories, is evident in another deceptively simple, first-person vignette: the poignant, humorous, and touching "Angels in My Hometown Church," from *The Way It Was*. Set in Puerto Rico, it explores the effects of a community's internalized racism as expressed by

parental social policing, church iconography, and a de-racializing cha-
rade for tourists, not to mention registering an initial sense of shock and
exclusion by a returned Puerto Rican migrant. The essay begins with
a childhood recollection of racial rejection, tempered by a satirically
comical, though also caricaturist, treatment of privileged women: "Doña
María Luisa Martínez de Rodríguez y Acevedo, mother of my best friend
Pedrito, shouted to her son from her balcony: "Pedritooooo...Pedrito.
..come over here immediately! You should not be playing in front of the
church with...that boy!" (1993, 53).

The narrator also implicates the role of societal institutions such as
the church, where after such repeated incidents during childhood he
sought solace at a statue of a Madonna overlooking brown and white
angels, but now finds the angels have all been painted white to appeal
to U.S. tourists. Upon returning to his hometown Cayey in 1965 after
living in New York for many years, he seeks that refuge where he recalls
he had gone as a child and "stood for a long time" because it "felt good,"
but now finds "coats of grey cement covered the space where the brown
and black..." (53–54). The paragraph ends abruptly with ellipses, leaving readers hanging to contemplate the range of his unspoken emotions.
Invoking class tensions again, the narrator appeals for an explanation to
a pious "well-dressed white lady with a fine silken shawl" in the church,
who responds: "You know Puerto Rico is becoming a great tourist center...You have been living in the United States for a very long time..."
(54). Set during a by-now firmly established Muñoz era, though not
directly invoked, the critique of the appeal to tourists can also infer
broader statist negotiations of power with the racial ideologies of U.S.
colonialism.

Taken together, these works illuminate how racism permeates everyday life in ways that Holton characterizes as "jumping frame," borrowing
a term from geography to show how Colón allows "readers to visualize the relationship of their experience to larger power structures" and
"to locate common cause among their diverse experiences" (2005, 15),
a move that also describes how the "moving back and forth between the
local and the global enables Colón to theorize the relationships between
various structures of power" (112). The following polemical essay republished in *The Way It Was* is an example par excellence from his *oeuvre*
of how such connections engaged insular discourses with oppositional
racial affiliations and with a sophisticated critical precision that enacts
the task Márquez outlines as an "unmasking of the more covert and
courtly class and racial protocols of Latin American convention" (19).
Hence this essay from Colón's later career surpasses the first-person
apprehensions in the vignettes and anecdotes and unpacks the discourses
themselves. Titled "The Negro in Puerto Rico Today," and published in
March 1960 in *The Worker*, the essay predates Arcadio Díaz Quiñones'

historicizing analysis of Tomás Blanco's sociological essay *El prejuicio racial en Puerto Rico* (1942, 1985). It holds the Muñoz-era intelligentsia accountable for persisting racial inequalities, theorizing a "coloniality of power" as inherent in the era's populism, a phrase Walter Mignolo uses to describe systemic internal colonialisms inherent to *Criollo*-managed post-independence Latin America (2000).[7]

The opening argument in Blanco's essay, as later also seen in Francisco Arriví's play *Vejigantes* (1958), contrasts Puerto Rico with the U.S. South to emphasize the incompatibility between Jim Crow racism, with its sadistic lynchings, and Puerto Rico's mixed-race legacy, minimizing local attitudes toward Puerto Rico's Afro-Caribbean legacy. Reading Blanco's seminal racial harmonizing discourses in Puerto Rico as managing Puerto Rican heterogeneity within a bourgeois homogenizing political project, Díaz Quiñones points to the silences, the omissions in Blanco's text, such as the political crisis the *Criollos*, whose power had been displaced by U.S. interests, found themselves in during the 1930s.[8] Díaz Quiñones contextualizes the publication of Blanco's essay as playing a key role in the cultural and racial debate emerging from the crisis period of the 1930s in Puerto Rico, rife with labor strikes and repressions against the burgeoning Nationalist movement, and in concert with canonical texts such as Antonio Pedreira's *Insularismo* (1934) and Luis Palés Matos' *Tuntún de pasa y grifería* (1937), which Díaz Quiñones posits as "pre-texts" to Blanco's essay. Blanco's essay, then, seeks to harmonize the racial conflicts those texts foregrounded, by renovating the era's enduring *gran familia* icon, by declaring the African presence fully Hispanicized, whitened, and assimilated, and by deeming social and racial conflicts imported. While racial *mestizaje* is celebrated, cultural *mestizaje* is denied (77), as Blanco claims a completely Hispanicized population. The unifying trope of the *gran familia*, while at least discursively reconciling conflict, preserves old orders of social hierarchy and paternalism, as Blanco and his ilk usher in the modernizing era in the 1940s and 1950s that would further insert Puerto Rico into the U.S. metropolitan apparatus under *criollo* tutelage.[9]

The year Luis Muñoz Marín was elected to his fourth and final gubernatorial term in office, in 1960, Colón's essay opens by noting the relatively scarce studies of racial prejudice at the time in Puerto Rico. Citing insular historical works on slavery, and assessing the few current ones that do exist, Colón states, "The bibliography on the Negro today in Puerto Rico is very poor," with two studies on the subject, including Blanco's, deemed "poor and vacillating" and Blanco's, in particular, as "inadequate" (1993, 93). I cite from Colón's ensuing arguments at length to demonstrate his understanding of how Eurocentrism operated in both U.S. and insular locations, and in collusion with each other, again illustrating Holton's use of "jumping frame." Also notable is the polemical tone of the essay, rather than first-person anecdote, and its replications of the poetic language of the era's cultural nationalism, such as the "soul" commonly invoked by Pedreira and Muñoz Marín. By now, Colón's critique of internal racism lies squarely with the intelligentsia elites who fashion a racial democracy in the name of autonomy, a cultural nationalism that Zilkia Janer aptly calls "colonial nationalism," which she defines as "a nationalism that validates colonialism and makes it stronger" (2). Indeed the work that such diasporic literature performs on both sides of the double margin it occupies, in both locations, may help disable a cultural nationalism that reproduces coloniality, or what Rey Chow calls "reproduction of Eurocentrism-in-the-name-of-the-other" (109). To demystify these discourses, Colón writes:

The fact that we in Puerto Rico have been "miscegenating" for the last four hundred years and more has created a series of illusions, if not downright hypocritical attitudes, that have been passed down as truth for many years.

One such illusion is that there is no such thing as race prejudice in Puerto Rico, that we are ALL Puerto Ricans, and that is all. No difference.

To believe this is to ignore the very origin of the white Puerto Ricans' and the Negro Puerto Ricans' ancestors, how they came to Puerto Rico, and the obligatory relationship of master and slave that was established right from the beginning. To believe this illusion is to ignore the tremendous pressure exerted by those in power under Spanish domination to make sure that all the lies of a "superior" and "inferior" race be perpetuated in life and in mind in order to justify their inhuman exploitation of slaves.

Then came American imperialism, using racism and discrimination to justify the exploitation of the Negro right here in the U.S.A. and of the other colonial and semi-colonial people all over the world. The U.S. representatives of the American imperialist *"way of life"* and its Puerto Rican stooges accelerated and perfected this process of catering to the racist ideas of the imperialist power.

Today, racial prejudice, racial discrimination and the barring of opportunities is practiced not crudely or openly. It is done suavely. With finesse. *WE are "civilized," you know.*

Today the imperialist "superior" race concept of the South permeates almost all of Washington and Wall Street, and dominates their policies. The bosses just insinuate. And the stooges do the dirty work.

Today, because growing racism in Puerto Rico is subtle, the aspiring young Negro is not branded with "El Carimbo" on his body. But he is branded in his soul, in his character, in his personality with "El Carimbo" of hypocrisy, of double talk, *of shallow, meaningless and useless sentimentality and poetry.* (94, emphasis added)

Though the rhetoric draws from a broader international socialist critique, it also inveighs against Puerto Rico's Free Associated State "Commonwealth" project, and may be responding sarcastically to a well-known speech Muñoz Marín delivered two months earlier to the Puerto Rico legislature, titled "¿Qué clase de civilización, de cultura y manera de vida quiere el pueblo de Puerto Rico?" (see *Mensajes al pueblo puertorriqueño* 1980; trans. as "A Good Civilization" 1974). For example, Colón's emphasis of "WE" and "civilized" questions the parameters and ideology of autonomist populism as a narrative of uplift and civilizational thinking, as suggested by the common translation of the *Mano a la Obra* industrialization project, Operation Bootstrap. The words Colón here emphasizes with capitalization and quotation marks were liberally invoked in Muñoz's speech, and the common rhetorical flourish "way of life," still loud in recent U.S. imperialist mandates, also echoes Muñoz's defense of Commonwealth status "as a means toward the ideal of the good life" (1974, 220–221). Colón also seems well aware, in the last line of this citation, of the role Afro-Caribbean poetry played in the populist intelligentsia's orchestration of a Puerto Rican racial harmony in contrast, rather than in cahoots, with U.S. racism.[10] Instead, Colón demonstrates the ideological connections, rather than the divergences, between the two.

When Colón here mentions "El Carimbo," the practice of branding slaves in Puerto Rico outlawed in 1784, as established in a previous column in the collection, published a month before this one ("The Negro in Puerto Rican History" 91), he also connects past practices to continuing prejudice in both locations. Colón categorically adopts the term "Negro," which resonates more forcefully at the time in the U.S. context of the period, and maintains it throughout, indicating, as elsewhere in this collection, a militant advocacy for the U.S. Civil Rights Movement, while here simultaneously aware of significations in an insular context.[11] He ends the column by forcefully illustrating proof of racial prejudice in Puerto Rico, citing an anti-discrimination law that the legislature had recently failed to pass, and closing by again holding Muñoz Marín accountable: "This happened on February 9, 1960, of the year of our...Luis Muñoz Marín" (95). Perhaps most curiously, the final line of the above citation, "But he is branded in his soul, in his character, in his personality with 'El Carimbo' of hypocrisy, of double talk, of shallow, meaningless and useless sentimentality and poetry," suggests a sophisticated critique of insular discursive practices that the stark simplicity of Colón's prose belies. The dangling addition of "poetry" to this list resonates with Díaz Quiñones' analysis of discursive architects of the Muñoz era's racial harmonizing discourses, including Tomás Blanco's promotion of Luis Palés Matos.

According to Díaz Quiñones, those including Pedreira, Muñoz Marin and Blanco managing the cultural and racial discourses consolidating a project of renewed homogeneity and hegemony in the context of a disrupted social order, looked to poetry to promote racial democracy and harmony (35). While obviously the role of poetry in public discourse has waned considerably today, of course then it was common for politicians, including Muñoz Marín, to be known as accomplished poets. During this era of Puerto Rican letters, Luis Palés Matos' groundbreaking Afro-Caribbean poetry put into relief the discursive struggle over the racial and linguistic representation of the nation, with a racial/linguistic aesthetic that confronted previous versions of the typical Puerto Rican as a white *jíbaro* speaking folksy Spanish. At first, Palés Matos' *Tuntún de pasa y grifería* (1937) met with sharp opposition and ridicule from *criollo* and vanguard sectors well before it was published, as prior publication of individual poems in insular magazines sparked controversy starting five years earlier (Díaz Quiñones 31; González 82–3). Blanco, however, attempted to smooth the racial divisions exposed by *Tuntún* and countered the critiques against it. Indeed, Palés Matos dedicated *Tuntún* to Blanco, who actively promoted Palés Matos' Afro-Caribbean aesthetics and themes as conciliatory rather than confrontational, and as proof of Puerto Rican racial harmony, in effect denying institutionalized racism for the sake of consolidating populist political power. Though Palés Matos called his work Antillean poetry, rather than black poetry, he publicly argued that, according to Mercedes López-Baralt's introduction to the third edition of *Tuntún,* the figures of the *jíbaro* and the *indio* served to hide blackness (94). An illuminating detail from this introduction is the citation of Palés Matos' family cook in the Afro-Puerto Rican coastal town of Guayama as one of his major sources, referred to here only as "la negra Lupe" (28).

Though Colón does not name Palés Matos beyond the reference to "shallow, meaningless and useless sentimentality and poetry," Colón's unpublished papers at the archives at Centro de Estudios Puertorriqueños, Hunter College, critically refer to "the question of so-called Negro poetry, Pales Matos to Fortunato Vizcarrondo," under an undated heading "Random Notes on Negro-Puerto Rican Unity in the United States," with accompanying notes comparing this poetry's "cultural caricature and degradation mockery [as] different from Langston Hughes, Phillis Wheatley, Dumbar [sic]. Contee Coulin [sic]." Judging from his archived papers, Colón's research, knowledge, and reflections on the history of race in Puerto Rico appear to be extensive, especially in a twenty-two-page typed formal outline titled "The Negro in Puerto Rican History," a detailed chronology spanning from the early sixteenth century to c. 1947.[12] His analysis of other poets, the archive suggests, for the most part do not seem to move beyond active appreciation (promoting contests and readings, collecting some poems and articles by or about Luis Llorens Torres and Julia de Burgos, with whom he also made appearances), yet the "Random Notes" cited above, display not only a knowledge of the most important canonical African American poets, ranging from Wheatley's slave era to the Harlem Renaissance, but also a nuanced reading that challenges the credibility of Puerto Rico's "so-called Negro" poetry and critiques its representations as "caricature" and "degrading mockery." Again, Colón's critical view of the island's "negroide" poetic tradition far anticipates later critiques,[13] though in some intelligentsia circles these poets are still celebrated acritically, despite the poetry's most obvious tendency to portray "mulata" women as stereotypically hypersexualized.

Indeed Afro-Caribbean poetry, populist theories of racial harmony, and works that deployed the trope of the hidden black grandparent interrupted, upheld, sought to manage, and confronted elite constructions of a national racial identity from at least the 1930s. As Duany has shown, the cultural nationalism of the 1950s was informed by canonical texts and ideological premises of the generation of the '30s (21, 125, 292f1). According to Duany, after the 1940s studies celebrating racial democracy in Puerto Rico, a critical perspective on insular racial exclusion and prejudice emerged in the late 1960s and early 1970s, but significantly waned in the following two decades (258). Colón's work, as part of a growing commitment to diaspora studies on the island, may then serve to help resurrect an important conversation on race in Puerto Rico. The literature expressing Colón's socialist internationalist, inter-ethnic, and transnational alliances with African Americans in particular calls into question migrations' accompanying processes of racialization in ways that destabilize dominant discourses in both nation-states. Indeed scholars such as Isar Godreau, Francisco L. Rivera-Batiz, and Duany interrogate the reasons why nearly 80 percent of Puerto Rican islanders identified as white in the 2000 Census, compared to nearly 36 percent of stateside Puerto Ricans who did so. Godreau's ethnography shows how black identifications are invoked to both distance from racialization as well as build racial solidarity, depending on the context; Rivera-Batiz suggests that once outside the country migrants equate national identity as a distinct race; while Duany deems the U.S. model of hypodescent, known informally as the one-drop rule, incommensurable to the island's concept of *mestizaje*. Yet others (Juan Flores, Victor M. Rodríguez) point out that inter-ethnic alliances between Puerto Ricans and African Americans and racializing experiences in the United States shifted self-identification.[14]

Colón's sustained engagement, and his sense of entangled and unstable U.S./Caribbean racial discourses suggest all those recent scholarly theories. In addition to theorizing a transnational Afro-*Latinidad* that perhaps also anticipated the current growth of that field, Colón's fierce opposition to racist colonial ideology fruitfully explicates the charged terrain and material impact of racist ideologies in deeply comparative U.S. and Puerto Rican contexts, pointing to insular discourses that have discursively vacated blackness, and exposing the different ways insular cultural nationalism denies and enacts Eurocentrism. Colón's writings, then, among other functions, and along with the broader corpus of diasporic Puerto Rican literature, document a consistent engagement with insular cultural nationalist discourses, regardless of whether insular discourses occluded the connection. Yet while literature of the diaspora has become increasingly accepted, the promulgation of Colón's work may face the persistent barrier of his having remained a Communist until his passing in 1974, as others have also observed.[15] In a visit to a graduate class at University of Puerto Rico, Río Piedras, in Spring 2007, Colón's niece, Olimpia Colón Aponte, who takes seriously her role as custodian of his legacy, noted that while fellow family members remember Colón with deep affection, they prefer not to be publicly associated with his political affiliations. This fear in Puerto Rico should not be underestimated, where such associations have historically been deadly, where political discrimination may well have as much or more repercussions as racial discrimination, and where teachers at every level of the public system are embattled by systematic labor woes.

The lack of awareness of Colón's legacy was evident in March 2007 when the highly regarded Bronx-based Pregones Theater brought its worthwhile show "The Red Rose," about Jesús Colón and starring Danny Rivera, to the recently opened, newly renovated (and venerated) Teatro at UPR's Río Piedras campus (then a focus of heated campus privatization protests). The audience in the 1,200-seat theater was so sparse, that UPR organizers gave away tickets at the door and refunded those who had paid $20 in advance. Some blamed faulty UPR publicity or speculated that students were not drawn to a show in English with Spanish subtitles or to the generational marquee status of Danny Rivera. But it couldn't have helped that so few in the university community know of Colón, which was reinforced by print and radio ads that barely mentioned him. This perhaps parallels that most Colón scholarship could be characterized as emergent, and that literature of the Puerto Rican diaspora in itself is still an emergent literature in much of Puerto Rico's curriculums.

Notes

I wish to thank two research assistants who helped me finalize the research for this essay, Naida Garcia and Ileana Cortes. I would also like to thank Roberto Marquéz for early encouragement after a presentation on this subject at the 2006 Latin American Studies Association annual conference, and Adalaine Holton for inviting me to a panel of scholars working on Jesús Colón at the American Studies Association annual conference in 2007. I am also indebted to all my undergraduate and graduate students who have over the years responded to Colón's writings in class discussions and assignments, as his work often elicits profound reflections. Of course I am solely responsible for this essay's contents.

1. There are notable exceptions of works published in Puerto Rico that have done this in the past, such as Barradas, Efraín, and Rafael Rodríguez. *Herejes y Mitificadores: Muestra de Poesía Puertorriqueña En Los Estados Unidos.* (San Juan: Ediciones Huracán, 1980.) And later Barradas, Efraín. *Partes de un Todo: Ensayos y Notas Sobre Literatura Puertorriqueña en los Estados Unidos.* (San Juan: Editorial de la Universidad de Puerto Rico, 1998.) Also López Adorno, Pedro. *Papiros De Babel: Antología De La Poesía Puertorriqueña En Nueva York.* (San Juan: Editorial de la Universidad de Puerto Rico, 1991.) As well as translations of Pedro Pietri by Alfredo Matilla Rivas: Pietri, Pedro. *Puerto Rican Obituary.* 1977. Trans. Alfredo Matilla Rivas. (San Juan: Isla Negra, 2000.) *The Masses are Asses/Las Massas Son Crasas.* Trans. Alfredo Matilla Rivas. (San Juan, PR: Instituto de Cultura Puertorriqueña, 1997.) Broader consideration of the literature by the diaspora by island intelligentsia has been gaining momentum in the past fifteen years, perhaps best illustrated by the publication of *Literatura Puertorriqueña del Siglo XX: Antología* (ed. Mercedes López-Baralt. San Juan: Editorial de la Universidad de Puerto Rico, 2004), which includes entries by Bernardo Vega, Pedro Pietri, Tato Laviera, and Esmeralda Santiago. In popular music, of course, the diaspora's influence is obvious, with Hector Lavoe as perhaps exemplary. That may suggest something about the class affiliations of those historically in a position to assess and disseminate these different spheres of cultural production.

2. To such groundbreaking and debated movements and statements in the Puerto Rico context such as the so-called negroide poetry and culture, its more critical offshoot antillanismo, the publication of Isabelo Zenón Cruz's *Narciso descubre su trasero* (1974), José Luis González's *El país de cuatro pisos* (1979), and Juan Flores' critique of Antonio Pedreira's canonical text *Insularismo e ideologia burguesa* (1979), literature of the Puerto Rican diaspora offers a potentially seminal intervention in discourses on race in Puerto Rico, also geographically and historically construed.

3. For readers not familiar with this icon from Puerto Rican national discourses, *jíbarismo* refers to the discourses surrounding the *jíbaro* or peasant, typically portrayed as rural, noble, humble, male, and white, and perhaps comparable to nation-building types such as the *guacho* in Argentina or in nineteenth-century United States to the figures of James Fenimore Cooper's Natty Bumpo, the legends of Davey Crocket and Daniel Boone, and later the hard-boiled characters of Hemingway and 1940s U.S. cinema noir. One study of how the rhetorical power of this emblem was harnessed by the Popular Democratic Party in the 1940s is: Nathaniel J. Cordova, "In His Image and Likeness: The Puerto Rican Jíbaro as Political Icon" *Centro* 7.2 (Fall 2005):171–191.

4. Elsewhere I complicate the term "Nuyorican," arguing that while the protest ethos of the Nuyorican school continues, particularly in spoken word performance, contemporary literature of the diaspora also departs from that tradition in the 1980s and 1990s, which I provisionally call post-Nuyorican (Maritza Stanchich, "Towards a Post-Nuyorican Literature." *Sargasso: The Floating Homeland/La Patria Flotante.* University of Puerto Rico. II [2005–2006]: 113–124). In addition, the characterization of Colón as "proto-Nuyorican" (e.g., in Frances Aparicio "From Ethnicity to Multiculturalism: An

Historical Overview of Puerto Rican Literature in the United States."
Handbook of Hispanic Cultures in the United States: Literature and Art. Ed.
Francisco Lomelí. Houston, TX: Arte Público Press, 1993. 19–39) is further
treated by David Vázquez's dissertation of how authors such as Colón represent early stages of insurgent U.S. Latino cultural nationalism (2004) and in a
recent essay showing how in particular Colón anticipates the militant cultural
nationalism of the 1960s Puerto Rican protest era in the United States (2009).

5. I thank Jesús Colón's niece, Olimpia Colón Aponte, who accepted the award on
her uncle's behalf at the invitation of the Schomburg Center for Black Culture,
for bringing this to my attention. Importantly, Olimpia Colón Aponte also
brought to my attention and produced documentation (Ellis Island passenger
record and *SS Carolina* ship manifest), that Jesús Colón did not arrive in New
York as a stowaway, as his first-person narrative, archived personal corre-
spondence and much subsequent scholarship has stated. According to Colón's
niece, it was Ramon Colón, his cousin and brother in-law, who arrived as a
stowaway. She also points out other semi-autobiographical moments in his
publications. Hence, in this essay I refer to first-person narrators rather than
assume strict autobiographical terms. Of course this opens up other considerations beyond my domain here (though David Vázquez's work also explores
the tensions between elements of *testimonio* and political autobiography in
Colón's *oeuvre*). I thank Prof. Colón Aponte for visiting our class, and for
fielding further questions from me later. I would also like to credit graduate
student Joshua King for inviting Prof. Colón Aponte to our class.

6. This history publication is usefully noted in the bibliography of the Edna
Acosta-Belén and Virginia Sánchez Korrol edited collection *The Way It Was
and Other Writings* (1993).

7. Mignolo uses this term following the Peruvian sociologist Anibal Quijano.
Ramón Grosfoguel also applies it in *Colonial Subjects: Puerto Ricans in a
Global Perspective* (Berkeley: University of California Press, 2003).

8. Blanco further compares slavery's abolition in both countries, juxtaposing
the U.S. Civil War with a paternalistically benevolent voluntary abolition
in Puerto Rico. Or as Díaz Quiñones comments, Blanco turns the story of
slavery into the story of abolition (41) and occludes the influence of the U.S.
abolitionist movement on Spanish abolitionism (51). In acknowledging the
existence of social barriers, he scapegoats women for perpetuating the attitudes of "marrying up" and posits *mulatas,* a common trope again repeated
here, as the accessible, exoticized site of class and racial mixing (130). At
least Blanco closes with a final footnote acknowledging that binaries may
not allow for exploration of the contradictions in between.

9. Anthropologist Arlene Torres concurs with Díaz Quiñones that the *mestizaje*
of the *gran familia* ideology at first promotes social integration, while still
hyperprivileging those recognized as phenotypically of European descent, in
"La Gran Familia Puertorriqueña 'Es Prieta De Belda,'" *Blackness in Latin
America and the Caribbean: Social Dynamics and Cultural Transformations.*
Vol. 2. Eds. Arlene Torres and Norman E. Whiten, Jr. (Bloomington: Indiana
University Press, 1998. 285–306).

10. The late Francisco Arrivi's well-known play *Vejigantes* performs a similar
move in depicting three generations of women in a family in which the

youngest, aptly named Clarita, whose name may signify whiteness but ends up suggesting mental clarity, becomes conscious of and confronts the internal racism that keeps her grandmother hidden by her mother. The action is precipitated by a government-sponsored *bomba* recording that Clarita brings home, and which her mother objects to, implying the role official cultural nationalism plays in ameliorating past erasures. The conflict over racist practices and discourses culminates with Clarita being courted by Bill (as in dollar?) from Alabama, whose segregationist ideology serves to highlight Puerto Rico's difference and relative corrective benevolence, with Clarita ultimately rejecting his proposals as resolution in the play. See also Jessica Adams' reading in *Just Below South: Intercultural Performance in the Caribbean and the U.S. South*, eds. Jessica Adams, Michael P. Bibler, and Cécile Accilien (University of Virginia Press 2007).

11. Delgado notes that for the second edition of *A Puerto Rican in New York* (republished in 1982), Colón "changed 'Negro' to 'black,' and 'American Negro,' to 'African American,' and suggested that his essay titled 'Puerto Rican Poet, Pachín Marín' be changed to 'Puerto Rican Black Poet, Pachín Marín' " (84). This reinforces my observation that here Colón is acutely aware of racial and poetic contexts in both locations.

12. I deduce this date from a reference later in the document to the baseball icon Jackie Robinson.

13. A helpful overview is Juan A. Giusti Cordero's "AfroPuerto Rican Cultural Studies: Beyond *cultura negroide* and antillanismo." *Centro Journal of the Center for Puerto Rican Studies*. (Vol. 8. 1&2 [1996]: 56–77).

14. Though the chief difference was in the "other race" category new to the 2000 Census, on the island nearly 10 percent identified as black, while stateside nearly 8 percent did.

15. As suggested by David Vázquez (2004, 21) and by historian Edgardo Pratt during a talk at "Foro didáctico cultural al rescate de un patriota...Arturo Alfonso Schomburg," a conference held January 24, 2008, at Centro de Estudios Avanzados de Puerto Rico y El Caribe in San Juan, as well as more strongly noted by Winston James (1996, f102).

Works Cited

Blanco, Tomás. *El Prejuicio Racial en Puerto Rico*. 1942. Rio Piedras, PR: Ediciones Huracán, 1985.

Chow, Rey. "In the Name of Comparative Literature." *Comparative Literature in the Age of Multiculturalism*. Ed. Charles Bernheimer. Baltimore: Johns Hopkins University Press, 1995. 107–116.

Colón, Jesús. *The Way It Was and Other Writings*. Eds. Edna Acosta-Belén, and Virginia Sánchez Korrol. Houston: Arte Público Press, 1993.

———. *A Puerto Rican in New York and Other Sketches*. 1961. New York: International, 1982.

———. *"Lo que el pueblo me dice..."* Crónicas de la colonia puertorriqueña en Nueva York. Ed. Edwin Karli Padilla Aponte. Houston: Arte Público, 2001.

Colón, Jesús. "Random Notes on Negro-PR Unity in the United States." Unpublished ts. Box 9, Folder 14. Jesús Colón papers. Centro de Estudios Puertorriqueños, New York.

———. "The Negro in Puerto Rican History." Unpublished ts. Box 12, Folder 12. Jesús Colón papers. Centro de Estudios Puertorriqueños, New York.

Colón, Jesús papers, Archives of the Puerto Rican Diaspora, Centro de Estudios *Puertorriqueños*, Hunter College, CUNY.

Cólon López, Joaquín. *Pioneros puertorriqueños en Nueva York: 1917–1947.* Houston: Arte Público Press, 2002.

Delgado, Linda C. "Jesús Colón and the Making of a New York City Community, 1917 to 1974." *The Puerto Rican Diaspora: Historical Perspectives.* Eds. Carmen Teresa Whalen and Víctor Vázquez-Hernández. Philadelphia: Temple University Press, 2005. 68–87.

Díaz Quiñones, Arcadio. Introduction. "Tomas Blanco: Racismo, Historia, Esclavitud." *El prejuicio racial en Puerto Rico.* 3rd ed. Rio Piedras, PR: Ediciones Huracán, 1985.

Duany, Jorge. *The Puerto Rican Nation on the Move: Identities on the Island and in the United States.* Chapel Hill, NC, and London: University of North Carolina Press, 2002.

Flores, Juan. "En torno a The Puerto Rican Nation on the Move." *Diálogo.* May (2003): 42.

Godreau, Isar P. "Slippery Semantics: Race Talk and Everyday Uses of Racial Terminology in Puerto Rico." *Centro Journal of the Center for Puerto Rican Studies.* 20.2 (Fall 2008): 5–33.

González, José Luis. *El País de Cuatro Pisos y Otros Ensayos.* 1980. Rio Piedras, P.R.: Ediciones Huracán, 1989.

Holton, Adalaine. *The Practices of Black Radical Print.* Ph.D. Diss. University of California, Santa Cruz. 2005.

James, Winston. "Afro-Puerto Rican Radicalism in the United States: Reflections on the Political Trajectories of Arturo Schomburgh and Jesús Colón." *Centro Journal of the Center of Puerto Rican Studies.* 8.1&2(1996) 92–127.

———. *Holding Aloft the Banner of Ethiopia.* New York: Verso, 1998.

Janer, Zilkia. *Puerto Rican Nation-Building Literature: Impossible Romance.* Gainesville, FL: University Press of Florida, 2005.

Márquez, Roberto. "Raza, Racismo, e Historia: 'Are All My Bones From There?' " *Latino(a) Research Review.* Winter 2000. 8–23.

Mignolo, Walter. *Local Histories/Global Designs: Coloniality, Subaltern Knowledges, and Border Thinking.* Princeton, NJ: Princeton University Press, 2000.

Muñoz Marín, Luis. "Mensaje XII: Martes, 19 de enero 1960." *Mensajes al pueblo puertorriqueño, pronuciados ante las cámaras legislativas 1949–64.* San Juan: Universidad Interamericana de Puerto Rico, 1980. 224–255.

———. "A Good Civilization, January 19, 1960." *Borinquen: An Anthology of Puerto Rican Literature.* Eds. María Teresa Babín and Stan Steiner. New York: Vintage, 1974. 200–228.

Palés Matos, Luis. *Tuntún de pasa y grifería.* 1937. San Juan, PR: Editorial del Instituto de Cultura Puertorriqueña, 1993.

Rivera-Batiz, Francisco. "Color in the Tropics: Race and Economic Outcomes in the Island of Puerto Rico." New York: Russell Sage Foundation, 2004.

Rodríguez, Victor M. *Latino Politics in the United States: Race, Ethnicity, Class, and Gender in the Mexican American and Puerto Rican Experience.* Dubuque, Iowa: Kendall/Hunt, 2005.

Vázquez, David J. "Jesús Colón and the Development of Insurgent Concsiousness." *Centro: Journal of the Center of Puerto Rican Studies.* XXI.1(Spring 2009) 78–99.

———. Representing the Self, Re-presenting the Nation: Nations, Nationalism, and the Latino/a Personal Narrative. Ph.D. Diss. University of California, Santa Barbara. June 2004.

Coloniality of Diasporas: Racialization of Negropolitans and Nuyoricans in Paris and New York

Yolanda Martínez-San Miguel

11.1   The Limits of Postcolonialism

Many of the countries of the Caribbean—such as Jamaica, Puerto Rico, Martinique, or the Dominican Republic—have large immigrant communities in a metropolitan country, such as Great Britain, the United States, France, or Spain, with which they had or still have colonial/imperial relationships. Given the significance of population displacements between colonies and metropoles for the production of foundational texts for postcolonial studies (such as the works of Frantz Fanon and Aimé Césaire), and given that in the United States the marginal status of some racial and ethnic minorities—like African Americans or Mexican Americans—has often been defined as an instance of "internal colonialism" (see Blauner; Carmichael and Hamilton; Cruse; Barrera, Muñoz, and Ornelas), the particular situation of colonial migrants merits further exploration to place the experiences of people of color in the United States within a broader context linking migratory and colonial/postcolonial perspectives.

But colonialism is a tricky term when we refer to the Caribbean. This region includes states that became independent between 1804 and 1983, colonies, incorporated territories, a few British and American "commonwealths," associated states, departments of France, and other overseas territories.[1] The wide variety of colonial, postcolonial, and neocolonial arrangements, as well as the existence of sustained migration flows from the Caribbean to North America and Western Europe, allows for a suitable comparative framework within a relatively small region to revisit the validity of the colonial and postcolonial debate.

Martinique and Puerto Rico share three major characteristics that will be the focus of my study. First, they currently have an active political relationship with their former/actual metropole enacted in the departmentalization of Martinique and Guadeloupe in 1946 and the creation of the *Estado Libre Asociado de Puerto Rico* in 1952. Second, they both have had a significant and institutionalized migratory relationship with their metropolitan counterparts through the BUMIDOM and the *División de la Migración*.[2] This is an interesting case within this region, since even though other countries—such as Jamaica or the Dominican Republic—have immigrant enclaves in countries with which they still have or had colonial/imperial ties, like the United Kingdom or Spain, most of them did not have an office to handle massive migrations to the metropole. Finally, in the two cases examined in this essay, the consistent exchange of populations between the island of origin and the continental territory of the metropole has produced a long-standing debate on the limits of the decolonization process from metropolitan societies. In both cases, Puerto Ricans and Martinicans migrate to the United States and France as citizens of the receiving country, yet they cross racial and cultural boundaries that make their experiences similar to other ethnic minorities and immigrant populations in metropolitan centers.[3] In this essay I use the term *intracolonial migrations* to refer to population displacements taking place between countries that have or had a colonial relationship that has not been resolved through the establishment of a sovereign state.[4]

I am interested in exploring the link between racism and colonialism, to study the textualization of a process of *racialization* of colonial subjects who become problematic members of the metropolitan societies to which they are migrating.[5] Robert Young summarizes some of the complexities of the intersection between colonial and imperial racial discourses:

> The ideology of race, a semiotic system in the guise of ethnology, "the science of races," from the 1840s onwards necessarily worked according to a doubled logic, according to which it both enforced and policed the differences between the whites and the non-whites, but at the same time focused fetishistically upon the product of the contacts between them. Colonialism was always locked into the machine of desire...(180–181)

Both nationalism and colonialism have been studied by focusing on how ethnoracial categories define political interaction in each one of these systems. Balibar's illuminating reflection on the nation as a fictive ethnicity is an excellent example of these studies (96). My thesis is that coloniality further complicates the conceptualization of ethnic identities in a post-colonial era, by producing subjects who are legal citizens, but who in fact function as marginalized and racialized ethnic minorities in the metropolitan centers of Western Europe and North America.[6] Thus, my work focuses on racialization, as a process that signals and emphasizes the differences between the ways in which ethnoracial identities are conceived in Caribbean societies that are supposedly postcolonial, and how they are imagined in their metropolitan counterparts, revealing the aporias of the modern state discourse in which the notion of citizenship is based.

I study two experiences of intracolonial diaspora, to analyze the process of visibilization of these subjectivities that are simultaneously included and excluded from metropolitan societies. I refer to two foundational texts for Francophone and Latino studies: *Peau noire, masques blancs* [*Black Skin, White Masks*][7] (1952) by Frantz Fanon and *Down These Mean Streets* (1967) by Piri Thomas. My analysis expands an important line of reading proposed by Arnaldo Cruz-Malavé, who establishes a dialogue between Fanon and Thomas, taking as a point of departure the intersections between masculinity and abjection through which both texts construct a Caribbean, diasporic, and black identity (330–335). My reading focuses, nonetheless, on how the process of racialization contributes to the articulation of a narrative about the constitution of subjectivities that are supposedly postcolonial, although they still function as colonized ethnoracial minorities within metropolitan societies. In both cases, it is important to note that these texts were produced after 1946 and 1952, key historical dates in the process of decolonization of these two countries. I am interested in developing further the provocative link established by Robert Young between desire and colonialism, to propose a reading that will focus on two fundamental strategies: (1) the visibilization of the racialization process as a foundational moment for the identity and narrative processes developed in these texts; and (2) the synthesis of this process of identification and disidentification of the colonial subject that is allegorized through a tense dialogue with metropolitan discourses, depicted as paternal and maternal interpellations.

11.2   Narrating Race: Nuyoricans and Negropolitans[8]

Both the Hispanic and the French Caribbean have produced a diversity of local notions and discourses to describe the formation and consolidation of their official cultures taking as a point of departure experiences of displacement, mixture, and hybridity.[9] In the French Caribbean, for example, the cultural movement of *créolité* refers to a hybrid identity that should not be confused with the Hispanic concept of *criollismo*.[10] At the same time, the aesthetic and ideological projects of *négritude* in the French colonies and *negrismo* in the Hispanic Caribbean complicate Paul Gilroy's argument in his book *The Black Atlantic*, by proposing two particular inflections of the Africanist debate in the insular Caribbean.[11] In the Hispanic Caribbean, on the other hand, terms such as *mestizaje*, *mulataje*, and *hispanismo* have functioned as metaphors that compete for the production of a Latin American and Caribbean discourse that has not become fully assimilated to what we currently define as Latin American and U.S. identities.[12] In both cases we find a dynamic coexistence of multiple modes of identification, in which Caribbean, Latin American, African, American, and Euro-American identity discourses interact and alternate. These ethnoracial discourses are already complex, but they become redefined by diasporic experiences, producing new categories, such as *Nuyorican* and *Negropolitan*, or even more recent terms such as African diaspora and *Latinidad*. It is precisely in this particular context that in this essay I would like to comment on a series of key scenes and subplots of *Black Skin, White Masks* and *Down These Mean Streets*, to analyze the centrality of migration to the metropole in the redefinition and deconstruction of ethnoracial subjectivities that live in metropolitan societies as second-class citizens.

Frantz Fanon (1925–1961) was born in Martinique and he met Aimé Césaire when he was a student in Fort-de-France. He was a French soldier during the Second World War, and returned to Martinique after he was injured in battle in 1944. After a short stay in his native island—during which he collaborated with the political campaign of his friend and mentor Césaire—Fanon left Martinique to study psychiatry in France. While practicing as a psychiatrist in France and Algeria, he deepened his political commitment with the struggle against French colonialism. *L'An Cinq, de la Révolution Algérienne* (1959) and *Les Damnés de la Terre* (1961) were two important texts he produced during the war between France and Algeria (1954–1962). In 1956, Fanon severed all his ties with the French government and became a member of the National Liberation Front; he participated actively in the struggle to free Algeria from French control. Fanon continued his political work until his death in 1961, a year before the independence of Algeria was achieved.[13]

Although most of his political, professional, and intellectual career took place in North Africa, Fanon's first book was written in France and was devoted to his experience as a Martinican in France. Patrick Williams insists on the Caribbeanness of *Black Skin, White Masks* (1952), and notes that in many of the postcolonial reappropriations of his work, the Francophone Caribbean background of this text is displaced by the importance assigned to Fanon's African experience (54–55).[14] This universalization and decontextualization of Fanon's work is surprising, especially if we take into account the clear definition of his locus of enunciation in the "Introduction" to his book: "Since I was born in the Antilles, my observations and my conclusions are valid only for the Antilles—at least concerning man at home" (14).[15] Throughout the book Fanon insists on the experience of men from the French Antilles (for another example, see his argumentation on pages 18–26).

Therefore, the now classical scene of the fifth chapter entitled "The Fact of Blackness," which narrates the process through which the narrator becomes a black man when a child sees him in the train, has a very particular context that is relevant for the reflection we are proposing here: this train is running in France, and the black man is a Martinican living in France as a French citizen. Thus, Fanon's text is not only about the rejection of the black man by the white world, but it is also a complex interrogation of the survival of colonial structures in supposedly *postcolonial* contexts:

> In the Antilles there was also that little gulf that exists among the almost-white, the mulatto, and the nigger. But I was satisfied with an intellectual understanding of these differences. It was not really dramatic. And then...
>
> And then the occasion arose when I had to meet the white man's eyes. An unfamiliar weight burdened me. The real world challenged my claims. In the white world the man of color encounters difficulties in the development of his bodily schema. Consciousness of the body is solely a negating activity. It is a third–person consciousness. The body is surrounded by an atmosphere of certain uncertainty. (110–111)

Fanon's description of the rearticulation of racial categories outside the French Antillean space—or his reflection about the process of racialization of a Martinican as a black man in France—produces a series of crucial interrogations. For example, the model of a Cartesian subject is undone by this scene of a body surrounded by an "atmosphere of certain uncertainty." The stability of what Balibar identifies as the "fictive ethnicity" is questioned when colonial/imperial conceptualizations of identity are produced as a result of the diasporic experience of a Caribbean subject that already confronts his origins as a problematic notion. This uncomfortable relationship with origins is a consequence of the fact that Antillean societies were constituted through a multiplicity of Asian, African, and European displacements (Hall, "Cultural Identity" 223–225; "Negotiating..." 4–8). This scene culminates with the recreation of colonial stereotypes as the iconic moment of acknowledgment and disavowal of difference, which, according to Homi Bhabha, "produces the colonized as a social reality which is at once an 'other' and yet entirely knowable and visible" (70–71). Nonetheless, what serves as a powerful background of this scene is the paradoxical situation of the *intracolonial migrations* produced by modern processes of decoloniza-tion. Recovering Fanon's Antillean and intracolonial locus of enunciation is crucial in order to perceive the complexity of the internal otherness described in this text:

> Where am I to be classified? Or, if you prefer, tucked away?
> "A Martinican, a native of 'our' old colonies."
> Where shall I hide?
> "Look at the nigger!...Mama, a Negro! Hell, he's getting mad....
> Take no notice, sir, he does not know that you are as civilized as we..."
> My body is given back to me sprawled out, distorted, recolored, clad in mourning in that white winter day. The Negro is an animal, the Negro is bad, the Negro is mean, the Negro is ugly; look, a nigger, it's cold, the nigger is shivering, the nigger is shivering because he is cold, the little boy is trembling because he is afraid of the nigger, the nigger is shivering with cold, that cold that goes through your bones, the handsome little boy is trembling because he thinks that the nig-ger is quivering with rage, the little white boy throws himself into his mother's arms: Mama, the nigger's going to eat me up. (113–114).

Recognition and misrecognition within the legal boundaries of French citizenship and coloniality—that is the central narrative of Fanon's book when we revitalize the Antillean dimension of his work. The narrative voice becomes unreadable/unintelligible (Butler 17) in the metropolitan context of this scene: the speaking subject is not white, but he is not only black; he is a French citizen, but he is Martinican too.[16] This is a subjectiv-ity that is simultaneously national and colonial, central and marginal, vis-ible and completely invisible, within the discursive matrix of a modernity that underlies national and postcolonial teleologies. This primary scene of Fanon's book illustrates the failure of the illusion of integration distinc-tive of French colonial policies, since even though departmentalization presupposes the complete juridical annexation of Martinique to France, this black subject that speaks in *Black Skin, White Masks* does not feel protected by the legal guarantees of citizenship because his racialization as a black man contradicts his condition as a citizen.

A similar motive is developed by Piri Thomas in his novel *Down These Mean Streets* (*DTMS*) (1967). This text explores the most intimate and subtle contradictions produced by the process of racialization through the narration of the tense and hostile relationship between the protago-nist of this novel, who conceives himself as a black man, and his father, who defends his Hispanic and Caribbean identity. John Peter Thomas, the author of this novel, was born in New York City in 1928; he is the son of a man who "left Cuba at the age 16 and worked his way to Puerto Rico on a small boat" (Hernández 173) and a Puerto Rican woman. His parents did not meet in Puerto Rico; they met in New York City, after Piri's father arrived in the United States on board the *SS Marine Tiger*, and once his mother moved with her older sister from the island of Puerto Rico to the island of Manhattan. Therefore, Piri was raised as a member of a translocal family, and this displacement between the Caribbean and the United States is represented through the relationship that this Puerto Rican child established with his parents as first-generation immigrants. It is interesting to note, nonetheless, that in the novel Thomas simplifies his family romance, since the narrator's fictional parents are both Puerto Ricans, although their marriage is an interracial one. Thomas' novel narrates his childhood and adolescence in Spanish Harlem (also known as "El Barrio"), in an Italian section of East Harlem, and finally in Babylon, Long Island. Contrary to Fanon, who became a psychiatrist, Piri begins to write from prison, after being convicted of armed robbery and felonious assault in a holdup in Greenwich Village.[17]

DTMS functions as a foundational narrative, both in terms of the autobiographical/*Bildungsroman* genre used to portray the experiences of a younger Piri (a topic studied by Cruz-Malavé, "Teaching," and Sánchez González), but also for the intriguing exploration of the invisibility of ethnic identities in a nation mythically imagined as a "melting pot." The foundational experience in Piri's case takes place when he goes to a job interview with a white Puerto Rican friend and realizes that he does not get an offer because he is considered a black man (103). This chapter, entitled "How to Be a Negro Without Really Trying," signals Piri's reconceptualization of his identity as a result of how he is seen in the metropolitan society. The chapter opens with a Piri who is not used to thinking in ethnoracial terms, and closes with the protagonist's realization that he has ceased to be a Puerto Rican to become an American "negro" (104). This topic becomes a central motive of the novel, and the text insists on the complexity of this process of racialization even in the title of some chapters—such as "Hung up Between Two Sticks" and "Brothers Under the Skin"—and sections of the novel, like "Down South."

As I mentioned before, the racial/ethnic question is explored in the novel through a very hostile and painful argument between the protagonist, Piri (who is struggling with binary notions of race and ethnicity in the United States and defines himself as black), and his father (who embraces an Antillean identity and rejects being conflated with African Americans):[18]

> "Son," Poppa, said, "there's a lot of things I'm right in and there's a lot of things you don't understand just yet. Maybe you see something in me I haven't seen yet, or maybe won't admit yet. I don't like feeling to

be a black man. Can you understand it's a pride to me being a Puerto Rican?"

"What kind, Poppa, black or white?" I didn't want to get mad, but couldn't help myself. I was trying to blame somebody for something that was hurting me, and I couldn't say it in words without getting mad. (150–151)[19]

Throughout the novel, Piri explores the invisibility of Puerto Ricans within the bipolar racial grid of the United States. As a mulatto, Piri feels *out of place* within his racially mixed family, and he goes to the South with his black friend Brew in search of a sense of belonging in U.S. society.[20]

A very powerful scene of the novel takes place when Piri arrives in Texas, tired of the "two-tone South" (186), and just after Brew disappears from the plot and the protagonist's life. In Texas, Piri experiences another inflection of the U.S. racial discourse, directly related to the presence of Mexicans as a third element unsettling the bipolar grid of racial identity. In this new context, Piri uses his Puerto Rican identity to pass as Hispanic and to have sex with a white prostitute:

Then I stepped in front of the mirror and put my jacket on. The broad was still on the bed, wondering if I was going to make her again. When I walked to the door, she smiled and said in broken Texas Spanish, did I like it and did I want more? I opened the door and said, "Baby, I just want you to know"—and I watched her smile fall off and a look of horror fill the empty space it left—"I just want you to know," I repeated, "that you just got fucked by a nigger, *by a black man!*" And I didn't wait to hear her gasp or to watch her jump out of that bed. I ran, I disappeared, because I learned a long time ago to hit and run right back to your turf...(189)

I would like to comment on the mirroring effect of this scene. Piri looks at his own reflection in the mirror, but he does not recognize himself until the look of horror of the prostitute locates him in his paradoxical place as a black Puerto Rican trying to find himself within the desiring/repulsive racial imaginary of the United States. The resemblance between this scene and Fanon's scene in the train is unsettling. What is particularly striking here is that Piri occupies his Puerto Rican/Antillean identity as a way to perform his blackness, and not to reclaim a different Boricua identity. Fanon, on the other hand, uses the visibility of his blackness to reflect on the contradictions of his colonial Antillean identity. At the end of the novel, Piri confirms his condition as a black Puerto Rican coming from a marginal *barrio*, living as a former drug addict and convict, who does not have any real hopes of becoming a member of mainstream of American society.

We should remember that this novel was written a few years after the U.S. Congress passed the Civil and Voting Rights Acts, eliminating legal racial segregation in educational institutions and restoring and securing the right to vote to the African American population.[21] Thus, Thomas' narrative interrogates the place of Puerto Ricans within the racial desegregation process in the United States, at the same time that it identifies the limits of these legal measures in the context of intracolonial migrations. Neither African American, nor Anglo American, nor a white Hispanic, Piri defines himself as an *unreadable* element within U.S. ethnic and racial minorities, and his works consistently resist a passive inscription within the tradition of Nuyorican or American ethnic minority discourses.[22]

11.3   Aporias of the *madre-patria* [Mother-Fatherland]

I would like to come back to two scenes that I have already analyzed in this essay to add another layer to my reading. The first one is Fanon's primary scene as a racialized subject in a Parisian train. In this case, the Antillean subject is racialized by the French child, who seeks refuge in his mother's arms to escape from the threatening corporality of the black man. The child's enunciation locates and fixes the Antillean subject in a racial condition that is foreign to Fanon. The mother intervenes in the scene to apologize for the child's behavior: "Take no notice, sir, he does not know that you are as civilized as we..." (113). This statement completes the scene, with the white mother reintroducing the Franco-Antillean identity into the French political and social signifying matrixes. The maternal intervention broadens and makes impossible the process of subjectivation of the Martinican as French when the metropolitan voice affirms that civilization is not conceived in the same way as race.

In Piri's case, the entire novel is produced through this tense dialogue with the father, a conversation that sometimes implies the invisibilization of the black child within Puerto Rican, Caribbean, and Antillean ethnoracial discourses represented through the father's voice. The novel begins, precisely, with an epigraph that signals this central dislocation with the paternal figure: "Pops, how come me and you is always on the outs?"(1). Piri frequently insists on his uncomfortable and distant interactions with his father, representing the paternal figure as a close relationship that promotes his sensation of being an outsider in his family circle because he is the darkest among his siblings. The argument between Piri and his father that I quoted in the previous section takes place in a chapter entitled "Funeral for a Prodigal Son," and after arguing with his father Piri abandons his home and goes to the south of the United States to explore his black identity. Once more, Piri feels singled out within his family and he only becomes visible when he assumes a black identity that distances him from his possible identification as an Antillean and Puerto Rican. His father constantly reminds him of his Antillean—and even Indian—condition in an effort to remove him from his black identification, but Piri cannot deny the visibility of his own blackness and how this racial condition dislocates his incorporation into his familiar context.

In both cases, the paterno-filial interpellation reinscribes the subject in a series of identity coordinates that complicate his inscription within a metropolitan context by insisting on the representation of Antillean identity as an excess. Antilleanity displaces blackness, in a gesture similar to the one developed in the *negrista* poetry written by Luis Palés Matos or Nicolás Guillén or the *antillanité* poetic developed by Glissant, but it cannot displace the prevalence of racial visibilization in the ways this Caribbean subject is identified within the metropolitan society, or within the domestic space of his translocal family. This allegorical representation of diaspora, entrance, and residency in the *madre-patria*—in Spanish literally meaning the mother-fatherland—defines the Antillean subject by producing a series of identity discourses through the axes of citizenship and metropolitanism that collide with insular and Caribbean discourses on identity. Therefore, for Fanon and Thomas, blackness becomes a metropolitan *discovery*, or a primary scene visibilizing the not-so-subtle links between colonialism and racism.

Fanon's and Thomas' texts depict the effects of the coloniality of diasporas just after the culmination of key decolonization processes in Martinique and Puerto Rico. Both writers assume a black identity as part of a racialization process of colonial citizens to reaffirm their vulnerable incorporation into the metropolitan societies that acknowledge Nuyoricans and Negropolitans only as second-class citizens. They also explore the unintelligibility of Antillean blackness within the limits of the notions of legality and citizenship of metropolitan societies. Even after a complete assimilation (in the case of Martinique's incorporation into France), or after the establishment of a semi-autonomous government (in the case of Puerto Rico), Puerto Ricans residing in the United States are still considered Nuyoricans, and Martinicans in France are still Negropolitans, intimate strangers within both metropolitan and Caribbean spaces.

Thomas and Fanon also explore the unintelligibility of their identities within the colonial/imperial logic that engendered them as racialized subjects, or as impossible juridical subjects. Their narratives subvert the value of citizenship as a crucial step for the constitution of subjects who belong legally to the metropolitan society, but not to its national imaginary. This situation reminds us of the famous legal oxymoron, "foreign in a domestic sense," used to refer to Puerto Rico and other unincorporated territories of the United States.[23] The maternal and paternal function in these narratives as a metaphor for the dyad metropole-nation, which is represented in a relation dominated by an internal tension that produces the racial asymmetries depicted and embodied by the two protagonists of these texts.

For the contemporary reader, on the other hand, Thomas and Fanon pose a question about how colonial citizenship and racialization become insurmountable obstacles for the globalizing fantasies constructed by avoiding the realities of a body stigmatized as black, and by erasing the legacies of colonialism in the configuration of transnational and post-colonial societies in the present time (Hall, "Cultural Identity..." 230–231). Even though nationalism is still anchored to fixed notions of racial and ethnic identity (Balibar 96), coloniality of diaspora complicates even more our current conception of ethnic identities by creating citizens who remain marginalized in the supposedly post-minoritarian societies of Western Europe and North America.

In these two cases, however, racialization locates the individual outside hegemonic identity discourses—metropolitan as well as Antillean—and outside legality itself, even though these subjects are citizens of the metropolitan societies. In Thomas' case, his *out of placeness* takes him to prison, drug abuse, and a criminal status. Fanon, on the other hand, breaks out of the metropolitan logic through his participation in the anticolonial struggle in Algeria. Caribbean nationalism was clearly not the answer for any of them. Their texts can be read as narratives about the limits of an incomplete postcoloniality that interrupts the master-narrative of a global, post-minoritarian, and postracial society, interrogating a metropolitan fantasy that crumbles beneath the undeniable embodiment of otherness depicted by these Antillean narrators.

Notes

This essay is part of a collaborative project with Jorge Duany (University of Puerto Rico) and Justin Daniel (Université des Antilles et de la Guyane) that compares the political and migratory history of Martinique and Puerto Rico to study the colonial circuits of Caribbean diasporas. Our work is part of a broader research initiative, entitled *Collaborative Writing on Translocal Flows in the Americas*, and designed by Marcial Godoy-Anativia. Our research group met in Bellagio in October 2004 and in Martinique in March 2005, with financial support from the Rockefeller Foundation, the Social Science Research Council, and the *Centre de Recherche sur les Pouvoirs Locaux dans la Caraïbe*.

1. A summary of the political status of the islands in the Caribbean can be seen in the following link: http://www.firstam.com/title-caribbean/2740.html.
2. BUMIDOM refers to the "Bureau pour le développement des migrations intéressant les Departments d'Outre Mer," an office that coordinated the

migration between France and its overseas departments between 1963 and 1981. Approximately 33,000 persons migrated between the French Caribbean and France as part of this program. In 1982, another office was created to handle this migration, the "Agence nationale pour l'insertion et la promotion des travailleurs d'outre-mer." For more information see Monique Milia's doctoral dissertation. In the case of Puerto Rico, there was also an "Information and Documentation Office for Puerto Ricans in New York" (1930–1941) that changed its name to "Identification Service of the Department of Agriculture and Commerce" in 1942. Later, the island's Labor Department opened the "Bureau of Employment and Migration" (1948–1951), which subsequently became the "Division of Migration" (1951–1988) and the "Department of Puerto Rican Community Affairs" (1989–). For more information see Jorge Duany, *The Puerto Rican Nation on the Move*, 166–184.

3. Other scholars who have compared Martinique and Puerto Rico in historical and political terms, are Ramón Grosfoguel, Monique Milia, Justin Daniel, and Edgardo Rodríguez Juliá.

4. On the debate about diaspora, identity, and citizenship in the Caribbean, see two essays by Stuart Hall, "Cultural Identity and Diaspora" and "Negotiating Caribbean Identities."

5. Racialization refers to "the extension of racial meaning to a previously racially unclassified relationship, social practice, or group" (Winant 59) and is a term coined by Michael Omi and Howard Winant in their book *Racial Formation in the United States*. According to Jorge Duany, "[racialization] involves imputing a hereditary origin to certain intellectual, emotional, or behavioral characteristics of an individual based on group membership" (535). Ana Yolanda Ramos links racialization to Puerto Rican and Latino studies in her books *National Performances*, and *Latino Crossings* (co-authored with De Genova). Duany has done an excellent critical review of the racialization process of Latinos in the United States in his essays "Ethnicity, Color, and Class among Dominicans in the United States and Puerto Rico" and "Race and Racialization among U.S. Latinos." He generously helped me to incorporate this notion into this essay.

6. I use Aníbal Quijano's notion of the "coloniality of power" as a point of departure for the theoretical framework proposed here. According to Quijano, the independence of Latin American countries was not simultaneously a decolonizing process because the white Creole elite did not share a common social and political project with the colonized and exploited *mestizo*, African-descendent, and indigenous workers. I develop this theoretical link in more detail in my essay entitled "Colonialidad de la diáspora: Puerto Rico y Martinica."

7. I am quoting from the English edition of the text published by Grove Weidenfeld and translated by Charles Lam Markmann.

8. In Puerto Rico, the first wave of emigrants were called Nuyoricans. This term was used to refer to the massive migration of Puerto Ricans to the United States that took place during the 1940s and 1950s, most of whom established their residency in New York City. More recently, this term has been replaced by "neorriqueño," Diasporican, or simply Rican, since Puerto Ricans now live in many U.S. cities besides New York. Negropolitans, on the other hand, is the term used in Martinique to refer to Martinicans

who have lived in France and who return to the Caribbean. Deborah Pacini Hernández made me aware of the fact that this second term may generally refer to diasporic colonial subjects in the French context, since the same term is used for African immigrants in France. See the reference to Parisian negropolitans in *Three Kilos of Coffee. An Autobiography* by Manu Dibango. For more information, see *Negropolitains et Euro-Blacks* by Tony Delsham and Michel Giraud's article, "Racisme colonial, ethnicité et citoyenneté."

9. Shalini Puri and Silvio Torres-Saillant discuss the currency and limitations of postcolonial theory to study the Caribbean.

10. "Criollo" and "créole" do not have the exact same meaning in the Hispanic and French Caribbean. In the Hispanic Caribbean, "criollo" refers to Spaniards born and raised in the Americas, although the term was originally adopted to refer to the offspring of African slaves born in the New World, and was later extended to refer to Spaniards in this same situation (Mazzotti 11). Since the end of the seventeenth century, creoles became an intermediary sector that was struggling to legitimate a hegemonic condition in the Americas vis-à-vis the peninsular functionaries who were usually appointed to the positions with more power and higher rank. See Martínez-San Miguel (*Saberes*), Mazzotti, Ross, and Higgings. "Créole," on the other hand, refers to the syncretized cultures and local dialects produced in the English and French Caribbean, in the form of "creoles," "pidgins," and papiamentos, and which in both cases are constituted by the diverse African, Asian, and European elements transplanted to the Antilles to produce the unique cultures and identities that define the zone today. For more information, see *Eloge de la créolité* by Bernabé, Chamoiseau, and Confiant, as well as Vevé Clark and Eduoard Glissant's texts on this topic. The anthology *Créolité and Creolization* edited by Enwezor *et al.* explores the links between the Anglo, French, Dutch, and Hispanic Caribbean taking créolité as a point of departure.

11. "Négritude" was a notion coined by Césaire in 1935 in the third issue of the journal *L'Étudiant Noir*, and it refers to the political and cultural movement developed in Paris by the future president of Senegal, Léopold Sédar Senghor, the Martinican poet Césaire, and the Guyanese poet Léon Damas. This African and Caribbean movement proposed the constitution of a unified black identity that conceived the African diaspora as a point of departure to resist the inherent racism of French colonialism. The main objective of the "Négritude" movement was not independence from France, but to promote a struggle to achieve equality for black citizens within French society. This movement has important links with black internationalism, including points of contact with the Harlem Renaissance and the "negrista" movement in the Hispanic Caribbean. For more information on these historical links, as well as distinctions among the Harlem Renaissance, "négritude," and Hispanic "negrismo," see the studies published by Brent Edwards, Frank Guridy, and Jerome Branche. For more information about the links between the racial debate in Puerto Rico and the "criollo" imaginary, see Magaly Roy-Féquière's book.

12. On Latin American "mestizaje," the foundational texts are Vasconcelos's *La raza cósmica* (1925) and José Martí's "Nuestra América" (1891). "Mulataje"

is a term coined by Gabriela Mistral (Fiol-Matta 18) and revived by José Buscaglia-Salgado in his book *Undoing Empire* as a counterpoint to the discourse on "mestizaje," because in the Caribbean miscegenation is mostly imagined as taking place between European whites and African blacks, while in Mexico this same process usually refers to the offspring produced from interracial relationships between European whites and indigenous subjects. Recent studies on "mestizaje" that can be useful are Serge Gruzinski's *The Mestizo Mind* and Rafael Perez Torres's *Mestizaje: Critical Uses of Race in Chicano Culture*.

13. Among the studies on Fanon that I have found more useful, I would like to mention the essays compiled in *Frantz Fanon: Critical Perspectives*, Ed. Anthony C. Alessandrini; *Fanon: A Critical Reader*, edited by Gordon, Sharpley-Whiting; and White, David Macey's *Frantz Fanon: A Biography*, as well as Williams's "Frantz Fanon: The Routes of Writing."

14. It is interesting to note that in the study of Fanon we find a similar situation to the way in which a thinker like Arturo Schomburg has been transformed into a central figure for the African American tradition in the United States, usually at the expense of his Puerto Rican identity. For more information on this unequal appropriation of the Antillean dimensions of Schomburg's work, see Jossianna Arroyo and Lisa Sánchez.

15. Excerpts from *Black Skin, White Masks* by Frantz Fanon, copyright 1967 by Grove Press, Inc. Used by permission of Grove/Atlantic, Inc.

16. I am using here Judith Butler's notion of what is "culturally inteligible" as presented in her book *Gender Trouble*: "...the 'coherence' and 'continuity' of 'the person' are not logical or analytic features of personhood, but, rather, socially instituted and maintained norms of intelligibility" (17). Butler uses this term to refer to the social construction of gender, while Fanon and Thomas focus on the intelligibility of race in the racialization processes produced and promoted by intracolonial diasporas.

17. For more information about Piri Thomas, see his text entitled "A Neorican in Puerto Rico: or Coming Home," as well as his webpage http://www.cheverote.com/piri.html/.

18. Several studies address the interaction and exchange between African American and Puerto Rican cultures, such as the books by Juan Flores and Raquel Rivera, and studies on the Puerto Rican community in Chicago conducted by Ana Yolanda Ramos in *National Performances* and the special issue of *Centro Journal* devoted to Puerto Ricans in Chicago (Fall 2001, 13.2). Another special issue of the *Centro Journal* dedicated to the study of race also includes important essays on Puerto Ricans and their relationship with other ethnic minorities (Spring 1996, 8.1–2). Nicolás C. Vaca has explored the tensions between the two communities in *The Presumed Alliance*.

19. Excerpts from *Down These Mean Streets* by Piri Thomas, copyright 1967 by Piri Thomas. Copyright renewed 1995 and 1997 by Piri Thomas. Used by permission of Vintage Books, a division of Random House, Inc.

20. Piri did not have the possibility of conceiving himself as "brown," a notion that was commonly used in the 1990s, and that functions as that space of uncomfortable tension and conflict in Richard Rodríguez's autobiographical text *Brown*.

21. I am referring to the case of racial desegregation decided in the courts in Brown v. Board of Education 1951–1954, and the two acts passed by congress, the Civil Rights Act of 1964 and the Voting Rights Act of 1965. These legal decisions granted basic civil rights, making racial discrimination illegal. They were approved after almost a decade of protests and marches, such as the 1955–1956 Montgomery bus boycott, the student-led sit-ins of the 1960s, and the huge March in Washington in 1963.
22. Thomas rejects being classified as a Nuyorican writer and questions this classification that was created after the publication of his first novel in the following interviews Hernández, Binder, Pacifico, and Stavans.
23. For more information, see the anthology edited by Christina Duffy Burnett and Burke Marshall, entitled precisely *Foreign in a Domestic Sense*.

Works Cited

Alessandrini, Anthony C., ed. *Frantz Fanon: Critical Perspectives*. New York: Routledge, 1999.

Arroyo, Jossianna. "Technologies: Transculturations of Race, Gender and Ethnicity in Arturo Schomburg's Masonic Writings." *Centro Journal* 17.1 (Spring 2005): 5–25.

Balibar, Etienne. "The Nation Form: History and Ideology." *Race, Nation, Class: Ambiguous Identities*. Ed. Etienne Balibar and Immanuel Wallerstein. New York: Verso, 1993. 86–106.

Barrera, Mario, Carlos Muñoz, and Charles Ornelas. "The Barrio as Internal Colony." *Urban Affairs Annual Review* 6 (1972).

Bernabé, Jean, Patrick Chamoiseau, and Raphaël Confiant. *In Praise of Creoleness*. Trans. M.B. Taleb-Khyar. Paris: Gallimard, 1993.

Bhabha, Homi. *The Location of Culture*. London and New York: Routledge 1994.

Binder, Wolfgang. "An Interview with Piri Thomas." *Minority Voices* 4.1 (1980): 63–78.

Blauner, Bob. *Still the Big News. Racial Oppresion in America*. Philadelphia: Temple University Press, 2001.

Branche, Jerome C. *Colonialism and Race in Luso-Hispanic Literature*. Columbia, London: U of Missouri Press, 2006.

Burnett, Christina Duffy, and Burke Marshall, eds. *Foreign in a Domestic Sense: Puerto Rico, American Expansion, and the Constitution*. Durham, NC: Duke University Press, 2001.

Buscaglia Salgado, José. *Undoing Empire: Race and Nation in the Mulatto Caribbean*. Minneapolis: University of Minnesota Press, 2003.

Butler, Judith. *Gender Trouble*. New York: Routledge, 1990.

Carmichael, Stokely, and Charles Hamilton. *Black Power*. New York: Vintage, 1967.

Clark, VêVê A. "Developing Diaspora Literacy and Marasa Consciousness." *Comparative American Identities*. Ed. Hortense Spillers. New York: Routledge, 1991. 40–61.

Cruse, Harold. *Rebellion or Revolution*. New York: William Morrow, 1968.

Cruz-Malavé, Arnaldo. "Teaching Puerto Rican Authors: Identity and Modernization in Nuyorican Texts." *ADE Bulletin*. 91 (Winter 1988): 45–51.

———. "'What a tangled web...!': Masculinidad y abyección y la fundación de la literatura puertorriqueña en Estados Unidos." *Revista de crítica literaria latinoamericana*. 23.45 (1997): 327–340.

Daniel, Justin. "Identidad cultural e identidad política en Martinica y en Puerto Rico: Mitos y realidades." *Revista de Ciencias Sociales* 7 (Nueva Epoca, 1999): 33–65.

De Genova, Nicholas, and Ana Yolanda Ramos-Zayas. *Latino Crossings: Mexicans, Puerto Ricans and the Politics of Race and Citizenship*. New York: Routledge, 2003.

Delsham, Tony. *Negropolitains et Euro-Blacks*. Fort-de-France, Martinique: Editions M.G.G., 2000.

Dibango, Manu. (with Danielle Rouard). *Three Kilos of Coffee. An Autobiography*. Chicago and London: University of Chicago Press, 1989.

Duany, Jorge. "Ethnicity, Color, and Class among Dominicans in the United States and Puerto Rico." *Latin American Perspectives* 25.3 (1998): 147–172.

———. "Race and Racialization." *The Oxford Encyclopedia of Latinos and Latinas in the United States*. Ed. Suzane Oboler and Deena J. González. New York: Oxford University Press, 2005. 535–544.

———. *The Puerto Rican Nation on the Move: Identities on the Island and in the United States*. Chapell Hill and London:The University of North Carolina Press, 2002.

Edwards, Brent. *The Practice of Diaspora*. Cambridge: Harvard University Press, 2003.

Enwezor, Okwui, *et al. Créolité and Creolization*. New York: Documenta 11_ Platform 3, 2003.

Fanon, Frantz. *Black Skin, White Masks*. New York: Grove Weidenfield, 1967.

Fiol-Matta, Licia. *A Queer Mother for the Nation*. Minneapolis: University of Minnesota Press, 2002.

Flores, Juan. *From Bomba to Hip-Hop. Puerto Rican Culture and Latino Identity*. New York: Columbia University Press, 2000.

Gilroy, Paul. *The Black Atlantic*. Cambridge: Harvard University Press, 1995.

Giraud, Michel. "Racisme colonial, ethnicité et citoyenneté: Les leçons des expériences migratoires antillaises et guyanaises." *Caribbean Studies* 32.1 (2004): 161–184.

Glissant, Edouard. *Caribbean Discourse*. Trans. J. Michael Dash. Charlottesville: University Press of Virginia, 1999.

Gordon, Lewis, T. Denean Sharpley-Whiting, and Renee T White. *Fanon. A Critical Reader*. New York and London: Blackwell, 1996.

Grosfoguel, Ramón. "Caribbean Colonial Immigrants in the Metropoles: A Research Agenda." *Centro* 7.1 (1994–1995): 82–95

Gruzinski, Serge. *The Mestizo Mind*. Trans. Deke Dusinberre. New York: Routledge, 2002.

Guridy, Frank. "From Solidarity to Cross-Fertilization: Afro-Cuban/African American Interaction during the 1930s and 1940s." *Radical History Review* 87 (Fall 2003): 19–48.

Hall, Stuart. "Cultural Identity and Diaspora." *Identity: Community, Culture, Difference*. Ed. Jonathan Rutherford. London: Lawrence & Wishart, 1990. 222–237.

———. "Negotiating Caribbean Identities." *New Left Review* 209: 3–14.

Hernández, Carmen Dolores. "Piri Thomas." *Puerto Rican Voices in English: Interviews with Writers*. Westport, Connecticut: Praeger Publishers, 1997. 171–185.

Higgings, Antony. *Constructing the Criollo Archive: Subjects of Knowledge in the* Biblioteca Mexicana *and the* Rusticatio Mexicana. Ohio: Purdue University Press, 2000.

Macey, David. *Frantz Fanon: A Biography*. New York: Picador, 2000.

Martí, José. "Nuestra América." *Prosa y poesía*. Buenos Aires: Kapelusz, 1968. 122–133.

Martínez-San Miguel, Yolanda. "Colonialidad de la diáspora: Puerto Rico y Martinica." *El ritmo incesante: Antonio Benítez Rojo y el Caribe fragmentado*. Ed. Rita Molinero. Forthcoming.

———. "Poéticas caribeñas de lo criollo: créole/criollo/creolité." *Poéticas de lo criollo: inestabilidad semántica y heterogeneidad identitaria*. Eds. David Solodkow and Juan Vitulli. Buenos Aires: Editorial Corregidor, 2009. 403–441.

———. *Saberes americanos: subalternidad y epistemología en los escritos de Sor Juana*. Pittsburgh: Instituto Internacional de Literatura Iberoamericana, 1999.

Mazzotti, José Antonio. "Las agencias criollas y la ambigüedad 'colonial' de las letras hispanoamericanas." *Agencias criollas*. Ed. José Antonio Mazzotti. Pittsburgh: Instituto Internacional de Literatura Iberoamericana, 2000. 7–35.

Milia, Monique Marie-Luce. "De l'autre-mer au continent: Étude comparée de l'émigration puertoricaine et antillo-guyanaise de l'aprés Guerre aux années 1960." Ph.D. dissertation, École des Hautes Études en Sciences Sociales, Paris, 2002.

Omi, Michael, and Howard Winant. *Racial Formation in the United States*. London: Routledge, 1994.

Pacifico, Patricia. "Piri Thomas Talks at Inter American University." *Revista/Review Interamericana* 7.1 (Spring 1977): 666–673.

Pérez-Torres, Rafael. *Mestizaje: Critical Uses of Race in Chicano Culture*. Minneapolis: University of Minnesota Press, 2006.

Puerto Rican Community in Chicago. Special Issue. *Centro Journal*. 13.2 (Fall 2001).

Puri, Shalini. *The Caribbean Postcolonial*. New York: Palgrave Macmillan, 2004.

Quijano, Aníbal. "Coloniality of Power, Eurocentrism, and Latin America." *Nepantla* 1.3 (2000): 533–580.

Race and Identity. Special Issue. *Centro Journal*. 8.1–2 (Spring 1996).

Ramos-Zayas, Ana Y. *National Performances: The Politics of Class, Race, and Space in Puerto Rican Chicago*. Chicago: University of Chicago Press, 2003.

Rivera, Raquel. *New York Ricans from the Hip Hop Zone*. New York: Palgrave, 2003.

Rodriguez, Richard. *Brown*. New York: Viking Adult, Penguin, 2002.

Rodríguez de Laguna, Asela. "Piri Thomas' *Down These Mean Streets*: Writing as a Nuyorican/Puerto Rican Strategy of Survival." *U.S. Latino Literature: A Critical Guide for Students and Teachers*. Ed. Harold Augenbraum and Margarite Fernández Olmos. Westport, CT: Greenwood Press, 2000. 21–29.

Rodríguez Juliá, Edgardo. *Caribeños*. San Juan: Instituto de Cultura Puertorriqueña, 2002.

Ross, Kathleen. *The Baroque Narrative of Carlos de Sigüenza y Góngora*. Cambridge: Cambridge University Press, 1993.

Roy-Féquière, Magaly. *Women, Creole Identity, and Intellectual Life in Early Twentieth-Century Puerto Rico*. Philadelphia: Temple University Press, 2004

Sánchez González, Lisa. *Boricua Literature: A Literary History of the Puerto Rican Diaspora*. New York: New York University Press, 2001.

Stavans, Ilans. "Race and Mercy: a Conversation with Piri Thomas." *The Massachusetts Review* 37.3 (Autumn 1996): 344–354.

Thomas, Piri. "A Neorican in Puerto Rico: Or Coming Home." *Images and Identities: The Puerto Rican in Two World Contexts*. Ed. Asela Rodríguez de Laguna. New Brunswick: Transaction Books, 1987. 153–156.

———. *Down These Mean Streets*. New York: Vintage Books, 1997.

———. *The World of Piri Thomas*. http://www.cheverote.com/piri.html/.

Torres-Saillant, Silvio. *An Intellectual History of the Caribbean*. New York: Palgrave, 2006.

Vaca, Nicolás C. *The Presumed Alliance: The Unspoken Conflict Between Latinos and Blacks and What It Means for America*. New York: Harper Collins, 2004.

Vasconcelos, José. *La raza cósmica*. México: Editorial Porrúa, 2001. [1925].

Williams, Patrick. "Frantz Fanon: The Routes of Writing." *An Introduction to Caribbean Francophone Writing*. Ed. Sam Haigh. New York: Berg, 1999. 51–68.

Winant, Howard. *Racial Conditions*. Minneapolis: University of Minnesota Press, 1994.

Young, Robert. *Colonial Desire*. Londres: Routledge, 1995.

12

The Dominican Diaspora Strikes Back: Cultural Archive and Race in Junot Díaz's *The Brief Wondrous Life of Oscar Wao*

Juanita Heredia

While scholars of African diasporic discourse such as Paul Gilroy and Stuart Hall have tended to focus on the historical and social relationships between Africa, the Anglophonic Caribbean, and Britain, much work still needs to be done by incorporating the Spanish Caribbean and its diaspora in the United States into the critical conversations of the triangular African/Black Atlantic.[1] Silvio Torres-Saillant, the prominent scholar of the Dominican diaspora, has contributed much critical and historical groundwork for understanding the connection between racial discourse and literature of the Dominican Republic and Dominican immigrants and their descendents, the diaspora, who arrived in waves, due to economic hardships, to the mainland United States in the 1970s and onward.[2]

Through critical articles, books, and interviews with writers like Junot Díaz, Torres-Saillant has begun a critical foundation for Dominican diasporic literature and culture in dialogue with the Dominican motherland, but he also considers the complexity of transnational history and race matters in the migrations between island and mainland. In this essay, I suggest that Torres-Saillant's preoccupation with Afro-Dominican diasporic identity is in direct dialogue with Gilroy's critical paradigm of the triangular "Black Atlantic" for both critics emphasize the significance of the African heritage/black presence in the Caribbean and the implications of its racial legacy in their diasporic communities in the United States or Britain. Similar to the West Indian community that arrived in England by the end of the 1940s (the Windward generation), the Afro-Dominican émigré population that landed in the east coast of the United States can be characterized by its working-class orientation that forms one of the labor forces in factories and public services following the Puerto Rican migratory trajectory of the 1950s. The children of these immigrants on the east coast are considered Dominican Americans or the Dominican diaspora, to which Junot Díaz belongs.[3] A writer who emerged in the 1990s, Díaz reveals in his fiction the inherent complications that, already in existence on the island, have affected displacement and migration to the United States. Torres-Saillant states,

> Whatever suffering Dominicans have endured in the foreign shores where despair has expelled them, they have also learned to see themselves more fully, more fairly, particularly in matters of race. The long struggles for equality and social justice by people of color in the United States have yielded invaluable lessons from which Dominican people in the diaspora and in the Dominican Republic have drawn and may continue to draw empowerment. The diaspora will render an inestimable service to the Dominican people if it can help to rid the country of white supremacist thought and negrophobic discourse, to whatever extent those aberrations may survive in Dominican society, and allow finally a celebration of our rich *African heritage*. (1109, my emphasis)

Similar to Gilroy's "transatlantic" voyages of communities crossing initially and involuntarily from Africa to the Caribbean eventually to England forming a "Black British" identity, Torres-Saillant suggests that the Dominican diaspora can play a crucial role in fomenting a new consciousness of what it means to be Afro-Dominican, a double diaspora, which consists of a two-part journey from Africa to Hispaniola (present Haiti and the Dominican Republic) and then to the United States.

The comparison of the two critical paradigms constructed by Gilroy and Torres-Saillant is important because Dominican history and the representation of race, or acknowledgment of the African heritage, has been suppressed or "deracialized" according to Torres-Saillant, so that to affirm any part of this cultural ancestry in this day and age translates into the birth of an Afro-Dominican diasporic renaissance, especially in Afro-Dominican letters in the United States and African diasporic literature at large.[4] In his Pulitzer Prize-winning first novel *The Brief Wondrous Life of Oscar Wao* (2007), Junot Díaz engages the cultural archive of African racial discourse that contests the dominance of U.S. imperialism and modern globalization.

In the long-awaited *The Brief Wondrous Life of Oscar Wao*, critically acclaimed Díaz introduces the multi-faceted world of the Afro-Dominican American protagonist, Oscar de León (a.k.a. Oscar Wao), through a reconfiguration of race and genealogy between Africa, the Dominican Republic and the United States to insist on an alternative masculinity to traditional gender roles. Best-known for his collection of short fiction *Drown* (1996), Díaz seduces the reading public with his latest *oeuvre* based on a young Afro-Latino adolescent coming of age in the world of science fiction and fantasy in Paterson, New Jersey. Díaz not only evokes sympathy for the character of Oscar, but he also demonstrates that young Latino males can aspire to pursue their dreams and enter imaginary worlds despite the odds against them in a New Jersey working-class *barrio*, a place that may not afford them many opportunities as they grow older. In *The Brief Wondrous Life of Oscar Wao*, Díaz offers a compelling narrative of how race and gender expectations in the representation of genealogy can influence self-perception and self-esteem in the social and intellectual formation of a young Afro-Latino student.

Díaz divides the novel into seven chapters, beginning with "Ghetto Nerd at the End of the World, 1974–1987" and ending with "The Final Voyage," jumping chronologically throughout the twentieth century. By incorporating a testimonial narrator in the voice of Yunior (also, a prevalent character as a young boy in many short stories of *Drown*), Díaz devises "an objective" perspective, familiar yet removed from the protagonist Oscar's family, to recount the youthful days of friendship between Yunior and Oscar de León, an outsider due to his overweight body image. Through a colloquial voice using both slang and eloquent vocabulary, Díaz constructs an "accessible" narrator in Yunior who has the ability to address a younger generation of urban readers but also appeals to audiences of all ages through his humor, irony, and stylistic influences.[5] Furthermore, Díaz's fast-paced linguistic technique permits the narrator to bond with a younger circle of readers on contemporary matters such as technological dependency, body image, and the search for the perfect love. In a footnote of the novel, the narrator captures the spirit of Oscar's persona, "You really want to know what being an X-Man feels like? Just be a smart bookish boy of color and in a contemporary U.S. ghetto. Mamma mia! Like having bat wings or a pair of tentacles growing out of your chest" (22). The fact that Díaz considers Oscar a boy of color suggests that the author wishes to enter a racial discourse in the United States.

12.1   Revision of a Transnational History

Throughout the novel, Díaz deftly illustrates the oppression of the social injustices in Dominican history, especially those suffered by people of African descent on the island and their descendents, the diaspora, in the United States. Rather than using official sources to present an alternative side of history, Díaz focuses on the stories of the people in the community, especially the memory of Oscar's family across transnational borders. In an interview with Ilan Stavans, Díaz explains, "It's thanks to my mother, simply because of where she came from, an arid, southern region of the Dominican Republic. People there are known for their *poca palabra*. My mother's terseness, her single-mindedness, her stoic attitude, had a strong impact on me. My sense of what language can do, how much you could communicate with few words, I owe to her" (48). In the narration as well as the dialogues in the novel, Díaz creates an effortless prose demonstrating how the migration from the island to the city transforms not only the location of geography but also the linguistic sensibility of the younger generation in the community. This social change is connected to Díaz's wish to conserve an urban edge to "the language of the streets," which makes his narrator identify with the African American working class as well but with a Dominican flair from island to urban spaces. By employing this linguistic technique, Díaz is also challenging the language of official discourse on the island and mainland by breaking with standardized English and Spanish to allow black, mulatto, and women of color to speak or "strike back."

While the narrator employs a colloquial, jovial voice with the poetic rhythm of hip-hop sounds and at times interjects a Caribbean Spanish to represent Oscar's genealogy, he also intervenes in official historical discourse through the use of footnotes.[6] By doing so, Díaz not only gives the impression that he presents historical facts "objectively," but he also critiques the abuse of authorial power in historical discourse, often written by male officials in power at the expense of the marginalized in Dominican and U.S. societies (e.g., blacks, mulattos, the poor, women). The narrator Yunior, an Afro-Dominican American male instructor of creative writing, we learn later, gives himself currency to reconfigure the dominant narrative of the nation, one often told by hegemonic forces, by decreasing its official validity to footnotes and by magnifying the traditionally silenced voices in the larger narration of the novel.

Furthermore, under the guise of the narrator Díaz exposes to a mainstream readership many unknown atrocities of the Trujillo dictatorship (1930–1960), especially inhumane activities associated with the government of this period, to critique indirectly the United States' involvement with the regime on the island and the negative consequences of imperial intervention for people of color. Díaz, as author, places Trujillo and his allies on trial for ordering the massacre of children, men, and women of color across transnational lines.[7] He suggests that by overtaking narrative power as author and through the eyes of the narrator Yunior (other times, Lola is the narrator), he allows himself to offer an alternative side to official history to dismantle the genocide committed against his ancestors and their descendents that affect his diasporic contemporaries.

One can further consider Díaz to be in a liminal position as critic. On one level, he attacks U.S. imperialism for monopolizing the lives of innocent people on the island by supporting Trujillo, his government, and the violence committed by them against humanity. U.S. support allowed Trujillo to instigate the massacre of thousands of Haitians and dark-skinned Dominicans at the national border between the islands in 1937 in order to "purify" or "Hispanicize" the Dominican Republic to eliminate any remnants of the African heritage.[8] Torres-Saillant discusses how this tragic historical event contributed to the "deracialization" of Dominican islanders that led to negrophobia, a racial denial of blackness by mulattos and mestizos in favor of the taíno/indigenous heritage and more acceptable lighter skin color. On another level, Díaz also repudiates U.S. institutions for their institutional racism and resistance to open friendly doors to people of color such as Afro-Dominican students to achieve "the American Dream," but rather sets them up for failure as illustrated in *The Brief Wondrous Life of Oscar Wao*.

Fully aware of the consequences of censorship under Trujillo's dictatorship, Díaz knows that he must be accountable to tell the story of the oppressed, the silenced, and the underprivileged. In other words, give voice to those who do not have access to political power, nor the written word, across the transnational border that divides the island from New Jersey, by deconstructing the narratives of empire in both, the U.S. and Dominican hegemonic contexts.[9] Torres-Saillant further notes that only by having Dominicans of African descent remember their ancestors and their traditions, transported from Africa to the Caribbean, can they point to a history that makes them visible. He explains, "The African-descended majority of the Dominican population will benefit greatly from a model that allows them to perceive their ancestors as the real protagonists of the epic of the Dominican experience" (1107).

One way that Díaz uncovers the silenced history of the marginalized Dominicans on the island and in the diaspora, is by returning to certain African beliefs and traditions such as the fukú, according to legend, a curse brought onto people of African descent with the arrival of Christopher Columbus. This spell can be a Pandora's Box that opens unforeseen unfortunate consequences. Similar to the marginalized under Trujillo's governments, Afro-Dominicans in the United States have been a neglected representation in history according to *The Brief Life of Oscar Wao*. Díaz contests the omission of perspectives and emphasizes the African diaspora's legacy and presence in the lives of Oscar's family history. From the beginning of the narrative, Díaz illustrates through the counter-discourse of memory how the fukú has influenced generations of Afro-Dominicans on the island and in the United States. Moreover, Díaz insinuates that the Afro-Dominican diaspora in the United States must come to terms with the past by recognizing the ghosts and legacy of the ancestors to combat the hardships of the present and persevere in the future as the protagonist Oscar attempts to do so.[10]

Díaz does not remain in the contemporary period of New Jersey, however, because he transports us to other geographies and temporalities: Africa through beliefs and the Dominican Republic through family migrations. Throughout the novel, Díaz demonstrates how the fukú, a symbol of bad luck, still lives in the daily lives of the protagonist Oscar and his family members in the twentieth century. Yet, with each triumph that Oscar and his ancestors experience, they must also retrocede one step back in a suffering, if not a tragedy. Thus, Díaz traces the fukú in a transnational genealogy that circulates the triangular Black Atlantic of Africa, the Dominican Republic, and the United States (New Jersey).[11] By examining three generations in Oscar's family from the Trujillo dictatorship in the Dominican Republic to immigration to the United States, Díaz uses the fukú as a trope of misfortune throughout Oscar's genealogy. One can further trace how race, black or mulatto, confines the family members to a doomed fate by disempowering each generation, particularly the characters of Abelard, Belicia, and Oscar on the island and mainland.

The Brief Wondrous Life of Oscar Wao may not follow a linear chronology of events in its genealogy, but Díaz brings coherence to the fragmentation of historical incidents affecting each member of Oscar's family. Even though the novel begins with the uncomfortable experiences from Oscar's adolescent years through his college days and thereafter, Díaz shifts spatially and temporally to show how previous generations, the grandfather Abelard and the mother Belicia, have had to contend with the challenges of the fukú, whether or not they believe in it. In each case, Díaz presents how the circumstances of the historical period dictate each family member's life and affects his destiny despite their will to resist the pitfalls of an unjust government that ironically imprisons rather than liberates its people who seek social justice on the island and mainland.

12.2   Race Matters and Its Legacy in the Twentieth Century

In The Brief Wondrous Life of Oscar Wao, Díaz illustrates how the cultural archive of race and genealogy disrupt the dominant discourse of the Trujillo dictatorship. Oscar's grandfather, the character of Abelard Luis de Cabral, is the first generation that is affected directly by the Trujillo regime in the Dominican Republic in the 1940s. Although Abelard holds a professional title as a medical physician and stands to inherit his family's fortune, he hardly has any political clout when it comes to exerting authorial control in society, much less in his own family.[12] His wife,

Socorro, who is a nurse, finds herself in a similar vulnerable position vis-à-vis the political figures in power. Abelard may be a model father to his two beautiful daughters, Astrid and Jacquelyn, who "often suffered from Mulatto Pigment Degradation Disorder, a.k.a. tans" and an exemplary husband, however, he cannot protect the women against the predatory efforts of Trujillo who permits himself to have any woman, regardless of age, class, legal status or race, that he desires (213). If Trujillo found young women in the Dominican Republic physically attractive, they were not immune from his insatiable sexual appetite. Such is the case with one of Abelard's daughters, Jacquelyn, who has hopes of studying at La Faculté de Medecine de Paris to become a physician like her father. As much as this character develops her mind and interiority, it is a fruitless deed under the dictatorship period in which they are living. Díaz explores this stigma of limited freedom for Abelard's family. Despite their education and class status, on the island, the authority of Trujillo dominated and took this family's liberties away. Díaz also infers that the family could only immigrate or exile to another nation since matters of personal freedom were beyond their control in the national homeland.

It is no wonder that Abelard Cabral attempts to keep his daughters "locked up" or "hidden" at home as much as possible, to be hidden from The Cattle Thief of Trujillo. Powerless and victim to the political system, the father attempts to protect his daughters, beautiful and mulatta, as best as he can. To live under such duress, Díaz notes, incarcerates rather than liberates progressive intellectuals and their families during this time, a paradox that speaks to the invalidity and hypocrisy of achieving a formal education and professional career in the Dominican Republic. Even though the family consents to Trujillo's orders to avoid problems, they must still endure political tyranny and death at the hands of a senseless dictator who manipulates the law to his own accord.

Once Trujillo notices the daughter Jacquelyn as an object of seduction, the fate of the Cabral family in this generation is sealed and transforms into a fukú. Trujillo tactfully begins with the imprisonment of the father Abelard who eventually dies tortured whereas the two daughters have "accidents": one whose body is found in the river while the other is mysteriously shot. Díaz insinuates that the legacy of the fukú lives on in this family's matters regardless of class status. After the two daughters Jacquelyn and Astrid die, Abelard's wife Socorro gives birth to a third daughter, Hypatía Belicia Cabral. Left orphaned and raised by her aunt, La Inca, after the death of her siblings and parents, Belicia becomes a symbol of resistance and survival of the Cabral family's honor.

In the chapter, "The Three Heartbreaks of Belicia Cabral, 1955–1962," Belicia Cabral represents the transnational generation as a Dominican who immigrates to the United States to find a better life for herself by escaping dictatorial torture and the curse of the fukú. Díaz dedicates a section of the novel solely to this character because her story serves as a testimony to the atrocious experiences committed against women in the Dominican Republic. Described as dark-skinned and naïve, Belicia must pay the consequences for her race, gender, and family's curse combined. Due to her romantic and idealistic inclinations, she falls victim to love three times, but her relationships end almost as soon as they begin, thereby cursed three times.

Although the aunt, La Inca, manages to send Belicia to a reputable school as an adolescent, Belicia earns a bad reputation because she becomes involved with the school's charmer, Jack Pujols, an upper-class young male with whom she disrobes. She participates in sexual games with him until they are literally caught one day. Expelled from school, she represents shame to her family's reputation and no hope for a better future. A woman's purity and virginity are intertwined and associated with the sexual excess of the body and therefore, must be disciplined and punished to protect the family honor. Infuriated and embarrassed by her niece's promiscuity, La Inca decides to place Belicia in a nun's school where she will be monitored and taught to be a decent lady. This institutional indoctrination of a woman's behavior affects Belicia in her adult years as seen with her daughter's upbringing. But Belicia has plans of her own when it comes to affairs of the heart for she continues to disobey her family on other occasions.

By falling in love with the Gangster, Trujillo's brother-in-law, on another occasion, Belicia treads dangerous waters as she enters her second romance as a young lady. Because she follows her heart, blind to political power and the machinations placed upon individuals not of the elite *criollo* class, Belicia must pay the consequences of this forbidden affair. She not only dreams of marrying this individual but she also risks her life by becoming pregnant for an unsure future. The jealous wife, Trujillo's ugly sister "la fea," threatens and pursues Belicia with the help of her brother's corrupt allies. Belicia, naïve and romantic, does not realize that she does not even have the police, much less the law, on her side. When she is almost kidnapped for the first time, Belicia can only depend on her former employers, Chinese owners of a restaurant where she worked. Belicia says, "Mis chinos, she told her daughter [Lola], saved my life" (142). Díaz demonstrates how different racial groups, even if marginalized, ally to help one another in a time of need.

However, the second time the gangsters, or Trujillo's men, tail her, Belicia is left to the mercy of fate. In fact, she is practically disfigured by these men when she is dragged into the sugar cane fields. The narrator recounts, "How she survived, I'll never know. They beat her like she was a slave. Like she was a dog...All that can be said was that it was the end of language, the end of hope. It was the sort of beating that breaks people, breaks them utterly" (147). In this instance, Díaz alludes to slavery in Dominican history when black women were treated as subhuman to the point that their spirit and bodies became disposable. This violence against Belicia's body and dignity demonstrates that patriarchal and racial abuses on women's rights, including those who are pregnant, validates the senselessness of a dictatorship and thus, critiques the nation for its lack of protective laws for disempowered women of color on the island. Nonetheless, Díaz decides to take a more hopeful turn in the narrative when he relocates Belicia outside the Dominican nation to the United States. When La Inca helps her niece immigrate to the United States at the age of sixteen, Belicia meets her future husband on the airplane, signaling another chance at love.

Belicia arrives in the United States to escape torture and violence on the island but little does she realize that what awaits her is the despair that every immigrant woman of color must experience, especially in the working-class neighborhoods of New Jersey.[13] To make matters worse, in her third romance, her husband leaves her and their children, Lola and Oscar, after two years in search of something better for himself.[14] The narrator foresees her future, "What she doesn't yet know: the cold, the backbreaking drudgery of the factorías, the loneliness of Diaspora, that she will never again live in Santo Domingo, her own heart...her third and final heartbreak, and she would never love again" (164). As a single mother and wage earner for her family, Belicia must enter the work force with limited skills in formal education and lack of command of the English language. All of these factors combined speak to this generation of immigrant women from the Dominican Republic who have problems reaching the "American dream," one that becomes more of a myth rather than a goal come true.

12.3   Transition to the Dominican American Generation: The Diaspora Strikes Back

Life for Belicia de León and her family takes an unexpected turn in Paterson, New Jersey, as they experience fragmentation rather than loyalty and unity. As she ages, Belicia develops health issues due to her job as a cleaning lady in New Jersey. She learns to sacrifice her time and body for the welfare of her children and their future. Women's bodies, especially those of the Dominican immigrant working class, cannot sustain a family forever and therefore, her children must work and earn scholarships to continue their higher education. At least in this area, Lola and Oscar manage to attain some level of competitiveness academically, for both are able to enter public universities (e.g., Rutgers University) and study a specialization of their choice, decisions their relatives on the island can only imagine.

The siblings, Lola and Oscar, symbolize the next generation like a *Star Trek* saga, the Dominican diaspora who look to the future in search of the "American Dream," through stability, and acceptance by society and perhaps a loved one to share one's life. They differ from their parents' generation in that they hold no nostalgia to live on the island because they travel or "return" to the Dominican Republic during vacation trips or moments of crisis, maintaining minimal contact with Dominican relatives. Díaz reveals in an interview, "Those in the diaspora haven't only changed as a result of their departure; they changed fundamentally the place they departed from" ("Driven" 50). He suggests that while the Dominican diaspora may return to the homeland culture by maintaining contact with relatives, their experiences are constantly changing as a consequence of migrations.

12.4   The Ugly Duckling, the Shy Latino

Oscar and Lola de León represent two different models of the Dominican diaspora generation that comes of age in the 1980s in search of happiness in the United States. The sister Lola, for example, embodies a gothic Latina who listens to alternative British rock bands such as the Smiths, consciously removing herself from the island's culture. Unlike a traditional Latina who stays within the confinements of her home, her family, and her neighborhood, Lola desires to travel to see the world by studying abroad or teaching English in Japan. Intelligent, independent, confident, and physically attractive, Lola is not afraid to break with family traditions which is why she ran away temporarily to live with her alternative boyfriend. With an absent father and working mother, Lola has set the rules for her life.

On the other hand, the younger brother Oscar is not only overweight at 307 pounds, but he is also shy which affects his ability to attract the opposite sex, an endeavor that he will pursue throughout his life. Thus, one notices a discrepancy between Oscar's interior and exterior worlds, his emotional state and physique. The lack of balance between his mind and body leads to mental depression that begins to bother Oscar in his early adolescence. Díaz paints the portrait of the shy Latino nerd as a young man to point out the inherent contradictions of living as a bicultural Latino intellectual in this day and age. The narrator comments, "The white kids looked at his black skin and his afro and treated him with inhuman cheeriness. The kids of color, upon hearing him speak and seeing him move his body, shook their heads. 'You're not Dominican.' And he said, over and over again, 'But I am. Soy Dominicano. Dominicano soy'" (49). Díaz uncovers the pressures that Oscar must endure as a result from being rejected by both peers, the dominant as well as the

Dominican, in his social circle. While the white students refuse to accept him due to his race, his fellow Domo pals are ashamed of his nerdiness and lack of Spanish on their terms. Where does Oscar belong in this modern tech age?

By no means is Oscar living a political torture under a ruthless dictatorship as his grandfather and mother experienced during Trujillo's regime, but he must confront peer pressure and recurring rejections in New Jersey from physically attractive girls such as the Afro-Peruvian Maritza and the Dominican prostitute Ybón who he met on one of his last trips to the Dominican Republic. Although his pal Yunior advises him to lose weight to attract girls, Oscar suffers from low self-esteem because he cannot even attain a simple deed such as a KISS, his one goal in life before he dies. Pathetic yet irresistible, Oscar embodies the contradictions that every young and overweight male of color experiences in an urban working-class *barrio*.

The absence of the father represents the lack of an immediate paternal and masculine model in Oscar's life, which makes him introspective, only being able to rely on himself. Therefore, he resorts to books (e.g., *Star Trek*), popular culture in the form of television programs such as the sci-fi serial *Doctor Who* or the comedy *What's Happening*, to develop an imaginative world rather than depend on the superficial materialism that most of his teenage peers do. In this sense, Díaz breaks with the representation of the stereotypical urban Latino teenage hoodlum in the *barrio* who is always getting into trouble because he is pursuing crime and drugs. Rather, this Dominicano teenager, Oscar, exposes his emotions and wears his heart on his sleeve when he associates with people, especially girls. His sensitive attitude also explains why Oscar always gets his heart broken when the pretty girls reject him. In this character, Díaz points to the complexity of understanding the "shy Latino," who inhabits a borderland position as he experiences a "double marginalization" within the mainstream as well as his *own* Dominican community. Because of his race, he does not belong with the dominant crowd; yet, because he becomes indoctrinated in American culture and values through education, he has grown distant from the communities that forged him. Díaz searches for a reconciliation between these two worlds for young males of color in a position similar to that of Oscar. Díaz asks how the African diaspora in the Spanish Caribbean survived and resisted monologic models of masculinity (e.g., dictator, helpless immigrant, drug dealer) when Oscar represents a departure from the limited models available to young males such as himself.

When romance enters Oscar's life in his adolescent years, though, his future is further complicated. Like a normal curious boy at his age, he spends his time by reading *Penthouse* magazines in hiding to playing Dungeons and Dragons for fun (26). Upon entering college, Oscar befriends the narrator of the novel, Yunior, who becomes his room-mate and protector at sister Lola's request while she studies abroad. Yunior only complies because he is in love with Lola, displaying his loyalty toward her rather than Oscar. Still overweight and unable to find a girl to take him seriously, Oscar despairs and attempts suicide while in college. His family is shocked and his mother Belicia decides to travel to the capital Santo Domingo, in the Dominican Republic, to visit family to bring Oscar back to his senses. By connecting Oscar to the land of his *antepasados,* his ancestors, Belicia believes that she may take pressure off Oscar and reconcile him with his roots on the island.

Even though Lola and Oscar feel out of place as Dominican diaspora on the island, it is not long before Oscar meets and falls in love with Ybón, a prostitute who is a gangster's girlfriend. Finally, Oscar finds someone who listens and pays attention to him, unlike his female peers in New Jersey. Because Oscar falls for an unrealistic mate, he is pur-sued, beaten up, and disfigured like Belicia in the cane fields, another allusion to slavery (296–299). A victim of love, this pattern resembles his mother's life or the strike of the fukú again in Oscar's family in the Dominican Republic. Ironically, Díaz seems to suggest that positive out-comes in formal education and career only occur in the United States, but the search for a true love can only happen on the island. In the end Oscar, like his mother who was chased by gangsters, sacrifices himself for love on a second return to the island. Unlike his mother, though, he dies a hopeless romantic, tragic hero, struck by the curse of the fukú, for he is killed. Why is this so?

In the development of the protagonist Oscar de León, Díaz explores the role of formal education and romance for students of color, particu-larly males, because young individuals like Oscar do not know where they belong. This is a double-edged sword because he achieves the "American Dream" of obtaining a decent education up to college, yet, he is considered a social outsider, because physically he is overweight, racially unaccepted by many groups and thus, unattractive to most of his female peers. The democratic side of the United States can only go so far, but other aspects of Oscar's life such as his mental stability haunt him. Despite his intelligence through his high level of vocabulary and computer wiz skills, education and society at large do not allow him to transcend into other areas, especially dating and attaining a certain sexual prowess expected of young Dominican/Latino males on the island as well as the mainland. The novel also demonstrates the challenges of the diaspora and the potential development that could occur, but we are left stagnant because Oscar can only progress so far. He is not good enough for acceptance by his peers, nor society. Díaz implies that some progress in the diaspora has been achieved in general, but there is still a long way to go for young people of color, especially shy males, to be fully understood. The illusion of the American Dream is real while the reality for young males like Oscar is crushing. Díaz explores the holes in the search for this goal for Oscar.

In spite of Oscar's death as a tragic hero, Yunior emerges as a narrator who holds the knowledge, or cultural archive, of the family's history. Through his voice, language, and perspective, he survives living in the *barrio* to tell of his deceased friend and others in the community to memorialize their experiences on paper, which is passed on to future generations such as Isis, Lola's daughter. By remembering Oscar's genealogy, renders it being imprinted in history and a testament to the sufferings by people of African ancestry as much in the Dominican Republic as in the United States. Díaz reverses the power balance of narration by using the fictitious genre of the novel to contest the "truth" of official history books to show multiple perspectives on the past.

In addition, Yunior exposes the violence and institutional racism committed against Oscar's family, a metaphor for the Afro-Dominican diaspora, raising awareness of the past to mobilize future generations to avoid repeating mistakes. In Yunior, we also witness an educator who holds knowledge, or cultural archive, and teaches creative writing to potential recorders of stories at a community college. He represents a generation of Dominican diasporic professionals graduating from university, a generation which lives and may open doors for younger generations by mediating between the working-class neighborhoods and the academic world, thereby reversing the stigma of the legacy of the fukú. In *The Brief Wondrous Life of Oscar Wao*, Díaz reclaims the Dominican diaspora to show that it can and does strike back.

Notes

1. For further elaboration on the Black Atlantic model of migrations, and diasporas, see Gilroy's *The Black Atlantic* (1993). He explains how modernity was formed as a result of colonial relationships between African, British, and the Anglophone Caribbean cultures. Consequently, African diasporic communities have been excluded from full social participation in England until recently.

2. The migrations by Dominicans to the United States in the twentieth century and thereafter, primarily fall into two groups: (1) the exile professional group which had political disagreements with Trujillo's government that was in power at the time; this group left in the 1950s and 1960s; and (2) working-class immigrants who left their homeland due to economic hardships under the Balaguer presidency in the 1970s and onward. In Haiti, racial threats also forced many to depart to the United States. Depending on class, race, and political orientation, many groups who left their homeland formed diasporas in the United States.

3. In addition to Junot Díaz, this generation of the Dominican diaspora consists of writers such as Angie Cruz, Nelly Rosario, and Maritza Loída Pérez, all of whom write about the relationship between the Dominican Republic and the United States with respect to race and gender.

4. In an interview with Céspedes and Torres-Saillant (2000), Díaz considers his fiction to be part of many literary traditions, including U.S. Latino, Caribbean, Dominican diaspora, and the African diaspora.

5. In her book review of *The Brief Wondrous Life of Oscar Wao*, Michiko Kakutani notes Junot Díaz's masterful ability to move between styles and worlds by describing his narrative as a mixture of influences, "Mario Vargas Llosa meets 'Star Trek' meets David Foster Wallace meets Kanye West."

6. Footnoted references to historical figures are reminiscent of Sandra Cisneros' critique of official history in her critically acclaimed novel *Caramelo* (2002). U.S. Latino writers employ this narrative strategy to make the audience aware of the subjectivity of representing the past not only in fiction, but also in "official" history. Like Cisneros, Díaz also uses irony to contest the dominant discourse in history.

7. In a footnote, for example, Díaz explores the intricate relationship of power between dictators and writers. He explains that a student is chased all the way to Columbia University in New York City to be returned and murdered on the island because he wrote a dissertation exposing Trujillo for committing inhumane atrocities against his fellowmen in the Dominican Republic (97).

8. When Haitians and dark-skinned Dominicans failed to pronounce the word, "perejil," (parsley) in a standard Spanish, they were identified as victims for the massacre of 1937. If they did not pass this linguistic test, they were sentenced to death.

9. Díaz exposes issues of the diaspora as a consequence of the Trujillo regime and massacre of 1937, one that is tied to the idea of how race and imperialism were crucial factors in the genocide of African-descent people in the Dominican Republic/Haiti borderlands. Díaz refers to Trujillo as a dictator who exploits people of color even though he, himself, is said to be mulatto. As the narrative progress, Díaz not only critiques Trujillo's violation of women's bodies and dignity that made him into a patriarchal dictator, but he also contests this masculine model as an option for younger male Dominicans, be it on the island or in the diaspora.

10. See Jenny Sharpe's *Ghosts of Slavery* for the role of memory of the ancestors and its presence through spirits for the African diaspora.

11. See the introduction of Paul Gilroy's *The Black Atlantic* (1993).

12. In de Moya's article, "Power Games and Totalitarian Masculinity in the Dominican Republic," he presents different examples of male models of power that have come to define manhood in the Dominican Republic.

13. In Chapter 6 of *The Tears of Hispaniola* (2007), Suárez discusses how the violence that was initiated on the Caribbean island for Dominican and Haitian diasporas may not altogether disappear with their migratory settlement in the United States (183).

14. This paternal figure resonates with the character of Yunior's father in *Drown*.

Works Cited

Céspedes, Diógenes & Silvio Torres-Saillant. "Fiction Is the Poor Man's Cinema: An Interview with Junot Díaz." *Callaloo* 23.2 (2000): 892–907.

Cisneros, Sandra. *Caramelo o Puro Cuento*. New York: Vintage, 2002.

de Moya, Antonio E. "Power Games and Totalitarian Masculinity in the Dominican Republic." *Interrogating Caribbean Masculinities: Theoretical and Empirical Analyses*. Ed. Rhoda E. Reddock. Kingston, Jamaica: University of the West Indies, 2004. 68–102.

Díaz, Junot. *Drown*. New York: Riverhead, 1996.

———. "Driven." *Conversations with Ilan Stavans*. Ed. Ilan Stavans. Tucson: University of Arizona Press, 2005. 47–51.

———. *The Brief Wondrous Life of Oscar Wao*. New York: Harcourt Books, 2007.

Gilroy, Paul. *The Black Atlantic: Modernity and Double Consciousness*. Cambridge, MA: Harvard University Press, 1993.

Kakutani, Michiko. "Travails of an Outcast." *The New York Times*. September 4, 2007.

Sharpe, Jenny. *Ghosts of Slavery: A Literary Archaeology of Black Women's Lives*. Minnesota: University of Minneapolis Press, 2003.

Suárez, Lucía. *The Tears of Hispaniola: Haitian and Dominican Diaspora Memory*. Gainesville: University Press of Florida. 2006.

Torres-Saillant, Silvio. "The Tribulations of Blackness: Stages in Dominican Racial Identity." *Callaloo* 23.3 (2000): 1086–1111.

Notes on Contributors

Lorgia García Peña obtained her Ph.D. in American culture from the University of Michigan. Currently she is the Future of Minority Studies Postdoctoral Fellow at Syracuse University. Her latest book project explores the significance of migration and transnational encounters in the formation of Dominican national discourse. Dr. García Peña is the recipient of the Ford Dissertation Fellowship (2006) and the Leslie Center for the Humanities Faculty Research Grant (2007). She has published various articles in important scholarly journals such as *Wadabagei*, *Xinesquema*, and *Revista Iberoamericana*.

Juanita Heredia is Associate Professor of Spanish at Northern Arizona University. She specializes in U.S. Latina/o and contemporary Latin American literatures and cultures. She is the author of *Transnational Latina Narratives of the Twenty-First Century: The Politics of Gender, Race and Migrations* (Palgrave Macmillan, 2009), and co-editor of *Latina Self-Portraits: Interviews with Contemporary Women Writers* (University of New Mexico Press, 2000). She has published widely on Latina narratives and popular culture in scholarly journals such as *Aztlán* and *Latino Studies*.

Ylce Irizarry is Assistant Professor of English at the University of South Florida. Her research areas include U.S. Latina/o and Chicana/o literature, Hispanic Caribbean historical fiction, narrative ethics, and *Testimonio*. Her work has appeared in journals such as *Antípodas* (2009), *Contemporary Literature* (2007), and *CAS: Comparative American Studies* (2006). Dr. Irizarry is currently working on a manuscript that explores how Latina/o and Chicana/o literatures have been increasingly concerned with the possibilities for empowerment within these cultural communities rather than with acculturation to the Anglo-American mainstream.

Laura Lomas is Associate Professor of English and Acting Director of the Women's Studies Program at Rutgers University, Newark, where she teaches ethnic and immigrant writing of the United States, literature of the Americas, and Latino(a) literature and culture. She is author of *Translating Empire: José Martí, Migrant Latino Subjects and American Modernities* (Duke University Press, 2008), which she completed with a fellowship from the National Endowment for the Humanities. Other recent publications include "José Martí's 'Evening of Emerson' and the United Statesian Literary Tradition," *Journal of American Studies* (2009), "Redefining the American Revolutionary: Gabriela Mistral on José Martí," *Comparative American Studies* (2008), and " 'The War Cut Out my Tongue': Foreign Wars, Domestic Violence and Translation in Demetria Martínez," *American Literature* (2006).

MÓNICA LLADÓ-ORTEGA is Assistant Professor of Spanish at the University of Puerto Rico at Carolina, where she teaches Puerto Rican, Latin American, and Caribbean literature. She has been Chair of the Department of Spanish and Associate Dean of Academic Affairs at the same institution. Her Ph.D. is in Spanish and Caribbean Literature from the University of Michigan, Ann Arbor. She has presented her work at numerous congresses including the annual conventions of the Latin American Studies Association, Modern Languages Association, and Puerto Rican Studies Association. Her research explores queer and gender studies as well as the literatures of the Caribbean and its diaspora. Currently her research projects focus on gender, autobiography, migration, and alternate notions of community building in Hispanic Caribbean Literature.

ANA BELÉN MARTÍN SEVILLANO is Assistant Professor of Spanish American literature at Queen's University, Kingston, Canada. Within the field of cultural studies, her research focuses on Spanish Caribbean cultural production. She has published several articles on contemporary Cuban arts and literature. She is the author of *Sociedad Civil y Arte en Cuba: Cuento y Artes Plásticas en el Cambio de Siglo* (Verbum, 2008). Currently she is working on projects that address issues of gender and race in contemporary Caribbean women's visual and literary works.

YOLANDA MARTÍNEZ-SAN MIGUEL is Professor of Latino studies and comparative literature at Rutgers University, New Brunswick. Her research focuses on Colonial Latin American discourses and contemporary Caribbean and Latino narratives, colonial and postcolonial theory, migration, and cultural studies. Professor Martínez-San Miguel is the author of *Saberes americanos: subalternidad y epistemología en los escritos de Sor Juana* (Instituto Internacional de Literatura Iberoamericana, 1999), *Caribe Two Ways: cultura de la migración en el Caribe insular hispánico* (Ediciones Callejón, 2003), and *From Lack to Excess: "Minor" Readings of Latin American Colonial Discourse* (Bucknell, 2008). She edited with Mabel Moraña the compilation of essays *Nictimene sacrílega: homenaje a Georgina Sabat de Rivers* (Iberoamericana and Claustro de Sor Juana, 2003). She is currently working on her fourth book project, a comparative study on internal Caribbean migrations between former/actual metropolis and colonies that questions transnational and postcolonial approaches to massive population displacements and their cultural productions.

VIVIAN NUN HALLORAN is Associate Professor of comparative literature and Associate Director of American Studies at Indiana University. Her research specialty is Caribbean literature and theory written in Spanish, English, and French. Professor Halloran is the author of *Exhibiting Slavery: The Caribbean Postmodern Novel as Museum* (University of Virginia, 2009). She has published articles on V.S. Naipaul, Caryl Phillips, and Jacques Derrida, and also works on postmodernism, life writing, and food and literature.

VANESSA PÉREZ ROSARIO is Assistant Professor of Puerto Rican and Latino studies at The City University of New York, Brooklyn College. Her research specialty is Caribbean literature and women's writing. She is co-editing with Aurora Levins Morales the forthcoming anthology *OtheRicans: Voices of the Greater Puerto Rican Diaspora*. She is currently working on a critical biographical study of Julia de Burgos that explores the ways that she functions simultaneously as a national cultural icon for Puerto Ricans on the island and for Latinos in the United States exploring new dimensions of scholarship on transnationalism, *Latinidad*, and the way that minority cultures self-identify.

MARITZA STANCHICH is Associate Professor of English in the College of Humanities at the University of Puerto Rico, Río Piedras, where she teaches U.S., Caribbean, and Latina/o literatures. Her work on literature of the Puerto Rican diaspora and on circum-Caribbean readings of Faulkner has appeared in the journals *Sargasso* and *Mississippi Quarterly*, respectively. She has also published in the collections *Prospero's Isles: The Presence of the Caribbean in the American Imaginary* (Macmillan Caribbean, Warwick University Caribbean Studies Series, 2004) and *Writing Of(f) the Hyphen: New Critical Perspectives on the Literature of the Puerto Rican Diaspora* (University of Washington Press, 2008). She previously worked as an award-winning newspaper journalist in New York, Washington, DC, and San Juan, and has also worked for academic unionization at the University of California, Santa Cruz, and with the Asociación Puertorriqueña de Profesores Universitarios (APPU) at UPR.

OMISE'EKE NATASHA TINSLEY is Assistant Professor of English and African American studies at the University of Minnesota, Twin Cities. Her forthcoming book, *Thiefing Sugar: Eroticism between Women in Caribbean*

Literature (Duke University Press, 2010), excavates and explores Dutch-, English-, and French-language Caribbean women's texts between 1900 and 1990, tracing how their queering of landscape-as-female-beloved metaphors imagines a poetics and erotics of decolonization.

CAROLYN WOLFENZON is a Visiting Assistant Professor at Bowdoin College where she teaches Latin American literature and Spanish. She obtained her Ph.D. from Cornell University in Latin American literature. Her areas of interest are the historical novel in Latin America, Colonial *crónicas* and *relaciones* de *Indias,* and migrant and diasporic cultures, especially in Latin American and Peninsular Jewish studies. Her under-graduate studies were in Peru at the Universidad de Lima where she studied communication science and worked as a journalist in different newspapers. Then she obtained her MA in Spanish from the University of Colorado at Boulder. She has published several articles in academic journals in England, Peru, Puerto Rico, and the United States.

Index